NOVEL IDEAS

NOVEL IDEAS

WRITING INNOVATIVE FICTION

PAUL WILLIAMS

© Paul Williams, under exclusive licence to Springer Nature Limited 2020

All rights reserved. No reproduction, copy or transmission of this publication may be made without written permission.

No portion of this publication may be reproduced, copied or transmitted save with written permission or in accordance with the provisions of the Copyright, Designs and Patents Act 1988, or under the terms of any licence permitting limited copying issued by the Copyright Licensing Agency, Saffron House, 6–10 Kirby Street, London EC1N 8TS.

Any person who does any unauthorized act in relation to this publication may be liable to criminal prosecution and civil claims for damages.

The author has asserted his right to be identified as the author of this work in accordance with the Copyright, Designs and Patents Act 1988.

First published 2020 by
RED GLOBE PRESS

Red Globe Press in the UK is an imprint of Springer Nature Limited, registered in England, company number 785998, of 4 Crinan Street, London, N1 9XW.

Red Globe Press® is a registered trademark in the United States, the United Kingdom, Europe and other countries.

ISBN 978-1-352-00848-7 hardback
ISBN 978-1-352-00844-9 paperback

This book is printed on paper suitable for recycling and made from fully managed and sustained forest sources. Logging, pulping and manufacturing processes are expected to conform to the environmental regulations of the country of origin.

A catalogue record for this book is available from the British Library.
A catalog record for this book is available from the Library of Congress.

*To the Creative Writing students at the
University of the Sunshine Coast,
who continue to push the boundaries
of fiction and make our classes
an exciting journey.*

*I would also like to thank my two
research assistants, Peter Moore
and Ebony Upshall, for their meticulous
help with this project and the University
of the Sunshine Coast for the
Publication Acceleration Grant which
made this book possible.*

CONTENTS

Dedication		v
	Introduction: The phenomenon of the novel	1
1.	Rise of the novel: It was a dark and stormy night	14
2.	Realism: The willing suspension of disbelief	30
3.	Modernism: The fragmentation of reality	42
4.	Minimalism: Less is more	58
5.	Magic realism: How flying carpets really fly	75
6.	Postmodernism: [De] Constructing 'Reality'	87
7.	Metafiction: Writing about the mirror	109
8.	The transgressive Novel: Writing with dark ink	127
9.	*Ecriture feminine*: Writing the body	142
10.	Postcolonialism: Writing back to empire	161
11.	The graphic novel and illustrated books	177
12.	Interactive narrative and digital possibilities	189
	Conclusion: Writing innovative fiction	197
Index		200

INTRODUCTION: THE PHENOMENON OF THE NOVEL

The novel has been declared dead so many times, no one believes it anymore. The novel has survived many attempts on its life, mainly because it is so pliable and can morph into whatever it needs to be. Modernism fragmented it, Postmodernism issued its death warrant, and e-publishing tried to eclipse it. Yet here it is – still in bookstores and still in hardback, in paperback, and on Kindle and still selling more than ever. The key to its resilience is perhaps in its name: something 'novel' has to keep reinventing itself.

Sitting on the London Underground tube train from Kensington to Piccadilly, I peer down the passageway and marvel at the sight of hundreds of commuters in rows… reading. Many are absorbed in their emails or perusing the free daily newspaper, but others are reading novels – in paperbacks, in hard cover, on iPads, on Kindle devices or on their phones.

I am always curious to know what books people read in public. To my left, a young woman is clutching a classic; on my right, an older man is reading a Young Adult novel; a woman hanging onto the rail is turning the pages of an erotic novel; further down the carriage, I spy a Jane Austen novel and a myriad of best-sellers.

People are all reading novels. Still.

Not much has changed since the Victorian Era when the station store sold 'penny blacks' and the latest instalment of a Charles Dickens novel, which commuters would read on the train – a steam locomotive back then. Others would likely have been reading romances or the latest Sherlock Holmes mystery. Then, like now, they would have been lost in literary worlds of a writer's making.

In our times, around 60,000 novel titles are published in the UK every year (Flood, 2014, n.p.). Best-sellers for the week line the shelves in WHSmith. The US publishes 100,000 novel titles per year (Wilkens, 2009, n.p.). Lee Child's Jack Reacher novels have sold a staggering 100 million copies to date – that's one copy every 9 seconds (Russell, 2018).

Almost every year, the top prizes in writing go to novelists. The Nobel Prize in Literature (Sweden), the Pulitzer (US) and the Man Booker (UK) celebrate the accomplishments of novelists who innovate with the novel form.

What is it about the novel's resilience and our fascination with this form of narrative that keeps it alive? A 'novel', as its name suggests, is always a new thing: it always strives to surprise, to take us further in our quest to understand the human psyche. There is something democratic about it too. There is a novel for everyone and by everyone.

Richard Flanagan, winner of the 2014 Man Booker Prize, calls the novel 'one of the great inventions of the human spirit' (Miller, 2014, n.p.).

People are consuming novels at a higher rate than ever before in history. They are also writing novels in unprecedented numbers. Creative Writing courses have mushroomed all over the world. Universities offer courses in novel writing. Whole shelves in bookshops are devoted to 'How to Write' books.

On the same train, in the same carriage as all those readers of novels, there is someone two seats away writing something that looks like a romance ('Her hand lingered in his just a second too long as they said goodbye') and one writer tapping on his laptop keyboard. If you peer over his shoulder, you'll see he is writing a chapter entitled 'Introduction: The Phenomenon of the Novel'.

> Everyone, the saying goes, has at least one book in them.
>
> What is the novel you always wanted to write? Jot down some ideas – is it memoir – your own life story? Or is it a sci-fi/mystery/thriller? Adventure? A plot line you thought would make a great story? Why do you want to write a novel? What is it about a 'novel' that captures what you want to say?

What does a novel do?

A novel is not merely a piece of entertainment. A novel gives us a window into the lived experience of another. We can never live another person's life or enter their thoughts but a novel allows us to approximate these experiences more closely than anything else. We can extend our empathy, we can be other people, and we can express ourselves and connect emotionally and intellectually to others in a form that allows this communication with other human beings. The novel allows us to explore our inner being and our past, present and future in ways that other forms do not.

Writing a novel is self-expression, self-actualisation, self-fulfilment and deep exploration of the world and our place in it.

Telling stories

Narrative is our way of making sense of our lived world. A novel tells stories, rehearses a self, fantasises, and speaks in a language of metaphor (like dreams do – more on this later). But a novel does not simply TELL a story – it enacts a life. In the writing of a novel, we perform ourselves.

It has always struck me as bizarre that at school and university we study novels, which are fundamentally fabrications. And in the last two decades, Creative Writing departments have burgeoned all over the world. In these departments, it is legitimate study to write a novel. Making something up, creating a world that perhaps bears no relationship to the 'real' world we inhabit every day, is a respectable area of research. The paradox is that we investigate truth by studying and writing made-up stories. Le Guin, in her 1969 introduction to *The Left Hand of Darkness*, expresses it this way:

> Fiction writers…, at least in their braver moments, do desire the truth: to know it, speak it, serve it. But they go about it in a peculiar and devious way, which consists of inventing persons, places, and events which never did and never will exist or occur, and telling about these fictions in detail and at length and with a great deal of emotion, and then when they are done writing down this pack of lies, they say, There! That's the truth!… I am an artist…and therefore a liar. Distrust everything I say. I am telling the truth (Le Guin, 1969, p. i).

When I was a child, 'telling stories' meant telling lies and always had a negative association. 'Paulie', my dad used to say, 'have you been telling stories? Whoppers?'

But somehow telling stories reveals truth or insight into the human condition. And this is the wonder of the novel. Welcome to its paradoxical world.

Keeping a journal

If writing a novel is learning to read and write a new language (of untruth, of metaphor and of self-actualisation), then the best way to articulate this subjective human condition is to keep a journal of your ideas, thoughts and practice. A journal is different from a blog, which is a public record of your life journey in words. A journal is a private space where you rehearse your life, with the door closed:

> Write with the door closed, rewrite with the door open. Your stuff starts out being just for you, in other words, but then it goes out. Once you know what the story is and get it right – as right as you can, anyway – it belongs to anyone who wants to read it (King, 2000, p. 57).

Practise your craft daily. It is a private word gym where you work out and exercise flabby linguistic muscles. It is a safe space to pour out and examine your most intimate and personal ideas. It is also a self-conscious way to pour out your rage, frustration, depression, inadequacy, triumph and joy, a method of articulating problems, and self-therapy. The more practice you have expressing your emotional and intellectual self in words and making visible your writing practice, the better your writing and the better your self-understanding.

I kept a journal for years and have a bookshelf of dated, hand-written journals and more recently electronic entries. Many a novel or short story or essay beginning has come from these scribblings. I take my journal wherever I go, for in the doctor's waiting room, in the middle of the night, or in the car, inspiration may strike. Most of all, my journal has helped me get into the habit of writing every day and shaping ideas into well-crafted sentences. Instead of spending too many hours a day on social media, I work out in my home word gym. Writing a novel is like long-distance running, and it is good to build muscles for the long-haul task. A journal will help channel your writing into this solitary but rewarding activity of 'talking to yourself'.

Freewriting

Peter Elbow coined the term 'freewriting' to describe a method to free yourself from the censor or editor in your head who prevents you from writing spontaneously. It is commonplace now for writers to use this method to get ideas down in an outpouring of stream of consciousness where the words flow without the hindrance of grammatical structure or punctuation. You cannot write as fast as you think, but freewriting allows your thoughts to flow relatively unhindered.

>  **VOCATION EXERCISE**
>
> What made you want to become a writer? Freewrite a paragraph where you analyse the desire/ache that pulled you into this vocation.
>
> Most people can trace their desire to four paths:
>
> 1. A mentor, teacher or some other person who inspired you to write – I want to be like this person!
> 2. Books or an author you read – I want to write like this!
> 3. How-to-write books: writing manuals and textbooks that helped you on the way
> 4. Creative Writing courses taken
>
> Which path did you take? Which teacher/mentor/book/course inspired you? Why?

Priest of the imagination

I became a writer because of a novel. I remember the exact moment. I was in high school in an English class and the teacher gave us a passage to read about an 'aha' moment of realisation. The passage was from James Joyce's novel *A Portrait of the Artist as a Young Man* (1916). The protagonist, Stephen Dedalus, is about to become a Catholic priest, but walking on the beach he sees a young woman swimming in the ocean. As she walks onto the shore, he has a revelation about beauty and art and life and decides at that moment to give up his calling as a priest of religion and to become an artist, a writer – what he calls a 'priest of the imagination':

> She was alone and still, gazing out to sea; and when she felt his presence and the worship of his eyes her eyes turned to him in quiet sufferance of his gaze, without shame or wantonness. Long, long she suffered his gaze and then quietly withdrew her eyes from his and bent them towards the stream, gently stirring the water with her foot hither and thither. The first faint noise of gently moving water broke the silence, low and faint and whispering, faint as the bells of sleep; hither and thither, hither and thither; and a faint flame trembled on her cheek.

—Heavenly God! cried Stephen's soul, in an outburst of profane joy.

He turned away from her suddenly and set off across the strand. His cheeks were aflame; his body was aglow; his limbs were trembling. On and on and on and on he strode, far out over the sands, singing wildly to the sea, crying to greet the advent of the life that had cried to him.

Her image had passed into his soul for ever and no word had broken the holy silence of his ecstasy. Her eyes had called him and his soul had leaped at the call. To live, to err, to fall, to triumph, to recreate life out of life! A wild angel had appeared to him, the angel of mortal youth and beauty, an envoy from the fair courts of life, to throw open before him in an instant of ecstasy the gates of all the ways of error and glory. On and on and on and on! (Joyce, 2010 (1916)).

My self-realisation moment came as a result of this passage. I knew then that I too wanted to be a writer, a novelist, an artist, a 'priest of the imagination'.

✏ 'PRIEST OF THE IMAGINATION' EXERCISE

Write about an 'aha' moment, a life-changing experience, or a transcendent awakening you have had. Use your senses and bring your own life and insights to bear in the piece.

What is a 'novel'?

The word comes from the Latin *novus*, meaning 'new'. We get the word 'novella' from the Italian word meaning 'new' or 'news' or 'short story of something new'. The French word for novel is *roman*, meaning romance (from the Romance language).

Novelists themselves find the novel difficult to define: E.M. Forster, in *Aspects of the Novel* (1927), describes a novel as 'a fiction in prose of a certain extent – over 50,000 words' (Forster, 1927, p. 17). Virginia Woolf calls it 'this most pliable of all forms' (2012 (1929), n.p.), and Terry Eagleton defines it by avoiding a definition altogether:

> The novel... eludes definitions..., actively undermines them. It is less a genre than an anti-genre. It cannibalizes other literary

modes and mixes the bits and pieces promiscuously together. You can find poetry and dramatic dialogue in the novel, along with epic, pastoral, satire, history, elegy, tragedy and any number of other literary modes (Eagleton, 2005, p. 1).

We generally recognise a novel as a long narrative in prose with

(a) a unified and plausible plot structure

(b) sharply individualised and believable characters

(c) a pervasive illusion of reality (verisimilitude)

(d) an intimacy of style

A novel is, of course, more than the sum of its parts. It aims for a comprehensive unified effect in which all of these elements of fiction intertwine to make a comment on the human condition. John Gardner puts it this way:

> A novel is like a symphony in that its closing movement echoes and resounds with all that has gone before.... Toward the close of a novel... unexpected connections begin to surface; hidden causes become plain; life becomes, however briefly and unstably, organized; the universe reveals itself, if only for the moment, as inexorably moral; the outcome of the various characters' actions is at last manifest; and we see the responsibility of free will (1983, p. 184).

We demand much of a novel. We want each narrative to surprise us in some way, to offer a unique way of seeing the world, or to have plot outcomes we do not expect or characters that are unusual. And the novel demands a lot of us as writers – everything in fact.

Innovation

The history of the novel is the history of its innovation and how it evolved to meet the needs of our ever-changing consciousness and environment. Innovation is not simply invention. It is more the bringing together of various new (or novel) ideas.

For example, the *Harry Potter* novels (1997–2007) are not a new idea. The ideas have been brought together from a long tradition of boarding school stories, wizard schools (Ursula Le Guin's 1968 *A Wizard of Earthsea*, for example), Roald Dahl humour, the idea of the Hero quest, a chosen orphan son who has to defeat the enemy, and a series of other 'borrowings'. But what makes *Harry Potter* innovative is the way J.K. Rowling brings all these elements together in a new and fresh way. Stephanie Meyer's *Twilight* series (2005–2008) is not new either. She did not invent vampires. Or the traditional *Romeo and Juliet* (1597) romance story either. But she made her vampire attractive and restrained, melding the two genres of romance and horror together and making this an innovative series.

In this book, we will explore how innovation works and find ways to bring together two disparate ideas and create new knowledge.

The spectrum of truth

In his introduction to a collection of short fiction (*Elements of Fiction*, 1968), Robert Scholes points out that there is not much difference between 'fact' (Latin: *facere* – 'to make or do') and 'fiction' (Latin: *fingere* – 'to make or shape'). Nor is there much difference between story (French: *histoire*) and history (French: *histoire*). He delineates the genres of narrative along what he calls the 'spectrum of truth', placing historical and journalistic writing on one side of the spectrum and fantasy on the other.

> Taking these two extremes as the opposite ends of a whole spectrum of fictional possibilities, between the infrared of pure history and the ultraviolet of pure imagination, we can distinguish many shades of coloration. But all are fragments of the white radiance of truth, which is present in both history books and fairy tales, but only partly present in each – fragmented by the prism of fiction, without which we should not be able to see it at all (Scholes, 1968, p. 4).

Scholes advocates for the primacy of fiction as the way of making sense of experience. It is not fact versus fiction, truth versus lies, or myth versus reality: everything we think or do is mediated with words, through language, through the storytelling devices in our brains.

> Fact, in order to survive, must become fiction. A thing done has no real existence once it has been done. It may have consequences, and there may be many records that point to its

former existence... but once it is done its existence is finished. A thing made (such as a fiction), on the other hand, exists until it is decayed or destroyed (ibid).

A genre is typically a category of literature, such as mystery, horror, speculative fiction, or non-fiction. This is not to be confused with format (such as a graphic novel) or literary techniques (such as stream of consciousness) or categories of fiction (such as young adult, children's, or adult). Genre fiction tends to be escapist fiction. It is reliant on plot twists and formulae and stock characters (such as the hero and the villain) in order to take us away from the worries and cares of everyday life and into a world of imagination.

Literary fiction

A literary fiction section in a bookstore or library may contain books that do not fit the genre categories or it may contain classics, or 'serious' works of literature. This unfortunate connotation relegates literary fiction to some sort of snobbish elitist space. Nothing is further from the truth. Some of the best genre fiction is literary fiction and vice versa. The classics were at one time genre fiction. This division implies too that genre fiction is somehow not 'literary' but more for mass entertainment, escapism and therefore somehow 'bad'.

What literary fiction does do is make a comment on society, politics, or the human condition. Literary fiction is more likely to be taught and discussed in schools and universities and win literary awards. We study literary fiction for its themes, its message, and its good writing style rather than for its plot. It builds on previous works of literature. It is deliberately written in dialogue with existing works and comments on them, builds on them, and creates innovation and new knowledge.

This book is mostly about literary fiction because literary fiction innovates and strives to be the best of whatever genre it inhabits. There are not many books on how to write literary fiction. Unlike genre, which follows formulae and therefore is easier to imitate, literary fiction is about an unquantifiable quality: your intelligence, your writing style, your skill with language and your experience in the world. It is about having something important and valuable to say. If literary fiction deals with the human condition and is 'deliberately written in dialogue with existing works', then to write it we must steep ourselves in the literary tradition. We must also seek wisdom and experience and strive to articulate them.

Dissecting myths

J.M. Coetzee, the Nobel prize–winning author, once wrote that his role as a writer was not to 'reinforce the myths of our time, but to dissect those myths' (Coetzee, 1988, p. 3).

A myth is a lie, an untruth, but it is also a story we tell ourselves to explain things. In some sense, a myth is a truth, an essential distillation of some concept we have come to believe. A myth is a paradigm, a world view, and a way of seeing the world. It is hard then to see what myths we live by since they have become naturalised and taken for granted. For example, we may believe that democracy is the best system of government to reflect the will of the people. But is it? We may believe that technology improves our lives for the better. But does it? Many novels question such 'myths'.

In Coetzee's post-apocalyptic novel set in Apartheid South Africa, *Life & Times of Michael K* (1983), war is a 'given', a myth of our time, a propaganda offensive to maintain white rule in Africa. But in one short exchange between two characters, this myth is dissected:

> "Also," I said, "can you remind me why we are fighting this war? I was told once, but that was long ago and I seem to have forgotten."
> "We are fighting this war," Noël said, "so that minorities will have a say in their destinies."
> We exchanged empty looks. Whatever my mood was, I could not get him to share it (Coetzee, 1983, p. 215).

The words 'we exchanged empty looks' undermine the whole belief system on which the conversation is predicated. Neither man believes in what he is saying.

When Coetzee observes that some writers reinforce the myths of their culture, in one sense he is talking about genre fiction. Reinforcing myths means that we perpetuate the stories already told, repeat the stereotypes and lull our readers into a safe space where our world view is unquestioned. The hero wins, the bad guy loses. The moral fabric of the world is intact. But to dissect those myths is what happens in literary fiction. In order to question our values, we need to deconstruct, demystify, expose the fault lines and the lies of what we consider to be 'the truth'.

> ✏️ **'MYTHS OF OUR TIME' EXERCISE**
>
> List some of the 'myths of our time' that are reinforced in the media or in novels you have read. Now list some of the 'myths of our time' that you feel need dissecting.

Huckleberry Finn

At eleven years old, I was hooked on the children's literature of the time, the genre fiction that reinforced the myths of that era. But my father decided to read to me one of his favourite books (the same novel his father had read to him as a boy), Mark Twain's *Huckleberry Finn* (1884). We were on his school-teacher's sabbatical, a three-month holiday in Italy over the summer, and we were bored, staying at my mother's relatives in the mountain village of Ciano d'Enza. During the day, we river-rafted down the Taro, explored ruined castles (like the *Castello di Rocca*) and ate huge three-course Italian meals. But in the hot afternoons of the *Ferie d'agosto* and on those long summer evenings, he would read me a chapter a day. I was entranced. I wanted to be Huck Finn and to have adventures on a raft down the Mississippi River, living a wild and carefree life away from civilisation.

   I learned at eleven years old about slavery, about the American Civil War, and about Shakespeare (the King and Duke who accompanied Jim and Huck on the raft on some of the journey were Shakespearean thespians and con artists). I learned about unreliable narrators and the distance between our understanding and that of poor Huck, who thought he was doing wrong by freeing a slave (caught in the myths of his time). I learned too about the phoniness of religion and how 'sivilization' (Twain, 2004 (1884), p. 354) was constructed. Yes, at eleven, I learned all that from one book. Italy did that to me too. I could tell the difference between my culture and Italian culture and measure the distance between the two civilisations.

   My father finished reading it to me in one month, and because I hadn't wanted it to end, I decided to read it again, this time by myself. I struggled with the language, the dialect (especially Jim's), but when I sounded it out loud, I got it. This was literary fiction at its best, but it was also a rollicking wild adventure story. I learned about the human condition and also how this novel dialogued with other books and literary concepts. I learned how Mark Twain was satirising Romantic genre fiction and sentimental poetry and pitting them against a gritty realism. I learned how to dissect the myths of Civil War America. 'It warn't real', Huck Finn said of a china bowl of fruit he found in the Grangerford house and that summed up a lot of what he discovered about his 'sivilization'.

Huckleberry Finn taught me what a novel can do. What a novel must do.

'THE NOVEL THAT CHANGED YOUR LIFE' EXERCISE

In 300 words, describe a novel that changed your life. What was it about this novel that changed your life/thinking? How did it change you?

Where we are going

Literary fiction is composed of the heart and soul of a writer's being and is experienced as an emotional journey through the symphony of words, leading to a stronger grasp of the universe and of ourselves.

My aim is that *Novel Ideas* will help you to become a better writer by harnessing your literary skills, life experience and personal wisdom and insight and forging that into a work of literary merit. The exercises are designed to assist you to dissect myths, chase innovation, create new knowledge, write about transcendent personal experience, dialogue with all that has gone before, and inhabit genres to create a novel that is the best it can possibly be. Please join me on a journey of self-discovery, self-fulfilment, self-actualisation and deep connection to a world of lived experience and to a deep relation to others and the world.

References

Coetzee, J.M. 1983. *Life & Times of Michael K.* London: Martin Secker & Warburg Ltd.
Coetzee, J.M. 1988. The Novel Today. *Upstream* 6, 1 (Summer): 2–5.
Eagleton, Terry. 2005. *The English Novel: An Introduction.* Oxford, UK: Blackwell.
Flood, Alison. 2014. UK publishes more books per capita than any other country, report shows. *The Guardian*, October 22. www.theguardian.com/books/2014/oct/22/uk-publishes-more-books-per-capita-million-report. Accessed 29 April 2017.

Forster, E.M. 1927. *Aspects of the Novel*. New York: Harcourt, Bruce and Company.

Gardner, John. 1983. *The Art of Fiction: Notes on Craft for Young Writers*. London: Vintage.

Joyce, James. 2010 (1916). *Portrait of an Artist as a Young Man*. London: Wordsworth Editions Ltd.

King, Stephen. 2000. *On Writing, a Memoir of the Craft*. New York: Scribner.

Le Guin, Ursula. 1969. *The Left Hand of Darkness*. New York: Ace Books.

Miller, Nick. 2014. Richard Flanagan wins 2014 Man Booker Prize for *The Narrow Road to the Deep North*. *The Sydney Morning Herald*, October 15. www.smh.com.au/entertainment/books/richard-flanagan-wins-2014-man-booker-prize-for-the-narrow-road-to-the-deep-north-20141014-1165ol.html. Accessed 29 April 2017.

Russell, Stephen A. 2018. 'Author Lee Child on the one person who can stop Jack Reacher with a cup of coffee', *The New Daily*, https://thenewdaily.com.au/entertainment/books/2018/11/23/lee-child-jack-reacher/?utm_source=Adestra&utm_medium=email&utm_campaign=Saturday%20News%20-%2020181124. Accessed 24 November 2018.

Scholes, Robert E. 1968. *Elements of Fiction*. New York: Oxford University Press.

Twain, Mark. 2004 (1884). *Huckleberry Finn*. London: Collector's Library.

Wilkens, Matthew. 2009. How Many New Novels are Published Each Year? https://mattwilkens.com/2009/10/14/how-many-novels-are-published-each-year/. Accessed 29 April 2017.

Woolf, Virginia. 2012 (1929). *A Room of One's Own*. Hertfordshire: Woodsworth.

1 RISE OF THE NOVEL: IT WAS A DARK AND STORMY NIGHT

The rise of the novel

While the Great Tradition has us believe that the novel was a white male invention and the likes of F.R. Leavis (1963) will point to *Don Quixote* (1615) or *Robinson Crusoe* (1719) as the first novel written, the candidate is more likely to be an 11th-century Japanese saga written by the female poet, Murasaki Shikibu. *The Tale of Genji* (1021) is a magnificent work whose chapters were written onto folded leaves of paper. It chronicles a dizzying array of hundreds of characters over generations. It was written for the entertainment of the court and offers a vicarious glimpse into the lives of courtiers at that time.

Another contender for the first novel is also by a woman, Aphra Behn, whose *Oroonoko* (1688) is the story of an African man tricked into slavery.

Or we could go back to *One Thousand and One Nights – Tales of the Arabian Nights* (1300s), in which the female narrator, Scheherazade, tells story after story to keep herself alive and escape femicide. Homer's *The Odyssey* (c. 700–800 BCE) is also an early embryo of the novel, an epic poem chronicling the picaresque adventures of Odysseus while his wife, Penelope, fights off suitors at home. The story is as much a test of her endurance, faithfulness and persistence in the belief in herself and her sovereignty as it is about her husband's swashbuckling adventures on the high seas. Stories keep us alive.

A similar theme holds together Boccaccio's frame tale *The Decameron* (1353). Stories told in a remote sanctuary keep the Black Plague at bay. A long pilgrimage in Chaucer's *The Canterbury Tales* (1387) is enlivened by stories in which characters tussle to be heard, trying to trump each other with rhetoric, crude shock tactics, authority and experience. The disruption occurs early on. The Knight has barely finished his proper tale based on the authority of tradition when the drunken Miller interrupts and tells a bawdy tale that undermines the values of the Knight's lofty idealisation of patriarchy, marriage and sex. The Wife of Bath too attacks patriarchy in a diatribe against her ex-husbands, arguing for women's need to 'have mastery' over men. Her tale is a reversal of the conventional quest myth. In 'The Wife of Bath's Tale', a knight has raped a woman, and in order to avoid execution in this land ruled by women, he embarks on a quest to find out what women truly desire.

It is from these frame tales that the word 'novel' originates. Today a novella is a short novel or a long short story. Put together a compilation of these *novelle* (*One Thousand and One Nights*, *The Decameron*, or *The Canterbury Tales*) and you get a 'novel'.

The earliest recorded literature in English (*Beowulf* (c. 700–1000) and *Sir Gawain and the Green Knight* (c. 1350–1400)) are epic poems that foreshadow the fantasy horror novel.

None of the authors would call these 'novels' and nor should we. The novel as we know it today came into being because of a number of confluences at a certain juncture of history, and the factors for its birth are crucial to understand what a novel is and what it does for writers.

Ian Watt, in *The Rise of the Novel* (2000 (1957)), lists several factors (paraphrased here):

1. Invention of the printing press – A novel is to be read by the masses, not by an elite. The novel is democracy in practice. Anyone can write, anyone can read a novel. Authors become free agents in the marketplace, and success is determined by sales, not status.

2. Equality – Anyone can be a character. The novel moves away from the aristocracy and the court and into the bustling streets of life.

3. The act of reading becomes a private act, a conversation between individual author and individual reader, a vicarious anti-solipsism, egalitarian in all senses.

4. The rise of the individual – In Medieval Europe, individuality would seem like a freak thing; your identity was fixed, before birth, to a wheel, family, feudal fiefdom, job function, class and sex. The concept of fluidity was heresy, and making your own way in the world would be a nonsensical idea. So this radical notion of a free agent working out his or her own destiny is a crucial aspect of the novel's revolutionary trajectory.

5. Realism – the move from a Platonic world view where the 'real' world is actually an illusion, a bad copy of a heavenly realm, to an Aristotelian world view where we need to observe our surroundings accurately. Verisimilitude matters. Readers want to experience the physical world through the novel – how it tastes, feels, smells and looks.

In summary, a novel is 'new', disruptive, democratic, fresh, and teeming with possibilities. In a novel, a writer can be someone else and go where no one has gone before.

> ✏️ **'DISRUPTIVE HERO' EXERCISE**
>
> A hero stands against society in some way. This is true even of popular heroes. Lee Child's Jack Reacher, for example, is a loner and an anarchist and fights against the mainstream. What novel can you think of that has a fluid mobile character liberated from his or her society? List the character traits of this hero. How is the novel 'disruptive'?

The early romances

The first popular novels were not great literary works. Yet they were disrupters in that they foreshadowed commercial fiction and the demand of the market. These early novels were 'sensational' fiction, pot boilers, pulp fiction, bodice rippers, trashy romances, horror stories. (So not much has changed!) But the exuberance of the new form is interesting to observe and freeing to read. Many of the first 'novels' were romances, and the words 'novel' and 'romance' were synonymous – the French called the new form a *roman*. In fact, most European languages use the word 'romance' instead of novel to describe an extended prose narrative.

The Romance (not to be confused with Romantic literature or the Romance genre) took the form of a Heroic or Chivalric narrative, filled with action and sword fighting and marvellous adventures of heroic knights errant on quests, often in pursuit of a lady's hand.

Originally written in poetic form, these romances began to be written in prose. An example of this heroic or chivalric romance novel is Thomas Malory's *Le Morte d'Arthur* (1470s). But soon these romances 'degenerated' into the popular romances we may begin to recognise as best-sellers when the focus shifted from upright courtly behaviour (high romance) to the bedroom antics and passions of ordinary men and women. We need only look at one example: García Montalvo's *Amadís de Gaula* (1508 (1304)), popular in 16th-century Spain, although its first version, much revised before printing, was written at the beginning of the 14th century. *Amadís de Gaula* was a runaway best-seller and paved the way for Romance novels. This novel is packed full of secret trysts, illegitimate secret children, abandoned babies who become princes and seek revenge, enchantresses and secret islands. For example, here's one plot line: the King of Gaul, already a sexually adventurous and amorous man, married to the King of Little Britain's voluptuous daughter, finds himself at a mysterious castle, belonging to the Count of Selandia. On his first night as guest, he awakes to find the Count's beautiful daughter at his bedside, in her revealing nightgown, offering her body to him. He resists her and she draws his sword, threatening to kill herself if he denies her pleasure. She holds the point of the sword to her throat and he knows she will carry out her threat of self-harm, so swiftly, passionately, he gathers her into his arms and they make love all night until dawn. The book is full of similar swooning secret passions, ecstasies of unbridled love and desire, and forbidden sexual union.

Gothic novels

Around 1800, the Romance novel began to look and feel very Gothic. Romances were often set in 'ruinous castles, gloomy churchyards, claustrophobic monasteries, and lonely mountain roads' (Richter, 1987, p. 151) and emphasised the supernatural. The name Gothic originates with Goths and later was associated with the 'ugliness' of Gothic (barbaric) architecture. Modern Gothic fashion, music and film are associated with this dark side, insanity and death. The Gothic was, and still is, a rebellion against the vanilla veneer of civilisation, exposing its ugly side. Gothic literature arose out of romance. Ann Radcliffe's *The Mysteries of Udolpho* (1794) and Matthew Lewis's *The Monk* (1796) are good examples of early Gothic fiction and, of course, Mary Shelley's *Frankenstein* (1823) and Bram Stoker's *Dracula* (1897) would follow.

Horace Walpole's *The Castle of Otranto* (1764) claims to be the very first Gothic novel. Its characteristics? Hyperbolic dramatic terror. And the style it is written in? Let's sample a slice:

> "Oh! my Lord, my Lord!" cried she; "we are all undone! it is come again! it is come again!"
> "What is come again?" cried Manfred amazed.
> "Oh! the hand! the Giant! the hand! – support me! I am terrified out of my senses," cried Bianca. "I will not sleep in the castle to-night. Where shall I go? my things may come after me tomorrow – would I had been content to wed Francesco! this comes of ambition!"
> "What has terrified thee thus, young woman?" said the Marquis.
> "Thou art safe here; be not alarmed" (Walpole, 2014 (1764)).

Today an editor would cut out all the exclamation marks and the hyperbolic histrionics of the characters. But this passage reveals how this genre functions.

Also worth reading is Lewis's *The Monk* (1796), a sensational and depraved tale of fornicating holy men, evil magic, dark secret passages, torture, madness and death. Again this would put some modern horror novels to shame.

What these early novels did well was melodrama. Writing teachers generally regard melodrama as a bad thing because it is a short cut, a cheat. Melodramatic writing exaggerates our emotions of dread and terror and sensation and relates sensational and thrilling action with four stock characters:

the Villain
the Hero
the Damsel in Distress
the Comic.

In the extract above, you can see the melodrama of these characters. Read the dialogue aloud and you'll see. You may find yourself flinging your arm across your forehead in an exaggerated pose.

Are we meant to avoid such melodramatic overwriting in our writing? 'Yes', the writing instructors will say. 'It's cliché. It's overwriting. It's telling the reader how to feel'.

But much of modern popular and sensational fiction is exactly that, and most Hollywood movies are staple melodrama and exaggerated sentiment.

Steven Spielberg, for example, admits that:

> in my work, everything is melodrama. I don't think I've ever not made a melodrama. *E.T.* is melodramatic, and so is *The Sugarland Express*. I mean, there's melodrama in life and I love it. It's heightened drama, taking things to histrionic extremes and squeezing out the tears a bit (Spielberg, 2005, p. 1).

Another example of the melodramatic, full of what we would now call clichés, is Edward Bulwer-Lytton's *Paul Clifford* (1830):

> It was a dark and stormy night; the rain fell in torrents, except at occasional intervals, when it was checked by a violent gust of wind which swept up the streets (for it is in London that our scene lies), rattling along the house-tops, and fiercely agitating the scanty flame of the lamps that struggled against the darkness (Bulwer-Lytton, 2010 (1830), p. 1).

Writing teachers nowadays warn us never to begin a story or novel with the words 'It was a dark and stormy night'. It's clichéd. But what if yours were the first to begin a novel this way?

>  **MELODRAMA EXERCISE**
>
> Take the above extracts from Horace Walpole's *The Castle of Otranto* and Edward Bulwer-Lytton's *Paul Clifford* and (1) identify what is melodramatic and clichéd about the style and content and (2) rewrite each extract, expunging the melodrama.

Early erotic and pornographic writing

If we are going to talk about counter-culture Gothic novels, the early novel also dabbled in other transgressive areas, such as the erotic and pornographic. *The Monk* is darkly erotic and transgressive, and soon a spate of writers poured out their own dark fantasies. Richard Head's *The English Rogue* (1665) is a hero's journey through various brothels, Aphra Behn created the *femme fatale*, and John Cleland's *Fanny Hill* (1748) introduced readers to the world of prostitution. Pierre Choderlos de Laclos's *Les Liaisons Dangereuses* (1782) reveals the debauchery of the aristocracy.

Here is a passage from *The Monk*: Ambrosio ('the ravisher') has drugged Antonia and locked her in a dungeon so that he can 'have his way with her'. Note the discreet language where body parts are not named and explicit sex is euphemised:

> He remained for some moments devouring those charms with his eyes which soon were to be subjected to his ill-regulated passions. Her mouth half-opened seem to solicit a kiss: he bent over her: he joined his lips to hers, and drew in the fragrance of her breath with rapture. This momentary pleasure increased his longing for still greater. His desires were raised to that frantic height by which brutes are agitated. He resolved not to delay for one instant longer the accomplishment of his wishes, and hastily proceeded to tear off those garments which impeded the gratification of his lust (Lewis, 1998 (1796), p. 260).

NOVEL IDEAS

The sentimental novel

Although the sentimental novel had its heyday later in the 19th century, its beginnings lie in the early formation of the novel in the 17th century. Sentimental novels, as their name suggests, are reliant on manipulating emotion, much in the way of a melodrama. The novel aims to elicit and prioritise emotion and not just any emotion but 'refined feeling' and 'sensitivity'. This was considered to be a mark of good breeding. The Prioress in Chaucer's *The Canterbury Tales* displays such characteristics:

> She was so charitable and solicitous
> That she would weep if she but saw a mouse
> Caught in a trap, whether it were dead or bled.
> She had some little dogs, that she fed
> On roasted flesh, or milk and fine white bread.
> But sorely she wept if one of them were dead,
> Or if men smote it with a stick to smart:
> Then pity ruled her, and her tender heart (Chaucer, 2005 (1387)).

Early examples of this genre of fiction are Samuel Richardson's *Pamela, or Virtue Rewarded* (1740) (whose aim is set out in the title page, which is primarily 'to cultivate the Principles of Virtue and Religion in the Minds of the Youth of Both Sexes'), Laurence Sterne's *A Sentimental Journey* (1768), Oliver Goldsmith's *The Vicar of Wakefield* (1766) and Henry Mackenzie's *The Man of Feeling* (1771). A later example is the immensely popular *Uncle Tom's Cabin* (1852), written by an abolitionist in order to elicit empathy for slaves in Confederate America. In her introduction to *Uncle Tom's Cabin*, Harriet Beecher Stowe writes that 'the poet, the painter, and the artist, now seek out and embellish the common and gentler humanities of life, and, under the allurements of fiction, breathe a humanizing and subduing influence, favourable to the development of the great principles of Christian brotherhood' (Stowe, 2014 (1852), p. 7).

Here is the tear-jerking passage that made every reader weep:

> "Dear papa," said the child, with a last effort, throwing her arms about his neck. In a moment they dropped again; and, as St. Clare raised his head, he saw a spasm of mortal agony pass over the face, – she struggled for breath, and threw up her little hands....
> "O, Eva, tell us what you see! What is it?" said her father.
> A bright, a glorious smile passed over her face, and she said, brokenly, – "O! love, – joy, – peace!" gave one sigh, and passed from death unto life!

"Farewell, beloved child! the bright, eternal doors have closed after thee; we shall see thy sweet face no more. O, woe for them who watched thy entrance into heaven, when they shall wake and find only the cold gray sky of daily life, and thou gone forever!" (Stowe 2014, (1852), p. 328).

TEAR-JERKING EXERCISE

Analyse the Stowe passage. Look for devices that she uses to squeeze the sentimentality out of her reader. How is it melodramatic? What emotion is being conveyed? What narrative devices are used to create this effect? Now write a scene that uses these devices and creates the same effect.

Pathos

Aristotle outlines three effective ways of persuading an audience: logos, pathos and ethos. Pathos is emotional persuasion, using rhetoric to move us emotionally to feel what the speaker wants us to feel. Advertising campaigns exploit this method, bypassing logic at times to get us to buy a product on impulse. Nowadays, however, writers are wary of sentimentalism: sentimentality is akin to false emotion. How often have you cried at the end of a movie or at some trivial plot line, engineered by swelling violin music, stock shots of teary faces, and so on and thought afterwards, why was I crying about that?

Is there room for sentimentality in writing novels today? Even Romance novelists try to steer clear of clichéd sentimentality. Of course, some popular novels (for example, the *Twilight* series) thrive on sentimental tropes to drive the plot along. Even at the time, writers took exception and countered what they saw as emotional exploitation of the reader. Henry Fielding wrote *Shamela* (1741) as a critique of Richardson's sentimentalist *Pamela*. Mark Twain wrote *Huckleberry Finn* (1884) partly in reaction to *Uncle Tom's Cabin* in order to expose what he saw as manipulative sentimentalism. Here, he parodies the sentimental artwork of Emmeline Grangerford, the deceased daughter of a host family Huck is staying with:

> They was different from any pictures I ever see before – blacker, mostly, than is common.... There was one where a young lady was at a window looking up at the moon, and tears running

> down her cheeks; and she had an open letter in one hand with black sealing wax showing on one edge of it, and she was mashing a locket with a chain to it against her mouth, and underneath the picture it said "And Art Thou Gone Yes Thou Art Gone Alas." These was all nice pictures, I reckon, but I didn't somehow seem to take to them, because if ever I was down a little they always give me the fan-tods (Twain, 2018 (1884), p. 106).

Sentimental novels have had a bad rap until recently because they have been relegated by male critics and a male literary establishment as 'women's fiction' (meaning inferior to 'real' male fiction). Maybe there has been a bias against emotion and sensitivity and maybe now is the time to re-examine 'sentimental' novels and redeem their reputation. There is no question that nostalgic sentimental novels like *Uncle Tom's Cabin*, *Gone with the Wind* (1936) and *The Bridges of Madison County* (1992) sell in the millions. Perhaps we like to escape into syrupy sweet, melodramatic tear-jerkers or maybe this conveys something fundamental about the human condition.

I have wrestled with this in my own writing. Here is an example from my novel *Soldier Blue* (2008) where I tackled a very emotional scene. The protagonist finds out that the childhood sweetheart he loves is engaged to someone else. The first time I wrote this, it was sickly sentimental:

> The trees echoed my feelings of despair. I was drowning in love. And she was the only one who could save me. I love you, I love you, every cell in my body shouted out to her. But the cruel ring on her finger was a knife cutting through my heart. She looked hesitant.
> "I'm so glad you're here. I have something to tell you."
> "You want to see me?" I spun dizzily, hungry for any morsel of her affection.
> "I want your advice." She looked even more nervous now. "Promise you'll still be my friend?"
> "I'll always be your friend, no matter what. You know that. Cross my heart and hope to die."
> "I want you to be the first to know."
> The birds in the tree above us were squawking so loudly and she was speaking so softly that I had to incline my head towards her and lip read. Her breath was warm on my face. I could hardly stand still, giddily swooning towards her. I wanted to hold her, touch her, kiss those sweet lips.

"I'm engaged."
I felt as if I had been sent to hell. Demons pulled me down into the depths of despair.
"Didn't you notice the ring?" She displayed the sparkling diamond set in the centre of blue amethysts as a sword, that same sparkling knife whose shafts of reflected light pierced me to the heart and left me bleeding and gutted on the ground.

Then I rewrote it, taking out all the devices, and it read much better – it still made me cringe but less so. Taking out all the emotion actually helped create a more emotionally laden scene.

Outside, in the cool of the trees, she twirled a ring around her finger, bit her lip.

"I'm so glad you're here. I have something to tell you."
"I'm all ears."
"I want your advice." Her left eyelid was fluttering. "Promise you'll still be my friend?"
"Cross my heart and hope to die."
"I also want you to be the first to know."
The birds in the tree above us were squawking so loudly and she was speaking so softly that I had to incline my head towards her and lip-read.
"I'm engaged."
A poem we had learned by heart in English the year before suddenly played in my head: a poem about the dead in hell listening to the smooth, silvery, sweet voice of an angel.
"Didn't you notice the ring?" She displayed the sparkling diamond set in the centre of blue amethysts as a sword, a knife whose shafts of reflected light glittered at me (Williams, 2008, pp. 273–274).

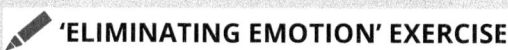 **'ELIMINATING EMOTION' EXERCISE**

Rewrite the sentimental scene from the previous exercise, eliminating all the tear-jerking devices you used.

Epistolary

> Dear Francesca,
> I hope this finds you well. I don't know when you'll receive it. Sometime after I'm gone. I'm sixty-five now, and it's been thirteen years ago today that we met when I came up your lane looking for directions. I'm gambling that this package won't upset your life in any way. I just couldn't bear to think of the cameras sitting in a second-hand case in a camera store or in some stranger's hands. They'll be in pretty rough shape by the time you get them. But, I have no one else to leave them to, and I apologize for putting you at risk by sending them to you.
> .... All the philosophic rationalizations I can conjure up do not keep me from wanting you, every day, every moment, the merciless wail of time, of time I can never spend with you, deep within my head.
> I love you, profoundly and completely. And I always will.
> The last cowboy,
> Robert.
> (Waller, 2014, p. 1)

Thus begins one of the sentimental best-sellers of the late 20th century... and it's epistolary. On her mother's death, a daughter finds secret letters which reveal an extramarital affair her mother had with a passing photographer.

One of the earliest narrative techniques to create verisimilitude in the novel was letter writing, or epistolary writing. The letter vouches for the authenticity of the document just as archived historical documents are deemed more authentic and to be trusted. Therefore, *Gulliver's Travels* (1726) opens with a letter vouching for Gulliver's character, followed by a terse disclaimer from Gulliver himself claiming that the facts had been falsified and exaggerated.

But epistolary writing is not only letter writing. It can be diary entries, newspaper clippings, emails, tweets, voice mail, grocery receipts, recipes, posters, reviews, footnotes, advertisements, road signs, or PowerPoint slides – anything to simulate veracity and journalistic truth.

In epistolary novels, the reader is a voyeur, eavesdropping on someone's conversation. It enables a simulation of honesty, a baring of the soul, intimacy, honesty, and confession. The first novel to exploit the form in a complex way was Behn's *Love-Letters Between a Nobleman and His Sister* (1684, 1685, 1687). Other early examples of epistolary novels in the 18th and

19th centuries are Richardson's *Pamela* (1740) and *Clarissa* (1749), Fielding's *Shamela* (1741), Mary Shelley's *Frankenstein* (1818) and Stoker's *Dracula* (1897).

Talking to yourself: diaries and journals

I have a whole shelf of exercise books in my office, crammed with my own writing. No one will ever see these books (I hope) because they are personal and written for no one else but me. Maybe not even for me. I have been writing journals since I was 16. In these journals are my thoughts, my frustrations, my anger, my attempts at style, my favourite quotes, my poems, my daily thoughts, my freewriting. I look back and can see the intellectual and emotional progress of my life, a parallel life in writing. It's a habit I took to easily, a compulsion. I had to express myself, talk out my problems and triumphs and work them out on paper.

A diary is similar – but is less internal and introspective – more an account of daily things done. I blend the two in my journals.

A blog is similar in form, but it is by nature public and meant to be shared.

Imagine if I had some secrets I wrote in my journals, and imagine if you broke into my office while I was away and read them. You would be a voyeur, an outsider with a window into someone's personal private life. The words are not meant for you, but you would find in them an honesty, perhaps, an unaffected style, rawness, because they were never meant for a market or public consumption.

So it is not surprising that the early forms of the novel imitated this voyeuristic practice of reading other people's diaries. Here is Stoker's *Dracula*:

> Jonathan Harker's Journal (Kept in shorthand) 3 May. Bistritz –Left Munich at 8:35 P.M., on 1st May, arriving at Vienna early next morning; should have arrived at 6:46, but train was an hour late. Buda-Pesth seems a wonderful place, from the glimpse which I got of it from the train and the little I could walk through the streets. I feared to go very far from the station, as we had arrived late and would start as near the correct time as possible (Stoker, 2003 (1897)).

And more contemporary, here is Helen Fielding's *Bridget Jones's Diary* (1996):

> January: An Exceptionally Bad Start
> Sunday 1 January

NOVEL IDEAS

> Noon. London: my flat. Ugh. The last thing on earth I feel physically, emotionally or mentally equipped to do is drive to Una and Geoffrey Alconbury's New Year's Day Turkey Curry Buffet in Grafton Underwood. Geoffrey and Una Alconbury are my parents' best friends and, as Uncle Geoffrey never tires of reminding me, have known me since I was running round the lawn with no clothes on. My mother rang up at 8:30 in the morning last August Bank Holiday and forced me to promise to go. She approached it via a cunningly circuitous route (Fielding 1996).

Or here is Sue Townsend's *The Secret Diary of Adrian Mole, Aged 13¾* (1982):

> **Wednesday January 14th**
>
> None of the teachers at school have noticed that I am an intellectual. They will be sorry when I am famous. There is a new girl in our class. She sits next to me in Geography. She is all right. Her name is Pandora, but she likes being called 'Box'. Don't ask me why. I might fall in love with her. It's time I fell in love, after all I am 13 3/4 years old (Townsend, 1982).

'DEAR DIARY' EXERCISE

Write the beginning of a story (300 words) that is told using a diary or journal or blog format.

Talking to others: monologic, dialogic, polylogic epistolary writing

> St. Petersburgh, Dec. 11th, 17 – TO Mrs. Saville, England
>
> You will rejoice to hear that no disaster has accompanied the commencement of an enterprise which you have regarded with such evil forebodings. I arrived here yesterday, and my first task is to assure my dear sister of my welfare and increasing confidence in the success of my undertaking (Shelley, 2003 (1823)).

In *Frankenstein*, Shelley employs the letter form to write her novel. I have often done this in real life – compiled emails from an old friend into a document that reads like an unfolding story. It could be monologic (just the emails written to me or the ones I wrote to her or him) or dialogic (alternate emails from me to her and her to me) or even polylogic (including emails from a third party or even a fourth party). Emails crucially leave out information and assume knowledge. That is, they have no overseeing guiding narrator to help the reader connect to the characters or email participants. Here, the characters speak for themselves, and the reader is left to construct the narrative between the gaps.

Here is an extract from one of the earliest English novels, written dialogically:

> LETTER I MISS ANNA HOWE, TO MISS CLARISSA HARLOWE JAN 10.
> I am extremely concerned, my dearest friend, for the disturbance that has happened in your family. I know how it must hurt you to become the subject of the public talk: and yet, upon an occasion so generally known, it is impossible but that whatever relates to a young lady, whose distinguished merits have made her the public care, should engage every body's attention. I long to have the particulars from yourself; and of the usage I am told you receive upon an accident you could not help; and in which, as far as I can learn, the sufferer was the aggressor. Mr. Diggs, the surgeon, whom I sent for at the first hearing of the encounter, to inquire, for your sake, how your brother was, told me, that there was no danger from the wound, if there were none from the fever; which it seems has been increased by the perturbation of his spirits.
>
> LETTER II MISS CLARISSA HARLOWE, TO MISS HOWE HARLOWE-PLACE, JAN. 13.
> How you oppress me, my dearest friend, with your politeness! I cannot doubt your sincerity; but you should take care, that you give me not reason from your kind partiality to call in question your judgment. You do not distinguish that I take many admirable hints from you, and have the art to pass them upon you for my own: for in all you do, in all you say, nay, in your very looks (so animated!) you give lessons to one who loves you and observes you as I love you and observe you, without knowing that you do – So pray, my dear, be more sparing of your praise for the future, lest after this confession

> we should suspect that you secretly intend to praise yourself, while you would be thought only to commend another (Richardson, 2004 (1748)).

Many lament the lost art of letter writing as electronic correspondence such as email, instant messaging, or texting is transient and can be deleted forever whereas letters can be preserved. I still have letters I have kept from childhood and teenage years.

The epistolary form enables what we call 'discrepant awareness' – the ability to read between the lines, to see what characters themselves do not see, and for authors to play with dramatic irony and unreliable narration. For example, we (hopefully) get the allusion to Pandora's box in the above example, but Adrian Mole does not. And here, for example, is Celia in *The Color Purple* (1982) (a polylogic, epistolary novel), an illiterate young woman who writes to God as she dare not tell anyone else her life story:

> Dear God
> I am fourteen years old. I am. I have always been a good girl. Maybe you can give me a sign letting me know what is happening to me (Walker, 1982, p. 1).

Other forms of epistolary writing can include newspaper articles (Stephen King's *Carrie* (1974) comprises narrative, news articles, journal articles and graffiti), PowerPoint slides (Jennifer Egan's *A Visit from the Goon Squad* (2010) includes a chapter using PowerPoint slides and one in textspeak), 'to do' lists and text messaging (Meg Cabot's *Boy Meets Girl* (2004)).

✎ EPISTOLARY EXERCISE

1. Write the beginning of a novel (300 words) that uses three epistolary devices (letters, emails, newspaper clippings, PowerPoint or a shopping list) and addresses the reader (narratee) directly without need for a mediating narrator.

2. Use monologic, dialogic or polylogic forms.

3. Use dramatic irony (discrepant awareness) to create effect.

Conclusion

The early novel played with strands that would later become genre fiction – romance, adventure, horror, erotica, and so on. The novel invented itself out of the struggle of the emerging individual, and popular novels tended to be sensationalist, melodramatic and sentimental. But because the form was still fluid, early novelists freely experimented with epistolary devices, sentimentalism, and the Gothic, and the phenomenon we now call the 'novel' began to take shape.

References

Bulwer-Lytton, Edward. 2010 (1830). *Paul Clifford*. London: Penguin.
Chaucer, Geoffrey. 2005 (1387). *The Canterbury Tales*. London: Penguin.
Fielding, Helen. 1996. *Bridget Jones's Diary*. London: Picador.
Leavis, F.R. 1963. *The Great Tradition*. New York: New York University Press.
Lewis, Matthew. 1998 (1796). *The Monk*. London: Penguin.
Richardson, Samuel. 2004 (1748). *Clarissa*. London: Penguin.
Richter, David H. 1987. Gothic Fantasia: The Monsters and The Myths: A Review-Article. *The Eighteenth Century* 28 (2): 149–170.
Shelley, Mary. 2003 (1823). *Frankenstein*. London: Penguin.
Spielberg, Steven. 2005. A Dialogue on Film with Steven Spielberg. *American Film Institute*. www.fathom.com/feature/122046. Accessed 14 August 2018.
Stoker, Bram. 2003 (1897). *Dracula*. London: Penguin.
Stowe, Harriet Beecher. 2014 (1852). *Uncle Tom's Cabin*. London: Vintage.
Townsend, Sue. 1982. *The Secret Diary of Adrian Mole, Aged 13¾*. London: Methuen Publishing.
Twain, Mark. 2018 (1884). *The Adventures of Huckleberry Finn*. London: Arcturus Publishing Limited.
Walker, Alice. 1982. *The Color Purple*. San Diego: Harcourt.
Waller, Robert James. 2014 (1992). *The Bridges of Madison County*. New York: Grand Central Publishing.
Walpole, Horace. 2014 (1764). *The Castle of Otranto*. Oxford: Oxford University Press.
Watt, Ian. 2000 (1957). *The Rise of the Novel*. London: Pimlico.
Williams, Paul. 2008. *Soldier Blue*. Cape Town: New Africa Books.

2 REALISM: THE WILLING SUSPENSION OF DISBELIEF

Ian Watt, in *The Rise of the Novel* (1957), argues that the novel's 'novelty' was its 'formal realism': the idea 'that the novel is a full and authentic report of human experience' (Watt, 2000 (1957), p. 21). Realism is 'the attempt to represent subject matter truthfully, without artificiality and avoiding artistic conventions, as well as implausible, exotic and supernatural elements' (ibid).

Walter Scott was the first to separate the two characteristics of the early novel: romance and realism. He defined the romance as 'a fictitious narrative in prose or verse; the interest of which turns upon marvellous and uncommon incidents', whereas in the novel, 'the events are accommodated to the ordinary train of human events and the modern state of society' (Scott, 2000 (1824), pp. 20–21).

The realist turn: Cervantes's *Don Quixote* (1615), Defoe's *Robinson Crusoe* (1719) and Swift's *Gulliver's Travels* (1726)

The rise of the novel as an alternative to the romance began with the publication of Cervantes's *Novelas Exemplares* (1613), as the author himself is delighted to point out:

> My genius and my inclination prompt me to this kind of writing; the more so as I consider (and with truth) that I am the first who has written novels in the Spanish language, though many have hitherto appeared among us, all of them translated from foreign authors. But these are my own, neither imitated nor stolen from anyone; my genius has engendered them, my pen has brought them forth, and they are growing up in the arms of the press (Cervantes, 1613).

Watt and most modern scholars, however, consider the first novel proper to be Cervantes's full-length narrative *The Ingenious Gentleman Don Quixote of La Mancha* (1615) because it made a turn: it consolidated what a novel is and does. *Don Quixote* critiques the romance novel in the light of the real world and deconstructs it:

> "Give me that helmet, my friend, for either I know little of adventures, or what I observe yonder is one that will, and does, call upon me to arm myself."
> [Sancho], on hearing this, looked in all directions, but could perceive nothing, except a cart coming towards them with two or three small flags, which led him to conclude it must be carrying treasure of the King's, and he said so to Don Quixote. He, however, would not believe him, being always persuaded and convinced that all that happened to him must be adventures and still more adventures; so he replied to the gentleman, "He who is prepared has his battle half fought; nothing is lost by my preparing myself, for I know by experience that I have enemies, visible and invisible, and I know not when, or where, or at what moment, or in what shapes they will attack me;" and turning to Sancho he called for his helmet; and Sancho, as he had no time to take out the curds, had to give it just as it was. Don Quixote took it, and without perceiving what was in it thrust it down in hot haste upon his head; but as the curds were pressed and squeezed the whey began to run all over his face and beard, whereat he was so startled that he cried out to Sancho:
> "Sancho, what's this? I think my head is softening, or my brains are melting, or I am sweating from head to foot! If I am sweating it is not indeed from fear. I am convinced beyond a doubt that the adventure which is about to befall me is a terrible one. Give me something to wipe myself with, if thou hast it, for this profuse sweat is blinding me" (Cervantes, 1615).

Cervantes here delivers his reader a healthy dose of curds and realism. He undermines the romantic illusion, idealisation and melodrama of previous novels by being a realist. Sancho provides the foil to what is real, and the delusion of a Romantic knight errant is exposed. Thus begins the novel we know today – the novel that exposes illusion, describes 'reality' and deconstructs and unmasks folly and illusion.

Though written much later, the *Adventures of Huckleberry Finn* (1884) is a touch of the cap to *Don Quixote* in the Confederation era of the

United States. Ostensibly a children's book, *Huckleberry Finn* deconstructs the myths of American colonial society (what Huck calls 'sivilisation') and he discovers that, like the imitation fruit he finds in a bowl on the Grangerford residence, 'it warn't real'. Huck and Jim are the paradisal Adam and Eve, the gullible innocents who fall victim to the schemes of con artists, Sunday-school teachers and even Tom Sawyer himself, who is the victim of Romance novels and world views. Huck is Sancho and Tom is Don Quixote:

> [Tom] had got secret news by his spies that next day a whole parcel of Spanish merchants and rich A-rabs was going to camp in Cave Hollow with two hundred elephants, and six hundred camels, and over a thousand "sumter" mules, all loaded down with di'monds, and they didn't have only a guard of four hundred soldiers, and so we would lay in ambuscade, as he called it, and kill the lot and scoop the things. He said we must slick up our swords and guns, and get ready.... But there warn't no Spaniards and A-rabs, and there warn't no camels nor no elephants. It warn't anything but a Sunday-school picnic, and only a primer-class at that (Twain, 2018 (1884), p. 9).

 **DON QUIXOTE EXERCISE**

Choose a prevalent romantic or other illusion and write a 300-word passage in which one character suffers from this delusion and the other character exposes it.

The second contender for the first novel is Daniel Defoe's (1719) *The Life and Strange Surprizing Adventures of Robinson Crusoe*, which is so meticulously descriptive and realistic that it created the standard for all novels to come. The details are so convincing and imitative of the travel yarns of the time that contemporary readers believed it to be a true historical account. Verisimilitude becomes the touchtone of the novel. Without it, our novelist ship is sunk.

How does Defoe create verisimilitude? First by making his narrator believable and trustworthy. We readers will take his word for it. He employs Aristotle's ethos, or credibility.

> I was born in the year 1632, in the city of York, of a good family, though not of that country, my father being a foreigner of Bremen, who settled first at Hull. He got a good estate by merchandise, and leaving off his trade lived afterward at York, from whence he had married my mother, whose relations were named Robinson, a good family in that country, and from whom I was called Robinson Kreutznear; but by the usual corruption of words in England we are now called, nay, we call ourselves, and write our name, Crusoe, and so my companions always called me (Defoe, 1995 (1719), p. 1).

Defoe also creates ethos by providing us with irrefutable photograph-like evidence of the reality of his protagonist's travels.

> I first got three of the seamen's chests, which I had broken open and emptied, and lowered them down upon my raft. The first of these I filled with provisions, viz., bread, rice, three Dutch cheeses, five pieces of dried goat's flesh, which we lived much upon, and a little remainder of European corn, which had been laid by for some fowls which we brought to sea with us, but the fowls were killed. There had been some barley and wheat together, but, to my great disappointment, I found afterwards that the rats had eaten or spoiled it all. As for liquors, I found several cases of bottles belonging to our skipper, in which were some cordial waters, and, in all, about five or six gallons of rack (Defoe, 1995 (1719), p. 19).

Defoe brings the shipwreck into close focus, and readers cannot help but believe in this conjuring trick. This is not autobiography or history but a fictional autobiography, a mimicking of a true historical account, a false document. The fundamental truth of novel writers is that we have to be good liars. Novelists are mimics of truth, creators of illusions, magicians who try to fool the public with conjuring tricks and sleight of hand. So what are this magician's secrets? In *Robinson Crusoe*, the English language takes on a scientific rational tone of facts and precise measurements. No longer are readers of novels satisfied with generalities or geographically disembodied settings. They demand real places, measured and detailed under close scrutiny. The novel reader expects journalistic detail. Defoe himself was a journalist before he became a novelist, and he brought with him the plain, unadorned style of the tabloid.

> ✏ **'STRANDED ON A DESERT ISLAND' EXERCISE**
>
> Write a 300-word descriptive passage about being stranded on a desert island. Use specific, accurate and concrete details that (a) convince your reader that you are a credible narrator (ethos) and (b) create verisimilitude.

The adventure genre began much earlier with Homer's *The Odyssey* (2003), but it finds its home in realism, in the resourcefulness and individual agency of the (male) hero, and in a British colonial context where adventure means exploring and conquering new worlds. The adventure story, and particularly *Robinson Crusoe*, is a metaphor for a new individualist mobility of a new class, providing people back home vicarious experience of the colonisation of other cultures, new frontiers, and a substitute experience for those in grey climates who were hungry for knowledge about the outside world. *Robinson Crusoe* begins a whole tradition of 'adventure' stories of empire and nation building – from H. Rider Haggard's *King Solomon's Mines* (1885) or its modern equivalent, Wilbur Smith's *The Leopard Hunts in Darkness* (1984), to the *Star Trek* series. Crusoe's resourcefulness enables him to recreate the whole of his civilisation on the island and subjugate an indigenous 'other' and teach him the 'correct' ways to behave, live and worship. As such, *Robinson Crusoe* becomes a tight allegory for the whole British colonial enterprise of empire building.

Jonathan Swift's *Gulliver's Travels* (1726) is a similarly detailed false account (fictional autobiography) of an adventure on the high seas and intrusion into foreign lands. The narrator likewise uses the same conjuring tricks as Defoe – first establishing his credibility and ethos…

> The author of these Travels, Mr. Lemuel Gulliver, is my ancient and intimate friend; there is likewise some relation between us on the mother's side. About three years ago, Mr. Gulliver growing weary of the concourse of curious people coming to him at his house in Redriff, made a small purchase of land, with a convenient house, near Newark, in Nottinghamshire, his native country; where he now lives retired, yet in good esteem among his neighbours (Swift, 2011 (1726), p. 2).

…and then using verisimilitude. Gulliver's detailed descriptions are, however, even more realistic and graphic than Crusoe's. Ironically, *Robinson Crusoe* is about a realistic shipwreck on an island, whereas *Gulliver's Travels* is a series of fantastic stories involving giants, floating islands and talking horses. Yet *Gulliver's Travels* is the more graphically realistic and therefore believable. Some readers actually believed the adventures of Lemuel Gulliver were real. Why? Because Swift is at pains to point out, for example, exactly how much excrement Gulliver produces in Lilliput:

> I had been for some hours extremely pressed by the necessities of nature; which was no wonder, it being almost two days since I had last disburdened myself. I was under great difficulties between urgency and shame. The best expedient I could think of, was to creep into my house, which I accordingly did; and shutting the gate after me, I went as far as the length of my chain would suffer, and discharged my body of that uneasy load […]; and due care was taken every morning before company came, that the offensive matter should be carried off in wheel-barrows, by two servants appointed for that purpose (Swift, 2011 (1726), p. 6).

Robinson Crusoe looks romantically hazy and idealistic by comparison. In *Gulliver's Travels*, as in 'real life', humans defecate, urinate, get pimples, and smell bad. *Gulliver's Travels* also undermines the notion of empire building that Defoe sets up in *Robinson Crusoe*. Swift uses a number of narrative devices to do this: 'A Voyage to Lilliput' asks the reader to look down the wrong end of telescope at Lilliput and see its petty diminished politics and human pride as vanity. 'A Voyage to Brobdingnag' asks us to look at human nature with a magnifying glass.

> Their skins appeared so coarse and uneven, so variously coloured, when I saw them near, with a mole here and there as broad as a trencher, and hairs hanging from it thicker than packthreads, to say nothing farther concerning the rest of their persons. Neither did they at all scruple, while I was by, to discharge what they had drank, to the quantity of at least two hogsheads, in a vessel that held above three tuns (Swift, 2011 (1726), p. 82).

Satire

Swift's purpose, however, is not simply to horrify but to satirise, and the novel is the perfect vehicle to do this.

> When a great office is vacant, either by death or disgrace (which often happens,) five or six of those candidates petition the emperor to entertain his majesty and the court with a dance on the rope; and whoever jumps the highest, without falling, succeeds in the office. Very often the chief ministers themselves are commanded to show their skill, and to convince the emperor that they have not lost their faculty. Flimnap, the treasurer, is allowed to cut a caper on the straight rope, at least an inch higher than any other lord in the whole empire. I have seen him do the summerset several times together, upon a trencher fixed on a rope which is no thicker than a common packthread in England. My friend Reldresal, principal secretary for private affairs, is, in my opinion, if I am not partial, the second after the treasurer; the rest of the great officers are much upon a par (Swift, 2011 (1726), p. 17).

 'NOT FOR THE SQUEAMISH GRAPHIC-REALIST' EXERCISE

In 300 words, describe a bodily function, activity or event as realistically as you can without sugar-coating it or using euphemism.

What life is really like

We know now that it is a fallacy to think of 'real life' as a static, objective truth we can reflect accurately or mirror in words. Equating narrative conventions with 'reality' is just a convention we have come to accept. Yet this is what the novel attempts: believability, verisimilitude and accuracy of detail. A novel should be like a photograph. Margaret Laurence begins her novel *The Diviners* (1974) with a description of a photograph and proceeds to describe what is behind the photograph, what is not visible, in order to deepen her realist portrait of her family.

> ✏️ **'PHOTOGRAPHIC REALISM' EXERCISE**
>
> Find an old family photograph and describe it exactly as you see it (appearance). Recall the emotions present – the smells, tastes, sounds as well as sights if possible (if you were present in the photo). Then write what is not seen, the 'reality' behind the photo.

Social and domestic realism

In contrast to the tales of adventure, romance and high drama with implausible plot lines, a new form of the novel began to emerge, one that aimed to depict the ordinary domestic and social reality of everyday lives. Jane Austen's fiction embodies such social and domestic realism, depicting characters in the throes of ordinary day-to-day struggles, such as finding husbands, dealing with financial instability, and catching colds. As Austen herself confesses:

> I could not sit seriously down to write a serious Romance under any other motive than to save my Life, & if it were indispensable for me to keep it up & never relax into laughing at myself or other people, I am sure I should be hung before I had finished the first Chapter (Sutherland, 2014, n.p.).

What Austen did was write what she knew. She wrote about a recognisable landscape with picnics and dances and familiar experiences that would resonate with readers and that reflected the range of possibilities and moral dilemmas they had to face. Walter Scott, high-flying adventure writer, praised Austen for her lack of plot (a good thing for a realist writer, apparently!): '*Emma* has even less story than [Jane Austen's] preceding novels' (ibid).

> ✏️ **'LACK OF PLOT' EXERCISE**
>
> Describe an ordinary domestic scene that depicts what life is 'really' like for you. Write what you know best, a familiar experience that reflects your daily life, possibly a scene with a moral dilemma that you had to face.

Victorian realism

Victorian writers, whom we now regard as rather over-obsessed with detail and clutter, strove to accurately portray the human experience by using what we now consider ornate prose. To some extent they succeeded. If you want to know what it was like to live in Victorian England, read a Victorian English novel, such as George Eliot's (1819–1880) *Middlemarch: A Study of Provincial Life* (1871), described by many as one of the greatest novels in the English language and a masterpiece of realism. Let's take a look at a passage:

> An eminent philosopher among my friends... has shown me this pregnant little fact. Your pier-glass or extensive surface of polished steel made to be rubbed by a housemaid, will be minutely and multitudinously scratched in all directions; but place now against it a lighted candle as a centre of illumination, and lo! the scratches will seem to arrange themselves in a fine series of concentric circles round that little sun. It is demonstrable that the scratches are going everywhere impartially, and it is only your candle which produces the flattering illusion of concentric arrangement, its light falling with an exclusive optical selection (Eliot, 1994 (1871), p. 269).

Victorian Realism is often (wrongly) said to be epitomised in Charles Dickens, whose immensely popular and prolific works illuminated and embodied the Victorian era for many. He wrote some fifteen novels, which were often serialised, and the characters and settings he created were so vivid (some say realistic) that they still echo in us today, so much so that we have a word – Dickensian – to describe this influence. *Great Expectations* (1861), for example, begins with a terrifying encounter by a winter graveyard graphically described:

> "Hold your noise!" cried a terrible voice, as a man started up from among the graves at the side of the church porch. "Keep still, you little devil, or I'll cut your throat!"
> A fearful man, all in coarse grey, with a great iron on his leg. A man with no hat, and with broken shoes, and with an old rag tied round his head. A man who had been soaked in water, and smothered in mud, and lamed by stones, and cut by flints, and

stung by nettles, and torn by briars; who limped, and shivered, and glared and growled; and whose teeth chattered in his head as he seized me by the chin.

"O! Don't cut my throat, sir," I pleaded in terror. "Pray don't do it, sir."

"Tell us your name!" said the man. "Quick!" (Dickens, 1992 (1861), p. 3).

How to create a Dickensian character

Dickens is not strictly a realist since his characters are exaggerations, types and caricatures and act melodramatically. But this is why they are hyper-real. He uses specific narrative techniques to create them so vividly:

1. Name: He gives his character a name that embodies their personality or that is onomatopoeic or alliterative, associative or symbolic, such as Miss Havisham (have, shame, sham) and Estella (star).

2. Synecdoche – Physical description: He selects one physical characteristic to represent the whole of that character. For example, the convict who assaults Pip is manacled with a leg iron.

3. Mannerism: Dickens singles out one tic or mannerism that is repeated by the character and is used to identify him or her. For example, Uriah Heep rubs his hands constantly.

4. The character has a particular manner of speech or saying that is repeated too. For example, Uriah Heep again is always 'umble'.

5. An article of clothing is metonymous with the character and his or her personality or profession. For example, Miss Havisham's tattered wedding dress represents her refusal to let time move on.

Here is the first description in *Great Expectations* of Mrs Joe Gargery, Pip's guardian sister. Look for each of these five elements in the following passage:

> My sister, Mrs. Joe Gargery, was more than twenty years older than I, and had established a great reputation with herself and the neighbours because she had brought me up "by hand." Having at that time to find out for myself what the expression meant, and knowing her to have a hard and heavy hand, and to be much in the habit of laying it upon her husband as well

as upon me, I supposed that Joe Gargery and I were both brought up by hand.

My sister, Mrs. Joe, with black hair and eyes, had such a prevailing redness of skin that I sometimes used to wonder whether it was possible she washed herself with a nutmeg-grater instead of soap. She was tall and bony, and almost always wore a coarse apron, fastened over her figure behind with two loops, and having a square impregnable bib in front, that was stuck full of pins and needles. She made it a powerful merit in herself, and a strong reproach against Joe, that she wore this apron so much. Though I really see no reason why she should have worn it at all: or why, if she did wear it at all, she should not have taken it off, every day of her life (Dickens, 1992 (1861), p. 8).

 'DICKENSIAN CHARACTERISATION' EXERCISE

Write a passage similar to the one above about a character and create all five of the Dickensian devices to bring them to life.

Conclusion

Literary Realism is the foundation of the novel, even if that novel is speculative or supernatural. Readers expect that a novel will represent ordinary everyday things, people and events as they are, without implausible or romanticised elements. The realist novel will tend to deconstruct or demystify and employ abundant details and accurate scientific 'objective information' in order to create verisimilitude. Writers therefore need to create credibility (ethos) by making characters, events and plots believable and by grounding ideas in specific times and places.

References

Aristotle. 1991 (1380). *The Art of Rhetoric*. London: Penguin.

Cervantes, Miguel de. 1615. *Don Quixote Part II, Chapter XVII* (e-book). www.spanisharts.com/books/quijote/2chapter17.htm. Accessed 15 August 2018.

Cervantes, Miguel de. 1613. *The Exemplary Novels of Cervantes Translated by Walter K. Kelly* (e-book). The Project Gutenberg. www.gutenberg.org/files/14420/14420-h/14420-h.htm. Accessed 15 August 2018.

Defoe, Daniel. 1995 (1719). *Robinson Crusoe*. Hertfordshire: Wordsworth.

Dickens, Charles. 1992 (1861). *Great Expectations*. Hertfordshire: Wordsworth.

Eliot, George. 1994 (1871). *Middlemarch*. Hertfordshire: Wordsworth.

Homer. 2003. *The Odyssey*. London: Penguin.

Scott, Walter. 2000 (1824). *The Norton Anthology of English Literature*, vol. 2, 7th edition, ed. M. H. Abrams, 20–21. New York: Norton.

Sutherland, Kathryn. 2014. 'Jane Austen: social realism and the novel'. *Discovering Literature: Romantics & Victorians*. www.bl.uk/romantics-and-victorians/articles/jane-austens-social-realism-and-the-novel. Accessed 27 June 2019.

Swift, Jonathan. 2011 (1726). *Gulliver's Travels*. New York: Dover Publications (Thrift Study Edition).

Twain, Mark. 2018 (1884). *Adventures of Huckleberry Finn*. London: Arcturus Publishing Limited.

Watt, Ian. 2000 (1957). *The Rise of the Novel*. London: Pimlico.

3 MODERNISM: THE FRAGMENTATION OF REALITY

Realism remains the foundation of novel building. Readers expect verisimilitude and all the conventions of realism we associate with how the 'real' world is. But that is not how we experience the world. Realism is a flat convention. It is an absolute, monolithic, fundamentalist view of truth and is built on faulty premises.

In the late 19th century, philosophers and scientists questioned the way we perceive the world, and artists and writers followed: James Joyce, Virginia Woolf and William Faulkner showed us that reality is not realism. Reality is not an unquestioned 'given' but a perception of the world, a construction of our subjective senses. We do not have a God-like view of the world. We have only our own first-hand faulty view and the second-hand perceptions of others. The movement that reacted to and questioned Realism is broadly called Modernism.

Modernism

Modernism flourished in the first decades of the 20th century, arising from this cultural crisis of seeing the world. Modernism rocked literature, the sciences, philosophy, psychology, anthropology, painting, music, sculpture and architecture. What was it that shook the Victorian realist world view? Marx and Darwin's radical views threatened humanist self-confidence and caused a feeling of ideological uncertainty and undermined the certainty that the world was as it appeared. In physics, it was Einstein on relativity (1905) and Planck on quantum theory (1900). In philosophy, it was Nietzsche on *The Will to Power* (1901) and Bergson on *Time and Free Will* (1889). In psychology, William James on emotions and inner time ('What is an Emotion?', 1884), Freud on the unconscious (*The Interpretation of Dreams*, 1900), Jung on the collective unconscious and, in linguistics, de Saussure. These thinkers showed us that the appearance of our world that we had been led to believe as true was naïve, and

MODERNISM: THE FRAGMENTATION OF REALITY

they asked us to demystify the false superstructure to see the underlying truth of how the world was 'really' constructed.

Probably the best way to understand the differences between Realism and Modernism is to study a realist painting such as Gustave Courbet's *Un enterrement à Ornans* (1849–50) and then to study an Impressionist painting such as Claude Monet's *Impression, soleil levant* (1872). The artists are doing the same thing – capturing what a scene is 'really' like. But the realist painter thinks he can use pigments and shapes to show directly what 'is'; the modernist painter to show us how we see what we think 'is'.

In Monet's painting, what do you see? Your first answer might be this: a sunrise, water, boats. But this is not what you really are seeing. You are seeing colours, lines and shapes, and your brain has constructed these as boats, water and a sunrise. The landscape is not in the painting but in our head. This is how we construct reality. It is not 'out there'. What is out there is only sense impressions. This is why we can get it so wrong. A shimmer on the road is not water but only a false sense impression. An example is the DUCK/RABBIT figure:

(Kaninchen and Ente, 2019)

What is it? We construct it as a duck or a rabbit or both, which means it is neither. So too the picture of the old/young lady.[1] So too Monet's

---

[1] The ambiguous figure of the old woman/young lady was first attributed to a 19th-century German illustrator. The British cartoonist William Ely Hill (1887–1962) created a later version in *Puck* (1915).

painting. We can observe our minds constructing reality from the impression, thereby smashing the illusion that reality is out there.

>  **DUCK/RABBIT EXERCISE**
>
> Find an example when you were mistaken about the reality of a situation because your senses deceived you. Describe what you think you experienced and then write about the moment you realised that this impression was false.

Realism naturalises the mechanism by which we construct reality and so is invisible. But Modernist writers have taken it upon themselves to expose this mechanism of how we construct reality.

Henry James, in 'The Art of Fiction', advocated for an impressionist rather than a realist literature: 'a novel is in its broadest definition a personal impression of life…. The analogy between the art of the painter and the art of the novelist is "complete" and they may learn from each other; they may explain and sustain each other' (James, 1884, p. 188).

Impressions

We come to knowledge through sense perception – the awareness or apprehension of things by sight, hearing, touch, smell and taste. Even so, this is not a direct and immediate access to reality, but an instrument. We have only impressions. And what is an impression? A sensory perception, yes, but more – a belief, a suspicion about something.

Probably the best example of a literary work of Impressionism is Henry James's novella *The Turn of the Screw* (1898), in which a governess is charged to look after two children at a country estate. Through the governess's account, we are given the impression that the castle is haunted by evil ghosts who are trying to kidnap the children and eventually succeed in murdering one of them by the end. But we can equally take the view that the governess is imagining the ghosts. The techniques James uses to build up impressions are the literary equivalent of Monet's impressionist techniques, but the ambiguity created in *The Turn of the Screw* is the literary equivalent of the old/young lady picture or the duck/rabbit. If we read the text one way or the other, we get different impressions.

The following passage reveals the governess's first impression of the ghost. The passage is painted in lines, colours and movements:

> I can't express what followed it save by saying that the silence itself-which was indeed in a manner an attestation of my strength-became the element into which I saw the figure disappear; in which I definitely saw it turn, as I might have seen the low wretch to which it had once belonged turn on receipt of an order, and pass, with my eyes on the villainous back that no hunch could have more disfigured, straight down the staircase and into the darkness in which the next bend was lost (James, Henry, 2011 (1898), p. 48).

Perhaps this needs to be translated into simple modern English to see what the governess is saying:

> I can't really describe what I saw, but – and this shows how strong I was – the figure disappeared into the silence around it; I saw it turn – just as the servant this figure once was might have turned to obey an order – and I saw it had a hunchback – as it went down the staircase and into the darkness at the bottom.

No disputing that impression, but the reality of it could be called into question. Is she imagining it? Mistaken about what she saw? Or is there really a ghost?

The novella embroils us in the governess's impressions that not only are the ghosts after the children but the children themselves are part of the conspiracy, communicate with the ghosts, but then feign innocence to the governess. Is this paranoia, or is she correct? All she has are her impressions which she communicates with the housekeeper, Mrs Grose:

> "They know – it's too monstrous: they know, they know!"
> "And what on earth – ?" I felt her incredulity as she held me.
> [...]
> She turned right and left in her distress. "How can you be sure?"
> This drew from me, in the state of my nerves, a flash of impatience. "Then ask Flora – she's sure!" But I had no sooner spoken than I caught myself up. "No, for God's sake, don't!" She'll say she isn't – she'll lie!" (James, Henry, 2011 (1898), p. 37).

This may feel furiously opaque to a modern reader. But here we see the broad brushstrokes of a master impressionist. Did the little girl (Flora) see the ghost? Is she concealing this fact? Or is the governess projecting her own fears and constructing a false reality? Interestingly, the first interpretations of this story were 'realist' – that the governess was simply and unproblematically describing what was 'really' happening. But then Edmund Wilson in 1934 came up with the 'mad governess theory' and this was followed by a myriad of interpretations, including New Critical, Freudian and Queer.

> ✏️ **'DISAPPEARING INTO THE SILENCE' EXERCISE**
>
> Using the extract from *The Turn of the Screw* as a model, write a 300-word scene about an encounter with a ghost or other entity and create an impression of a 'reality' that could be interpreted another way.

Henry James maintains that a fiction writer's goal is to 'gather impressions'. All we have are what we can glean from our five senses and from our 'inner landscape' (what we think and feel) and out of these we construct theories about what we believe and what is out there with which we construct a narrative.

> ✏️ **IMPRESSIONIST EXERCISE**
>
> Freewrite an impression of someone. Give ONLY your sense impressions. What you see (think of Monet's Sunrise). Then write about your other impressions – what you feel, think and suspect about this person.

Stream of consciousness

We apprehend 'reality' through impressions, but we think not in a collage of impressions but in what William James, pioneering American psychologist and philosopher brother to novelist Henry James, called a 'stream of consciousness'. We do not think in sentences or realist descriptions but in an organic flow of thoughts.

> Consciousness, then, does not appear to itself chopped up in bits. Such words as 'chain' or 'train' do not describe it fitly as it

> presents itself in the first instance. It is nothing jointed; it flows. A 'river' or a 'stream' are the metaphors by which it is most naturally described. In talking of it hereafter let us call it the stream of thought, of consciousness, or of subjective life" (James, William, 1950 (1890, p. 239).

Stream of consciousness is a metaphor that describes that continuous flow of sensations, impressions, images, memories and thoughts in our minds.

Following William James, early Modernist writers wrote stream-of-consciousness narrative in order to provide a textual equivalent to the way we think and perceive the world. Such narratives create the impression that the reader is eavesdropping on the flow of conscious experience in the character's mind. They use narrative devices such as psycho-narration, free indirect style, associative and dissociative leaps in content, and creative use of punctuation.

James Joyce's succession of novels *A Portrait of the Artist as a Young Man* (1916), *Ulysses* (1920) and *Finnegan's Wake* (1939) experiment with this "stream". In *A Portrait of the Artist as a Young Man*, we see the world from the streamed consciousness of Stephen Dedalus at school:

> They all laughed again. Stephen tried to laugh with them. He felt his whole body hot and confused in a moment. What was the right answer to the question? He had given two and still Wells laughed. But Wells must know the right answer for he was in third of grammar. He tried to think of Wells's mother but he did not dare to raise his eyes to Wells's face. It was Wells who had shouldered him into the square ditch the day before because he would not swap his little snuffbox for Wells's seasoned hacking chestnut, the conqueror of forty. It was a mean thing to do; all the fellows said it was. And how cold and slimy the water had been! And a fellow had once seen a big rat jump plop into the scum (Joyce, 2000 (1916), p. 11).

In *Ulysses*, Joyce presents the reader with the raw interior consciousness of Leopold Bloom:

> if his nose bleeds youd think it was O tragic and that dying looking one off the south circular when he sprained his foot at the choir party at the sugarloaf Mountain the day I wore that

> dress Miss Stack bringing him flowers the worst old ones she could find at the bottom of the basket anything at all to get into a mans bedroom with her old maids voice trying to imagine he was dying on account of her to sever see thy face again though he looked more like a man with his beard a bit grown in the bed father was the same besides I hate bandaging and dosing when he cut his toe with the razor paring his corns afraid hed get blood poisoning (Joyce, 2010 (1922), p. 641).

Virginia Woolf's writing style incorporates a sophisticated form of stream of consciousness, and she argues that impressions are more like a shower of atoms:

> Examine for a moment an ordinary mind on an ordinary day. The mind receives a myriad impressions – trivial, fantastic, evanescent, or engraved with the sharpness of steel. From all sides they come, an incessant shower of innumerable atoms; and as they fall, as they shape themselves into the life of Monday or Tuesday, the accent falls differently from of old (Woolf, 2016, n.p. 1925).

In her novels, Woolf presents the reader with such incessant showers of impressions in her attempt to mimic the unstructured free flow of thought. Here, for example, is a moment of an ordinary mind on an ordinary day in the life of Mrs Dalloway:

> Such fools we all are, she thought, crossing Victoria Street. For Heaven only knows why one loves it so, how one sees it so, making it up, building it round one, tumbling it, creating it every moment afresh; but the veriest frumps, the most dejected of miseries sitting on doorsteps (drink their downfall) do the same; can't be dealt with, she felt positive, by Acts of Parliament for that very reason: they love life. In people's eyes, in the swing, tramp, trudge; in the bellow and the uproar; the carriages, motor cars, omnibuses, vans, sandwich men shuffling and swinging; brass bands; barrel organs; in the triumph and the jingle and the strange high singing of some aeroplane overhead was what she loved; life; London; this moment of June (Woolf, 2000 (1925), p. 4).

> ✏️ **'STREAM OF CONSCIOUSNESS' EXERCISE**
>
> Write down a stream of free-flowing consciousness for five minutes and observe how you wonder and wander and flow. Try to record (or imitate) in words exactly what is happening in your mind. Observe your thinking/consciousness/self-consciousness/awareness of self-consciousness. Time travel in past, present and future. Let your reader experience your thoughts and feelings and meanderings – your aliveness.

Interior monologue, free indirect discourse, and non-subordinating style

Here are some techniques that writers use to give us the impression of a stream of consciousness:

(a) interior monologue was first used extensively by Édouard Dujardin in *Les Lauriers sont coupés* (1887) to represent thoughts passing through the minds of the protagonists (organised by passing freely associated impressions), a conversation with oneself (as we do with speech rehearsal), or a soliloquy (talking to oneself).

> ✏️ **'TALKING TO YOURSELF' EXERCISE**
>
> Interior monologue – write down a real or imagined conversation you have had with yourself.

(b) free indirect discourse is a third-person narration that weaves in and out of characters' thoughts. The narrator (like an omniscient narrator) can access the consciousness of his or her character (be the character) and report as well as comment using the essential qualities and features of first-person direct speech but using the features of third-person indirect speech. The narrator takes on the mindset of a character and parrots his or her thoughts, sometimes making it difficult to tell the difference between the thoughts of the narrator and those of another character. A type of free indirect discourse is when the narrator's voice acquires the emotions and way of speaking of other characters, so that a deeper aspect of those characters is revealed. The difference between this and omniscient is that in the latter, the narrator can see into the minds of all the characters but stands outside of all of them whereas in free indirect discourse, the narrator inhabits each character intimately.

Oscar Wilde used free indirect discourse frequently in *The Picture of Dorian Gray* (1890). In the following paragraph, the narrator tells the reader what Lord Henry sees, perhaps even what Lord Henry thinks, but the reader cannot tell with complete assurance. Has the narrator merely described the direction Lord Henry is looking or entered Lord Henry's mind or has the focalisation shifted to Lord Henry?

> From the corner of the divan of Persian saddle-bags on which he was lying, smoking, as was his custom, innumerable cigarettes, Lord Henry Wotton could just catch the gleam of the honey-sweet and honey-coloured blossoms of a laburnum, whose tremulous branches seemed hardly able to bear the burden of a beauty so flame-like as theirs; and now and then the fantastic shadows of birds in flight flitted across the long tussore-silk curtains that were stretched in front of the huge window, producing a kind of momentary Japanese effect, and making him think of those pallid jade faced painters of Tokio who, through the medium of art that is necessarily immobile, seek to convey the sense of swiftness and motion. The sullen murmur of bees shouldering their way through the long unmown grass, circling with monotonous insistence round the dusty gilt horns of the straggling woodbine, seemed to make the stillness more oppressive. The dim roar of London was like the bourdon note of a distant organ (Wilde, 2001 (1890), p. 7).

✏ 'FREE INDIRECT DISCOURSE' EXERCISE

In a 300-word scene, be a narrator who can enter the minds of several characters and tell us what they are thinking.

(c) Non-subordinating style: Subordination means that all phrases in a sentence and all sentences in a paragraph should follow logically.

The sun is shining, and it has been shining all day. But stream of consciousness will break this pattern deliberately, and phrases that follow each other are not logically connected. This is in order to imitate the way the mind will suddenly switch from one topic to another, even in mid-sentence, by free association.

Stanley Fish marvels at how Woolf's non-subordinating style can 'stop on a dime, arrest action, freeze the frame, stay still at the same time the reader moves linearly' (Fish, 2012):

> She was now formidable to behold, and it was only in silence, looking up from their plates, after she had spoken so severely about Charles Tansley, that her daughters, Prue, Nancy, Rose – could sport with infidel ideas which they had brewed for themselves of a life different from hers: in Paris, perhaps; a wilder life; not always taking care of some man or other; for there was in all their minds a mute questioning of deference and chivalry, of the Bank of England and the Indian Empire, of ringed fingers and lace, though to them all there was something in this of the essence of beauty, which called out the manliness in their girlish hearts, and made them, as they sat at table beneath their mother's eyes, honour her strange severity, her extreme courtesy, like a queen's raising from the mud a beggar's dirty foot and washing it, when she thus admonished them so severely about that wretched atheist who had chased them to – or, speaking accurately, been invited to stay with them in – the Isles of Skye (Woolf, 1994 (1927), p. 3).

'Words', says Woolf (2015 (1942), n.p.), 'have a need of change ... because the truth they try to catch is many-sided, and they convey it by being themselves many-sided, flashing this way, then that'.

Erich Auerbach comments that Woolf attempts 'to render the flow and the play of consciousness adrift in the current of changing impressions' (Auerbach, 2013 (1946), p. 535). She has reversed the usual relationship between interior events and narrative events, where the former has always been subordinate to the latter and where inner thoughts comment on or prepare the ground for the movement of plot. But, in Woolf's case, the external events have lost their hegemony. They serve to release and interpret inner events.

> ✏️ **'MANY-SIDED TRUTH' EXERCISE**
>
> Imitate the above passage in a 300-word narrative in which external events are subordinate to inner events. Attempt to portray the changing impressions of a character's mind.

Kaleidoscopic stream of consciousness

Across the pond, American writers were also experimenting with stream of consciousness: William Faulkner used the technique in a kaleidoscopic way, presenting his readers with a myriad of impressions from different perspectives. *As I Lay Dying* (1930) is the story of a funeral told from many streams or perspectives. *The Sound and the Fury* (1929) tells a story from four points of view, converging to give us an overall impression of life on the farm. Here is a passage of Benjy's thinking (Benjy is disabled and cannot speak):

> Caddy uncaught me and we crawled through. Uncle Maury said to not let anybody see us, so we better stoop over, Caddy said. Stoop over, Benjy. Like this, see. We stooped over and crossed the garden, where the flowers rasped and rattled against us. The ground was hard. We climbed the fence, where the pigs were grunting and snuffing. I expect they're sorry because one of them got killed today, Caddy said. The ground was hard, churned and knotted. Keep your hands in your pockets, Caddy said. Or they'll get froze. You dont want your hands froze on Christmas, do you (Faulkner, 1995 (1929), p. 2).

Fictional autobiography

In Chapter 2, we examined the fictional autobiography of *Robinson Crusoe* (1719), *Gulliver's Travels* (1726) and Charles Dickens's *Great Expectations* (1861). Dickens's novels in the Realist tradition would often give us a first-person account of a life but told in retrospect to give it objectivity. Here, for example, is the beginning of Dickens's *David Copperfield* (1850):

> To begin my life with the beginning of my life, I record that I was born (as I have been informed and believe) on a Friday, at

twelve o'clock at night. It was remarked that the clock began to strike, and I began to cry, simultaneously. In consideration of the day and hour of my birth, it was declared by the nurse, and by some sage women in the neighbourhood who had taken a lively interest in me several months before there was any possibility of our becoming personally acquainted, first, that I was destined to be unlucky in life; and secondly, that I was privileged to see ghosts and spirits; both these gifts inevitably attaching, as they believed, to all unlucky infants of either gender, born towards the small hours on a Friday night (Dickens, 1992 (1850), p. 1).

But that is not how we live our lives. A modernist fictional autobiography would look and feel very different. How then would an impressionist narrative read of the same subject matter? Joyce's modernist fictional autobiography *A Portrait of the Artist as a Young Man* finds the sense impressions that a young child would have and presents these unmediated to the reader as memory:

> Once upon a time and a very good time it was there was a moocow coming down along the road and this moocow that was coming down along the road met a nicens little boy named baby tuckoo
> His father told him that story: his father looked at him through a glass: he had a hairy face.
> He was baby tuckoo. The moocow came down the road where Betty Byrne lived: she sold lemon platt.
> O, the wild rose blossoms
> On the little green place.
> He sang that song. That was his song.
> O, the green wothe botheth.
> When you wet the bed first it is warm then it gets cold. His mother put on the oilsheet. That had the queer smell.
> His mother had a nicer smell than his father. She played on the piano the sailor's hornpipe for him to dance. He danced:
> Tralala lala,
> Tralala tralaladdy,
> Tralala lala,
> Tralala lala (Joyce, 2000 (1916), p. 3).

> ✏️ **BABY TUCKOO EXERCISE**
>
> Write a 300-word passage that describes an early memory from your childhood, told as a series of impressions, as Joyce does in the above extract.

The unconscious

The idea that there is a vast unknown territory to be explored beneath the surface of what we thought was all known utterly transformed art and culture in the early 20th century.

Sigmund Freud (1856–1938), Austrian psychologist and psychotherapist, proposed the (then) preposterous theory that most of our mind is not accessible to us and has been deliberately hidden in order to protect us from our deepest traumas and forbidden desires. His method of investigating this unconscious mind was psychotherapy, through analysis of dreams and free association.

> The unconscious system may therefore be compared to a large ante-room, in which the various mental excitations are crowding upon one another, like individual beings. Adjoining there is a second, smaller appartment, a sort of reception-room, in which consciousness resides. But on the threshold between the two there stands a personage with the office of door-keeper, who examines the various mental excitations, censors them, and denies them admittance to the reception-room when he disapproves of them (Freud, 1996, p. 566).

Woolf, in particular, was excited by this metaphor, vowing to penetrate into 'the source beneath the surface, the very oyster within the shell' (Woolf, 2015 (1942), p. 15) and to explore 'the upper' and 'the under' of our minds (Ibid, p. 163).

Carl G. Jung (1875–1961), Swiss psychiatrist, influential thinker and the founder of analytical psychology, went further in understanding the psyche through exploring dreams, art mythology, world religion and philosophy, coining the phrase the 'collective unconscious' as a cultural memory containing myths and beliefs of the human race which work at a symbolic level.

Modernist writers grew interested in dreams as access to the unconscious to the reality beneath our repressed egos and experimented with methods to access this vast reserve of subjective creativity. Later in the century, writers would advocate for an automatic or spontaneous writing to tap into the unconscious. Jack Kerouac, for example, practised 'spontaneous prose':

> If possible write "without consciousness" in semi-trance (as Yeats' later "trance writing") allowing subconscious to admit in own uninhibited interesting necessary and so "modern" language what conscious art would censor, and write excitedly, swiftly, with writing-or-typing-cramps, in accordance (as from center to periphery) with laws of orgasm, Reich's "beclouding of consciousness." Come from within, out-to relaxed and said (Kerouac, 1958, n.p.).

Time

The French philosopher Henri Bergson (1858–1941) examined the notion of time and made some interesting claims: time is mobile and incomplete; for the individual, time speeds up or slows down; and in order to explore 'real' time, we need to explore the inner life of man [sic]. Time is a construct and duration can be grasped only through intuition and imagination.

Time in realist novels is taken for granted as linear, regular and durable. But modernist writers began to play with notions of the fluidity of time and the awareness of time.

Marcel Proust, for example, in *In Search of Lost Time (À la recherche du temps perdu)*, considered one of the most influential novels in the 20th century, attempts to 'capture' time in memory and, more importantly, in words. Here is the famed passage where he realises that through describing a memory, time can be captured or at least relived:

> No sooner had the warm liquid mixed with the crumbs touched my palate than a shudder ran through me and I stopped, intent upon the extraordinary thing that was happening to me. An exquisite pleasure had invaded my senses, something isolated, detached, with no suggestion of its origin. And at once the vicissitudes of life had become indifferent to

> me, its disasters innocuous, its brevity illusory – this new sensation having had on me the effect which love has of filling me with a precious essence; or rather this essence was not in me it was me. ... Whence did it come? What did it mean? How could I seize and apprehend it? ... And suddenly the memory revealed itself. The taste was that of the little piece of madeleine which on Sunday mornings at Combray (because on those mornings I did not go out before mass), when I went to say good morning to her in her bedroom, my aunt Léonie used to give me, dipping it first in her own cup of tea or tisane. The sight of the little madeleine had recalled nothing to my mind before I tasted it. And all from my cup of tea (Proust, 2003 (1908), p. 48).

Another example is Woolf's *To the Lighthouse*. In the central section of the novel, 'Time Passes', the narrative rushes through time as a sped-up movie would. In this section, told in an omniscient point of view, ten years pass:

> then again silence fell; and then, night after night, and sometimes in plain midday when the roses were bright and light turned on the wall its shape clearly there seemed to drop into this silence this indifference, this integrity, the thud of something falling.
> [A shell exploded. Twenty or thirty young men were blown up in France, among them Andrew Ramsay, whose death, mercifully, was instantaneous.] (Woolf, 1994 (1927), p. 207).

Following Bergson's principles, modernist writers inhabited the space and time of stream of consciousness as subjective fluid time. No longer the past-present-future, time is simultaneous: 'the knowledge of some other part of the stream, past or future, near or remote, is always mixed in with our knowledge of the present thing' (James, William, 1892, pp. 396–397).

'TIME FLUID' EXERCISE

Using the Proust example above, capture a moment in time by describing in a 300-word passage a memory of a specific sensual event.

Conclusion

Modernist texts are overtly experimental in their attempt to expose the conventions of perception, time, the conscious, and narrative. These texts are often characterised by their lack of traditional chronological narrative (discontinuous narrative), breaking of narrative frames (fragmentation), multiple narrative points of view, use of interior monologue/stream-of-consciousness technique, and their perspectivism: locating meaning in the viewpoint of the individual and the subjective rather than the omniscient, 'objective'. Modernist texts will prioritise impressions and imitate the texture of lived experience and examine how we know and perceive the world.

References

Auerbach, Erich. 2013 (1946). *Mimesis: The Representation of Reality in Western Literature*. Oxfordshire: Princeton University Press.

Dickens, Charles. 1992 (1850). *David Copperfield*. Hertfordshire: Wordsworth.

Faulkner, William. 1995 (1929). *The Sound and the Fury*. London: Vintage.

Fish, Stanley. 2012. *How to Write a Sentence: And How to Read One*. New York: Harpercollins Publishing.

Freud, Sigmund. 1996. *The Major Works of Sigmund Freud*. Chicago: Encyclopedia Britannica.

James, Henry. 2011 (1898). *The Turn of the Screw*. London: Penguin Classics.

James, Henry. 1884. 'The Art of Fiction', *Longman's Magazine* 4, September.

James, William. 1950 (1890). The Stream of Consciousness. *The Principles of Psychology*. New York: Dover Publications, Inc.

Joyce, James. 2000 (1916). *A Portrait of the Artist as a Young Man*. London: Penguin.

Joyce, James. 2010 (1922). *Ulysses*. Hertfordshire: Wordsworth.

Kaninchen and Ente. 2019. https://commons.wikimedia.org/wiki/File:Kaninchen_und_Ente.png. Accessed 30 June 2019.

Kerouac, Jack. 1958. Essentials of Spontaneous Prose. *Evergreen Review*. www.writing.upenn.edu/~afilreis/88/kerouac-spontaneous.html. Accessed 16 August 2018.

Proust, Marcel. 2003 (1908). *In Search of Lost Time (À la recherche du temps perdu)*. London: Penguin.

Wilde, Oscar. 2001 (1890). *The Picture of Dorian Gray*. Hertfordshire: Wordsworth.

Woolf, Virginia. 2000 (1925). *Mrs Dalloway*. London: Penguin.

Woolf, Virginia. 1994 (1927). *To the Lighthouse*. London: Wordsworth.

Woolf, Virginia. 2016 (1921). *The Common Reader* https://ebooks.adelaide.edu.au/w/woolf/virginia/w91c/chapter13.html.

Woolf, Virginia. 2015 (1942). *The Death of the Moth, and other essays*. Adelaide: eBooks@Adelaide. https://ebooks.adelaide.edu.au/w/woolf/virginia/w91d/chapter24.html. Accessed 16 August 2018.

4 MINIMALISM: LESS IS MORE

'Minimalism' is a relatively new term. It began to be applied to literary works in the second half of the 20th century, but the minimalist movement has been around much longer. It was led by an eclectic group of vigilant artists who sought to curb the flowery exuberances of the Romantics and Modernists and melodramatists and overwriters of every age. It is essentially a realist movement that endeavoured to purge language of excess.

Recently, Minimalism has come to mean leading a simple lifestyle and avoiding excessive consumerism. But Minimalism as an art movement began in the early 20th century.

Minimalism in visual art and music

Perhaps the most extreme example of minimalism is John Cage's 3'44" (1952), a piece of 'music' in which not one note is played. Or the near monochrome paintings of Ad Reinhardt (1975), who declared: 'The more stuff in it, the busier the work of art, the worse it is. More is less. Less is more' (Reinhardt, 1992 (1975), p. 204).

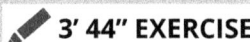 **3' 44" EXERCISE**

Listen to John Cage's piece and freewrite for the entire 3 minutes and 44 seconds to fill the silence with your own thoughts about minimalism.

For writers, Minimalism is a useful tool to help us become better at our craft. It is largely the method employed in writing workshops. If you have ever been in a creative writing workshop, you will have noticed that it operates under often assumed hidden assumptions, that of an I.A. Richards model of practical criticism (the text is sufficient to produce meaning), and a set of minimalist practices: show don't tell, less is more, cut it out, the adverb is not your friend, make the verbs work. Cut, cut, cut.

Fancy versus plain prose

Annie Dillard divides contemporary prose styles into two simplistic strands: fancy and plain. She praises plain style as clear, unambiguous and even 'democratic':

> [Plain style] does not explain events in all their ramifications; it does not color a scene emotionally so that a reader knows what he should feel. This prose is humble. It does not call attention to itself but to the world. It is intimate with character; it is sympathetic and may be democratic [...] It praises the world by seeing it (Dillard, 1981, p. 120).
> She characterises this minimalist style as prose which avoids too much punctuation, complex imagery and vocabulary and 'is not an end in itself but a means' (ibid, pp. 116–117).

Dillard's manifesto, one that extols the virtues of bare, simple, honest prose, has been repeated throughout the 20th century as the model for good writing.

Haiku

Perhaps we need to go back a thousand years to get to the root of minimalism. Haiku (literally 'cutting') is a Japanese poetic form that juxtaposes two images or ideas with a *kireji* [cutting word] between them. The effect is to create a gap in which the reader or listener must create the meaning. The images juxtaposed are usually everyday objects or occurrences. For example, here's the master of the haiku, Bashō Matsuo:

> Old pond
> frogs jumped in
> sound of water
> (Matsuo, 1686).

An English-language haiku has the following characteristics:

1. 17 total syllables
2. three lines of 5-7-5 syllables (or breaths)
3. Two simple subjects are often placed in juxtaposition and often separated by punctuation. The first part is the set up and the second part is the 'punchline'.
4. A keen or unusual observation is made by comparing the two subjects.
5. often contains a seasonal reference, about the natural world

Another example is Murakami Kijo:

> First autumn morning:
> the mirror I stare into
> shows my father's face (Kijo, 1917).

> **🖋 'UNEXPECTED LEAP' EXERCISE**
>
> **Write a Haiku in this format, focusing on two simple subjects while providing an unexpected perspective. This will help you find the exact word, be minimalist and create the gap between the words.**

The imagists: an instant of time

In the early 20th century, the Imagists sought to do a similar thing. They were at the forefront of the Modernist movement and reacted against Romanticism and ornate Victorian poetry, emphasising simplicity, clarity of expression, and precision, using the 'exact' visual image.

Imagism was founded by English poet T.E. Hulme, who in his essay 'Romanticism and Classicism' argued for accuracy and simplicity. For Hulme, the language of poetry is a 'visual concrete one […] Images in verse are not mere decoration, but the very essence' and what he called the 'hard, dry image' (Hulme, 2003 (1924), p. 68).

Imagism resembled haiku in its concise, simple and concrete images and its minimalism and its capture of a simple moment. Ezra Pound argued that the image 'presents an intellectual and emotional complex in an instant of time' (Pound, 1913a, 1913b, p. 200). See, for example, his

Imagist poem, 'In a Station of the Metro' or fellow Imagist William Carlos Williams's 'The Red Wheelbarrow' (1923).

In March 1913, the Imagist manifesto, which included the following aims, was published:

1. To use the language of common speech, but to employ the exact word, not the nearly-exact, nor the merely decorative word […].

2. To present an image. We are not a school of painters, but we believe that poetry should render particulars exactly and not deal in vague generalities, however magnificent and sonorous. It is for this reason that we oppose the cosmic poet, who seems to us to shirk the real difficulties of his art.

3. To produce a poetry that is hard and clear, never blurred nor indefinite.

4. Finally, most of us believe that concentration is of the very essence of poetry (Lowell, 1917, n.p.).

> ✎ **'SO MUCH DEPENDS' EXERCISE**
>
> Write an Imagist poem. Present one simple image in words, simply, using the language of common speech, the exact word, rendering details particularly, concentrated, like a red wheelbarrow or a metro crowd scene.

Le mot juste

Imagism has roots in 19th-century French realism in prose writers like Gustav Flaubert, who argued that 'the exact word' or *le mot juste* was necessary to give writing its power: 'All talent for writing consists, after all, of nothing more than choosing words. It's precision that gives writing power' (Flaubert, 1856 cited in Hamrick, 2017, n.p.). We need only to read an excerpt from Flaubert's celebrated novel *Madame Bovary* (1856) to see this power at work:

> Seen from close, her eyes appeared larger than life, especially when she opened and shut her eyelids several times on awakening: black when looked at in the shadow, dark blue in bright light, they seemed to contain layer upon layer

of color, thicker and cloudier beneath, lighter and more transparent toward the lustrous surface (Flaubert, 1994 (1856), p. 76).

Flaubert's 'right word' is unsullied by sentimentality, his prose *lisse comme un marbre et furieux comme un tigre* (hard as marble on the surface and furious as a tiger' (Byatt, 2002, n.p.).

So following ('underneath') the description of Madame Bovary is this:

Deep down, all the while, she was waiting for something to happen. Like a sailor in distress, she kept casting desperate glances over the solitary waster of her life, seeking some white sail in the distant mists of the horizon. She had no idea by what wind it would reach her, toward what shore it would bear her, or what kind of craft it would be – tiny boat or towering vessel, laden with heartbreaks or filled to the gunwales with rapture. But every morning when she awoke she hoped that today would be the day; she listened for every sound, gave sudden starts, was surprised when nothing happened; and then, sadder with each succeeding sunset, she longed for tomorrow (Flaubert, 1994 (1856), p. 76).

'HARD AS MARBLE' EXERCISE

Write a 100-word description of a person, thing or place and choose your words carefully to avoid sentimentality. Use precision. Now add a 200-word 'underneath' passage that reveals what is bubbling underneath this description.

Strunk and White: make every word tell

In the 20th century, such Flaubertian precision of words, simple language and minimalist style prevailed and were synonymous with 'good' writing (this assumption will be deconstructed in Chapter 9). This style of writing owes its popularity to two men: William Strunk (1869–1946) and E.B. White (author of *Charlotte's Web* (1952) and *Stuart Little* (1945)). In 1920, Strunk published a style guide, a book which became the bible of writing style. In 1959, White expanded the book and it has been used ever since in many English departments, schools and writing guides as the practical golden standard for all writing. In 2011, *Time* named it one of the 100 best and most influential books written in English since 1923.

Our prejudices about what constitutes good writing – that simple is best and that adverbs and adjectives are unnecessary verbiage – derive mostly from this book. Creative writing pedagogy shamelessly lifted these tenets for its model of how to write: 'the adverb is not your friend' (King, 2010, p. 118); 'semicolons are transvestite hermaphrodites representing absolutely nothing' (Vonnegut cited in Dolnick, 2012).

The philosophy behind *The Elements of Style* (2014 (1918)) – that the 'right word' is necessary to give writing power – is Minimalism. Omit needless words. Use the active voice. Write plain English:

> Vigorous writing is concise. A sentence should contain no unnecessary words, a paragraph no unnecessary sentences, for the same reason that a drawing should have no unnecessary lines and a machine no unnecessary parts. This requires not that the writer make all his sentences short, or that he avoid all detail and treat his subjects only in outline, but that he make every word tell (Strunk and White, 2014 (1918), p. 24).

The aim, Strunk insists, is simply 'to write plain English adequate for everyday uses' (Strunk and White, 2014 (1918)).

> **'PLAIN ENGLISH' EXERCISE**
>
> Take one of your earlier pieces of writing, such as a chapter from a novel, and apply Strunk and White's rules to rewrite your prose in simple plain English.

Orwell's newspeak

Plain, simple, Minimalist writing became the norm in 20th- and 21st-century textbooks on how to write. But it was George Orwell who in 1948 pointed out the underlying ideological and political reasons why simple writing was imperative. Imprecise English was dangerous.

> You think, I dare say, that our chief job is inventing new words. But not a bit of it! We're destroying words – scores of them, hundreds

of them, every day. We're cutting the language down to the bone. The Eleventh Edition won't contain a single word that will become obsolete before the year 2050... (Orwell, 2008 (1949), p. 54).

In Orwell's novel *1984* (1949), Big Brother's project is to limit thought:

> Don't you see that the whole aim of Newspeak is to narrow the range of thought? In the end we shall make thoughtcrime literally impossible, because there will be no words in which to express it. Every concept that can ever be needed, will be expressed by exactly one word, with its meaning rigidly defined and all its subsidiary meanings rubbed out and forgotten... Every year fewer and fewer words, and the range of consciousness always a little smaller (ibid, p. 55).

In these passages, it appears as if Orwell is arguing that such Minimalist reduction of the English language is destructive. But he is arguing that such language is manipulative and obfuscating. Linguistic decline occurs when governments use language to serve their ideologies. Newspeak narrows the range of thought and renders dissent 'literally impossible, because there will be no words in which to express it' (ibid).

1984 saw a resurgence in its popularity in the US in 2016 when Donald Trump came to power. It was a *New York Times* number-one bestseller along with apocalyptic novels about censorship and restricting free speech. Why? Because people recognised the way Newspeak was being resurrected in right-wing media, such as Fox News, and anything contrary to the monolithic discourse was seen as 'fake news'.

1984 also exposed the notion of 'doublethink', which is the

> power of holding two contradictory beliefs in one's mind simultaneously, and accepting both of them... To tell deliberate lies while genuinely believing in them, to forget any fact that has become inconvenient, and then, when it becomes necessary again, to draw it back from oblivion for just as long as it is needed, to deny the existence of objective reality and all the while to take account of the reality which one denies – all this is indispensably necessary (ibid, p. 223).

Orwell's ideas and the roots of his concept of Newspeak are articulated in his seminal 1946 essay 'Politics and the English Language', which criticises the 'ugly and inaccurate' English being disseminated through the media of his time. Orwell connects political oppression with the manipulation of words into propaganda. Political language 'is designed to make lies sound truthful and murder respectable, and to give an appearance of solidity to pure wind' (Orwell, 2010 (1946), n.p.). Unclear prose is used by political instruments to hide the truth rather than express it, a 'contagion', a 'packet of aspirins always at one's elbow' (ibid).

The remedy? Concreteness and clarity, outlined in his six 'rules', which, similar to Strunk's, suggest avoiding complex wording, passive construction of sentences, clichéd imagery, and obscure phrasing.

Ernest Hemingway's masculine, muscular prose

> If a man writes clearly enough any one can see if he fakes. If he mystifies to avoid a straight statement, which is very different from breaking so-called rules of syntax or grammar to make an effect which can be obtained in no other way, the writer takes a longer time to be known as a fake and other writers who are afflicted by the same necessity will praise him in their own defence.... (Hemingway, 2000 (1932), pp. 53–54).

Ernest Hemingway, the literary child of Flaubert, seeks 'straight', 'true' and 'competent' writing: 'All you have to do is write one true sentence', he goes. 'Write the truest sentence that you know' (Hemingway, 2010 (1960), p. 12).

His Nobel prize–winning 1952 novella *The Old Man and the Sea* shows best his attempt to do this. It is a simple tale but reveals his Minimalist method:

> He looked across the sea and knew how along he was now. But he could see the prisms in the deep dark water and the line stretching ahead and the strange undulation of calm. The clouds were building up now or the trade wind and he looked ahead and saw a flight of wild ducks etching themselves against the sky over the water, then blurring, then etching again and he knew no man was ever alone on the sea (Hemingway, 2000 (1952), p. 67).

Note the absence of figurative imagery, the hypotaxis (and... and... and), simple English, lack of adjectives and adverbs (the only one used is 'strange'), the Imagist style of presenting concrete images, physical descriptions, and the Haiku leap across a gap to a conclusion that reveals the tiger underneath.

David Lodge notes that Hemingway's minimalism, like Orwell's, arises from a belief that simple language denotes actual things and gives us true experience of the world:

> 'fine writing' falsified experience, and strove to 'put down what really happened in action, what the actual things were which produced the emotion that you experienced' by using simple, denotative language purged of stylistic decoration (Lodge, 2011 (1992), p. 90).

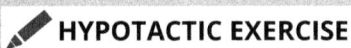

HYPOTACTIC EXERCISE

Write a 300-word narrative that imitates the above passage. Avoid figurative imagery and adjectives and adverbs. Use hypotaxis (and... and... and), simple English, concrete images, and physical descriptions. Then write a final sentence that makes the haiku leap.

Omission

Hemingway does more than simply describe true experience. His minimalist techniques involve 'literary omission'. He argues that:

> as long as the writer omitted "important things or events" deliberately and with a profound knowledge of the omitted content, the story would be strengthened by the omission because readers would "feel something more than they understood" (Hemingway cited in Johnston, 1984, p. 68).

Simple language is deceptive: the 'surface detail of the story rests upon and grows out of foundations of hidden, though imperative information' (Johnston, 1984, p. 69). An iceberg's power, Hemingway argues, is that most of it is under water.

Therefore, readers need to deduce the underlying 'true' story under the surface simplicity of the words. The writer must use 'indirection, suggestion and implication, rather than outright omission' (Johnston, 1984, p. 69) and 'dispassionate and understated prose'. Just as Freud's unconscious is buried under the surface, Hemingway argues that minimalist writing helps expose 'things of a shocking nature' that have been 'omitted'. For example, *Hills Like White Elephants* (1927) tells the surface story of a conversation between a couple, omitting the underlying issue.

> 'It's really an awfully simple operation, Jig', the man said. 'It's not really an operation at all.'
> The girl looked at the ground the table legs rested on.
> 'I know you wouldn't mind it, Jig. It's really not anything. It's just to let the air in.'
> The girl did not say anything (Hemingway, 1955 (1927), p. 52).

This has been interpreted to be a decision about abortion yet it is never mentioned and is left to the reader to infer.

Overwriting, a common problem with writers, is telling the reader too much. The following exercise will help eliminate overwriting.

✎ 'LETTING THE AIR IN' EXERCISE

Using the Hemingway example above, write a 300-word scene about an issue, a decision to be made, or a conflict between two people and omit the essential details. To help the reader deduce the underlying 'true' story under the surface simplicity of the words, ensure that the story is not too obscure.

Raymond Carver's 'aesthetic delight'

The American short story writer Raymond Carver carried the minimalist torch into the latter part of the 20th century, advocating commonplace but precise language as the way to give direct access not only to 'true' experience but to 'aesthetic delight':

> It's possible, in a poem or a short story, to write about commonplace things and objects using commonplace but

precise language, and to endow those things – a chair, a window curtain, a fork, a stone, a woman's earring – with immense, even startling power. It is possible to write a line of seemingly innocuous dialogue and have it send a chill along the reader's spine – the source of artistic delight, as Nabokov would have it. That's the kind of writing that most interests me. I hate sloppy or haphazard writing whether it flies under the banner of experimentation or else is just clumsily rendered realism. In Isaac Babel's wonderful short story, "Guy de Maupassant", the narrator has this to say about the writing of fiction: "No iron can pierce the heart with such force as a period [or full stop] put just at the right place" (Carver, 1981, n.p.).

Look, for example, at this passage of Carver's where he uses Hemingway's simple English:

> I was in bed when I heard the gate. I listened carefully. I didn't hear anything else. But I heard that. I tried to wake Cliff. He was passed out. So I got up and went to the window. A big moon was laid over the mountains that went around the city. It was a white moon and covered with scars. Any damn fool could imagine a face there (Carver, 2003 (1981), p. 26).

If we look at an earlier version of this story (Carver was renowned for editing his stories even after they were published), we see how he has pared down the details even more from this version:

> I was in bed when I heard the gate unlatch. I listened carefully. I didn't hear anything else. But I had heard that. I tried to wake cliff, but he was passed out. So I got up and went to the window. A big moon hung over the mountains that surrounded the city. It was a white moon and covered with scars, easy enough to imagine a face there – eye sockets, nose, even the lips.

The moon here is the object that can send a chill along the reader's spine. That is the source of artistic delight.

> **'SEND A CHILL ALONG THE READER'S SPINE' EXERCISE**
>
> Take a passage or chapter of a novel you are writing and edit it as Carver has done in the above example. Use precise words and make sure the punctuation is in the right place. Try to 'send a chill along the reader's spine'.

Cormac McCarthy: the sacred idiom shorn of its referents

Cormac McCarthy takes the minimalist baton and runs with it. In *The Road* (2006), he demonstrates why his pared-back prose is appropriate for his gritty violent realist stories. In a post-apocalyptic world where the objects are disappearing, the words for those objects are also disappearing. The style of his novel reflects this:

> The world shrinking down about a raw core of parsible entities. The names of things slowly following those things into oblivion. Colors. The names of birds. Things to eat. Finally the names of things one believed to be true. More fragile than he would have thought. How much was gone already? The sacred idiom shorn of its referents and so of its reality (McCarthy, 2009 (2006), p. 93).

McCarthy alludes to de Saussure's notion that the sign (the word) and its referent (the thing in the world that a word or phrase denotes or stands for) are only arbitrarily connected. de Saussure states that the relationship between a sign and the real-world thing it denotes is an arbitrary one. There is not a natural relationship between a word and the object it refers to, nor is there a causal relationship between the inherent properties of the object and the nature of the sign used to denote it. The sign relation is dyadic, consisting only of a form of the sign (the signifier) and its meaning (the signified). de Saussure saw this relation as being essentially arbitrary, motivated only by social convention.

This undermines previous Realist writers' claims that they can reproduce the real world accurately with simple words that correspond in a one-to-one relation and thereby give us the 'truth'. There is no simple connection. Furthermore, without the real thing, the word will disappear too.

The Road echoes this loss of words. The novel is composed mostly of sentence fragments and sentences which are broken and static. Apostrophes are shorn off, so we have dialogues with 'dont', 'wont' and so on. Sentences, when complete, are often parataxical and hypotaxical, stretched to reveal the void underneath them, or blunted to show that they will take us nowhere.

> When he got back the boy was still asleep. He pulled the blue plastic tarp off of him and folded it and carried it out to the grocery cart and packed it and came back with their plates and some cornmeal cakes in a plastic bag and a plastic bottle of syrup. He spread the small tarp they used for a table on the ground and laid everything out and he took the pistol from his belt and laid it on the cloth and then he just sat watching the boy sleep...The boy turned in the blankets. Then he opened his eyes. Hi, Papa, he said.
>
> I'm right here.
> I know (McCarthy, 2009 (2006), p. 3).

 'SHORN OF ITS REFERENTS' EXERCISE

Write a 300-word McCarthy-style passage in which you experiment with Minimalist form:

1. Use sentence fragments and parataxis interspersed with long hypotaxical sentences.
2. Avoid apostrophes where possible.
3. Avoid speech tags and the use of quotations marks.
4. Use simple, dry, plain minimalist prose.

Problems with minimalism

Minimalism is a method more than a movement and has insidiously corkscrewed its way into our culture as 'good' writing. At school, we are taught to use adverbs and adjectives; at university and college writing programs, we are taught to take them out. 'Fancy', complicated prose is pejorative. Simple equals honest, straightforward and plain equal truth. There is merit in this method as a cure for overwriting, and if you have ever participated in a writing workshop, you have probably been trained in this style. Minimalism, however, appears to be a very 'masculine' way of being in the world, and all the examples of Minimalist writers in this chapter have been men.

Critics of Minimalism charge that it is reductive, detached and unemotional. Orwell's criticism of linguistic manipulation for political ends may itself be a charge against Minimalism.

> The primary aim of Newspeak is to reduce the meaning of language as well as the number of words possible. To this end, Newspeak removes all synonyms and antonyms.... Synonyms do not exist; words like satisfying, great, or excellent, for example, would all revert merely to some form of the word good.... Comparative and superlative adjectives are dispatched in a similar manner: for example, there is no word for better or best in Newspeak.... By reducing the number of words available, as well as reducing the intensity and emotion behind the words that people in Nineteen Eighty-Four can use, The Party is able to further suppress their population's thought and emotions....By limiting the number of ways to describe the world, The Party is able to limit the population's very perception of the world (Orwell, 2008 (1949), p.23).

So too de Saussure's separation of sign and referent makes us question claims by Hemingway and Flaubert that minimalist writing gets to the 'truth', to 'real' things.

Masculine prose

You may have noticed that much of what is considered good writing in this book or 'Great literature' is overtly gendered. Hemingway's 'muscular', 'macho', masculine prose, for example, is a brutally minimalist, unemotional, and objective style. As expected, his prose divides things into neat binaries:

> He always thought of the sea as la mar which is what people call her in Spanish when they love her. Sometimes those who love her say bad things of her but they are always said as though she were a woman. Some of the younger fishermen...

> spoke of her as el mar which is masculine. They spoke of her as a contestant or a place or even an enemy. But the old man always thought of her as feminine and as something that gave or withheld great favours, and if she did wild or wicked things it was because she could not help them. The moon affects her as it does a woman, he thought (Hemingway, 2000 (1952), p. 10).

Similarly, Chuck Palahniuk sets out in *Fight Club* (1996) to create a masculine space in opposition, and reaction, to the feminine, a 'man-cave' of a novel that advocates masculine self-actualisation:

> Bookstores were full of books like the Joy Luck Club and the Divine Secrets of the Ya-Ya Sisterhood and How to Make an American Quilt. These were all novels that presented a social model for women to be together. But there was no novel that presented a new social model for men to share their lives (Palahniuk, 2006 (1996), p. 214).

'Good' writing as gendered writing

A common binary occurs in our own writing backyard. 'Good' writing is most often promoted and taught in creative writing programs as strong hard prose and muscular straightforward minimalism, whereas 'bad' writing is flowery, emotional and spontaneous.

However, 'affectation itself', Stephen King argues, 'beginning with the need to define some sorts of writing as "good" and other sorts as "bad", is fearful behavior' (2000, p. 128). Theodor Adorno goes further: 'lucidity, objectivity, and concise precision', he claims, are 'invented ideologies for [editors and writers'] own accommodation [...] for the sake of their incomes' (1990, p. 303). The concept of 'good' writing has been constructed by a power group, and membership into that power group is dictated by following certain rules.

Minimalism breeds its own style of bad writing. If bad writing is in part laziness in observation of details, derivative in that it imitates, bad writing can also be disengagement with the sensual, the sensible and the corporeal. Often, minimalist writing creates a flawless style but lacks substance and gravitas. How many workshops have you attended where the perfect story has been workshopped and clinically styled but still leaves the reader with a sense of disengagement and 'so what'-ness? Critics of minimalism argue that this style of sparse limited prose focuses on the mundane and mediocre and that 'its pared down and…inexplicit aesthetic necessarily inculcates an…impoverished and ultimately valueless effect upon its reader' (Greany, 2012, n.p.). Madison Smartt Bell disputes the idea of 'less is more' and suggests quite adamantly that 'less is less' (1986). John Aldridge labels minimalism 'assembly-line' fiction and calls it 'unoriginal, homogenised and ultimately of little value' (1992, p. 7). Minimalism, by privileging form over content, becomes empty, 'banal, trivial and inconsequential' (ibid).

References

Bell, Madison Smartt. 1986. Less is less: The dwindling American short story. *Harper's Magazine*. April: 64–69. https://harpers.org/archive/1986/04/less-is-less/. Accessed 1 October 2018.

Byatt, AS. 2002. Scenes from a provincial life. *The Guardian* [online], July 27. www.theguardian.com/books/2002/jul/27/classics.asbyatt. Accessed 18 August 2018.

Carver, Raymond. 1981. A Storyteller's Shop Talk, *New York Times* [online], February 15. https://archive.nytimes.com/www.nytimes.com/books/01/01/21/specials/carver-shoptalk.html?_r=1&oref=slogin. Accessed 18 August 2018.

Carver, Raymond. 2003 (1981). *What We Talk About When We Talk About Love*. London: Vintage.

Dillard, Annie. 1981. Contemporary Prose Styles. *Twentieth Century Literature*, vol. 27, no. 23, pp. 207–222.

Dolnick, Ben. 2012. Semicolons: A Love Story. *New York Times* [online], July 2. https://opinionator.blogs.nytimes.com/2012/07/02/semicolons-a-love-story/. Accessed 18 August 2018.

Flaubert, Gustave. 1994 (1856). *Madame Bovary*. Hertfordshire: Wordsworth.

Greany, Phil. 2012. "An Introduction to Literary Minimalism in the American Short Story," what we've got (blog), February 7. https://philgreaney.wordpress.com. Accessed 12 October 2019.

Hamrick, Catherine. 2017. On Writing: The Power of the Exact Word. https://catherinehamrick.com/2017/04/16/on-writing-the-power-of-the-exact-word/. Accessed 19 August 2018.

Hemingway, Ernest. 1955 (1927). *Men Without Women*. New York: Scribner.

Hemingway, Ernest. 2000 (1932). *Death in the Afternoon*. London: Vintage.

Hemingway, Ernest. 2000 (1952). *The Old Man and the Sea*. London: Vintage.

Hemingway, Ernest. 2010 (1960). *A Moveable Feast*. New York: Scribner.

Hulme, T.E. 2003 (1909-1917). *Selected Writing: T.E. Hulme*. Manchester: Carcanet Press Limited.

Johnston, Kenneth. 1984. Hemingway and Freud: The Tip of the Iceberg. *The Journal of Narrative Technique*, vol. 14, no. 1, pp. 68–73. www.jstor.org/stable/30225083?seq=1#page_scan_tab_contents. Accessed 18 August 2018.

Kijo, Murukami. 1917. *First Autumn Morning*. www.poemofquotes.com/famous-haiku/murakami.php. Accessed 18 August 2018.

King, Stephen. 2010. *On Writing: A Memoir of the Craft*. New York: Scribner.

Lodge, David. 2011 (1992). *The Art of Fiction*. London: Vintage.

Lowell, Amy. 1917. On Imagism. *Tendencies in Modern American Poetry*. New York: Macmillan Company. www.english.illinois.edu/maps/poets/g_l/amylowell/imagism.htm. Accessed 04 January 2018.

Matsuo, Bashō. 1686. 'Frog Poem', Translated , Lafcadio Hearn (1898). https://en.wikisource.org/wiki/Frog_Poem_(Hearn). Accessed 26 June 2019.

McCarthy, Cormac. 2009 (2006). *The Road*. London: Picador.

Orwell, George. 2010 (1946). *Politics and the English Language*. London: Penguin. www.orwell.ru/library/essays/politics/english/e_polit. Accessed 18 August 2018

Orwell, George. 2008 (1949). *Nineteen Eighty-Four*. London: Penguin Group.

Palahniuk, Chuck. 2006 (1996). *Fight Club*. London: Vintage.

Pound, Ezra. 1913a. 'A Few Don'ts by an Imagiste', *Poetry Magazine*, March. www.poetryfoundation.org/poetrymagazine/articles/58900/a-few-donts-by-an-imagiste. Accessed 17 October 2018.

Pound, Ezra. 1913b. *In a Station of the Metro*. www.poetryfoundation.org/poetrymagazine/poems/12675/in-a-station-of-the-metro. Accessed 8 August 2018.

Reinhardt, Ad. 1992 (1975). *Art as Art: The Selected Writing of Ad Reinhardt*. California: University of California Press.

Strunk, William and E.B. White. 2014 (1918). *The Elements of Style*. Essex: Pearson Education Limited.

Williams, William Carlos. 1923. "XXII", *Spring and All*. New York: Contact Editions / Dijon: Maurice Darantière.

5 MAGIC REALISM: HOW FLYING CARPETS REALLY FLY

By day, we live realist lives. For most of us, nothing 'magical' happens. The sun comes up, we go to work, and everything that seems out of the ordinary has a rational explanation, even that creak of the floorboards in the spooky house we live in is not a restless ghost but elementary physics – the house contracts and expands according to temperature fluctuations. But at night, monsters prowl our dreams, dead friends long gone are alive once more, we merge into other people, animals speak, we can fly by simply willing our bodies upwards, fantastic things happen to us, and we don't even blink an eye – well, strictly we do because we are in REM (rapid eye movement) sleep. We accept illogical, irrational images in our sleep as normal. We are at home swimming in our unconscious, which is filled with strange creatures, weird settings and bizarre events.

Even in the light of day, we do not escape: when we get restless and bored with the mundanity of our material existence or when we want to escape its hardships and joylessness, we snuggle up with a good book about other worlds, magic and dragons or we pay to watch movies about a man who has scissors for hands or snakes for hair.

We spend more than 30 per cent of our life in fantasy worlds. Yes, we do live in a material world, and we have banished our ghosts of the ages, gods or demons or magic. We can scientifically explain everything. Realism aims to reflect that world. But Realism is based on the assumption that the material world is the primary content of our lives, that this is how we apprehend experience.

But the pendulum swings back and forth. Now that romanticism has been banished, there is a reaction against verisimilitude, and minimalism in particular, and along come fabulism, surrealism, magic realism and fantasy to challenge realism and invigorate it with older forms such as the fable (hence the name fabulism), the tale, the legend, the myth, allegory and parable.

In our dreams, we accept fantastical qualities quite readily. We all do it. We may remember our dreams only partially or not at all, as our brain deliberately means for us to forget them, but we can develop techniques to help us remember them.

The language of the unconscious

We dream in what are common fictional narrative techniques – simile, symbol, metaphor, analogy, metonymy, synecdoche and allegory. Our unconscious mind uses figurative language to tell fantastic stories at night in order to process our daily lives, our problems, our traumas and our experiences. Sometimes the dreams are realist (but also still fictional).

> **'LANGUAGE OF THE UNCONSCIOUS' EXERCISE**
>
> Write down a dream you remember in which the impossible happened and you accepted it as 'real'.

Surrealism: Beautiful as the chance meeting on a dissecting table of a sewing machine and an umbrella

The precursor to Magic Realism was Surrealism, a movement of the early 20th century, mainly in the visual arts, that sought to tap into the unconscious (Chapter 3) and to 'resolve the previously contradictory conditions of dream and reality into an absolute reality, a super-reality' (Breton, 1971 (1924), p. 26).

Surrealist works, like dreams, juxtapose illogical, irrational images and events in the language of the unconscious. Look, for example, at a Surrealist painting such as Salvador Dali's *The Persistence of Memory* (1931). The irreality is depicted realistically and, as in a dream, given as normal.

Surreal automatic writing techniques

1. Surrealist automatism

The first Surrealist work is commonly accepted to be André Breton and Philippe Soupault's *Les Champs magnétiques* (1920). It is a novel written in the technique of automatic writing, which Breton argues is a route to a 'higher reality'. Automatic writing, like freewriting, attempts to bypass the censor and to let the unconscious speak. In what is now called 'Surrealist automatism', the artist abandons conscious control and the unconscious mind to speak. Here is an example from the novel:

> The bird in this cage makes the dedicated-to-blue pretty child cry. Her father is an explorer. The new-born kitties rotate. There are in those woods pale flowers that make those who pluck them die. The whole family is prosperous and gathers under this lime-tree after mealtime (Breton and Soupault, 1920).

Other elements, such a juxtaposition, collage and non sequiturs, are also used to create surrealist writing.

2. 'Exquisite corpse', also known as 'exquisite cadaver' (French: *cadavre exquis*)

This is a collaborative or collective method of writing, in which each writer adds a line to the story and passes this on to another writer to add to it. You may have played this game as a child: you wrote a line, folded over the paper and passed it to someone else, who wrote the next line.

3. 'The cut-up method'

William Burroughs and Brion Gysin (1977) advocated for a form of random/automatic writing in their work. 'The cut-up method' involves taking texts (your own or 'found' texts from books, newspapers and so on), cutting them up with scissors, and piecing them back together in random ways.

4. 'Spontaneous prose'

Jack Kerouac, Beat poet of the fifties and author of *On the Road* (1957), which he wrote (he claims) 'spontaneously' and on a continuous roll of paper, suggests writing quickly and 'unconsciously' and never editing what you have written. To allow a free flow of ideas and a free random associative flow of ideas, his method involves no punctuation and no 'afterthinking' or editing (Melehy, 2017).

The idea is appealing. Let randomly generated thoughts disrupt the rational, left-brain thinking and let our 'creative side' tap into the unconscious where our creative power lies. But the problems are also immediately apparent. Is what we write gibberish, inaccessible to people, useless? What can this be but simply an experiment?

Peter Elbow

Elbow advocates a type of automatic writing which has become standard practice in creative writing courses to free up the creator in us and silence the critic:

> The idea is simply to write for ten minutes (later on, perhaps fifteen or twenty). Don't stop for anything. Go quickly without rushing. Never stop to look back, to cross something out, to wonder how to spell something, to wonder what word or thought to use, or to think about what you are doing. If you can't think of a word or a spelling, just use a squiggle or else write "I can't think what to say, I can't think what to say" as many times as you want; or repeat the last word you wrote over and over again; or anything else. The only requirement is that you never stop (Elbow, 1998 (1973), p. 3).

Elbow argues that this type of 'jabbering' or 'babbling' exercise enables our authentic voice to emerge:

> The habit of compulsive, premature editing doesn't just make writing hard. It also makes writing dead. Your voice is damped out by all the interruptions, changes, and hesitations between the consciousness and the page. In your natural way of producing words there is a sound, a texture, a rhythm – a voice – which is the main source of power in your writing. I don't know how it works, but this voice is the force that will make a reader listen to you. Maybe you don't like your voice; maybe people have made fun of it. But it's the only voice you've got. It's your only source of power. You better get back into it, no matter what you think of it. If you keep writing in it, it may change into something you like better. But if you abandon it, you'll likely never have a voice and never be heard (Elbow, 1998 (1973), pp. 6–7).

Freewriting is a means to an end. Once we have allowed our creative side out, Elbow argues, we then invite the editor back in and shape our scribbles into something coherent.

> ### ✏️ 'AUTOMATIC WRITING' EXERCISES
>
> Try all four methods:
>
> 1. Surrealist automatism: Write for a minute at a liminal stage, either as soon as you wake up or in half sleep, and attempt to abandon control of the conscious mind.
>
> 2. Exquisite corpse: With a writing partner or two, add a line to a story and pass it on to another writer to add to it.
>
> 3. The cut-up method: Cut and paste words and letters from magazines and newspapers and form whatever story presents itself.
>
> 4. Spontaneous prose: Write for five minutes and free-associate your thoughts. Ignore punctuation and follow a spontaneous flow, invoking a 'semi-trance'.
>
> In all these methods, do not let the censor/editor in. Let your thoughts roam freely and allow juxtaposition, collage and non sequiturs. This should happen 'automatically'. Then read back the writing and see whether it has allowed your unconscious to emerge. Is there anything of merit here? What do you see of the unconscious?

The Kafkaesque

Perhaps the first magical realist was Franz Kafka (1883–1924), whose modernist, bizarre and surrealist tales created a new word in the English language ('Kafkaesque') in their fusion of nightmare and reality, magic and realism. In Kafka's stories, a man is turned into a beetle, shaming his family; a circus artist starves himself for the entertainment of the crowds; a man is put on trial for no reason. Kafka's works are so realistic that we are viscerally plunged into their nightmare worlds and experience the alienation, absurdity and existentialist angst of life.

For example, here is the beginning of *The Metamorphosis* (1915):

> One morning, as Gregor Samsa was waking up from anxious dreams, he discovered that in his bed he had been changed into a monstrous verminous bug. He lay on his armour-hard back and saw, as he lifted his head up a little, his brown, arched abdomen divided up into rigid bow-like sections. From this height the blanket, just about ready to slide off completely, could hardly stay in place. His numerous legs, pitifully thin in comparison to the rest of his circumference, flickered helplessly before his eyes.
> "What's happened to me," he thought. It was no dream (Kafka, 2015 (1915), p. 5).

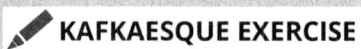

KAFKAESQUE EXERCISE

Read the suggested Kafka stories referenced at the end of this chapter, analyse the narrative techniques he uses (realist form and surrealist content) to make them Kafkaesque, then attempt to write a 500-word short story using these techniques so that the real and the dream world are one.

Magical realism

The term Magic Realism or Magical Realism was first used and is associated primarily with Latin American literature, in particular that of Jorge Luis Borges, Gabriel García Márquez and Isabel Allende. It is also almost always postcolonial and deconstructs colonial discourse and its ties to mainstream realism.

Magic Realism's accolades include prize-winning novels such as Salman Rushdie's *Midnight's Children* (1981), Allende's *The House of the Spirits* (1982), Toni Morrison's *Beloved* (1987), Ben Okri's *The Famished Road* (1991), Arundhati Roy's *The God of Small Things* (1997), and Tim Winton's *Cloudstreet* (1991), all on the fringes of the Western literary mainstream.

García Márquez, in his Nobel Prize acceptance speech for his Magic Realist tales, claims that the challenge for Latin American writers was to make their 'outsized' world believable. 'My most important problem was destroying the lines of demarcation that separates what seems real from what seems fantastic' (García Márquez, 1982).

Magic Realism aims to resolve the previously contradictory conditions of dream and reality and is characterised by two things:

1. A narrative technique that blurs the distinction between fantasy and reality.
2. An equal acceptance of the ordinary and the extraordinary. Narrators and characters accept supernatural magical events as natural, even ordinary and unremarkable.

How do magic carpets fly?

Often Magic Realism is confused with fantasy. What is the difference? Think of a magic carpet. In the Disney movie *Aladdin* (1992), we see Aladdin on his flying carpet, which has a personality of its own. This is fantasy. We do not question its reality, as we know it is not meant to be realistic. This fantasy world has its own rules. In our 'real' world, we know that carpets do not fly or have personalities. But in one of Salman Rushdie's magic realist novels, we read about a real flying carpet:

> People tend to focus on the "magic" more than the "realism." But, like all fiction, fantasy arrives at truth via the road of untruth. The moment you decide you're going to have a rug that flies through the air... you must immediately ask yourself realistic questions about it. What would that be like? If you were standing on a carpet that levitated, would it be difficult to keep your balance? Would the carpet be rigid or would the movement of air under the carpet make the carpet undulate? If you flew very high, would it get very cold? How do you keep warm on a flying carpet? And I think the moment you start asking yourself those kinds of practical or real world questions, the flying carpet becomes believable – it becomes a thing that might exist. And if it existed, it would function like this (Rushdie, 2010).

>  **'FLYING CARPET' EXERCISE**
>
> Take a fantasy concept like a flying carpet or a time machine and make it realistic, ask scientific questions of it and write a magic realist paragraph that renders the magic 'real'.
>
> 1. Establish the familiar, then lift the veil.
> 2. Make your magical world REAL.
> 3. Push yourself over the edge.
> 4. Suspend disbelief and believe what you write.
> 5. Don't be afraid to leave the door open.
> 6. Make sure that you are writing Magic Realism and NOT fantasy.

Gabriel García Márquez

In the seminal novel *One Hundred Years of Solitude* (1967), García Márquez's masterpiece of Magic Realism, magic is matter of fact. For example, the village decides to give up sleeping so they can have an extra eight hours to work.

Two iconic García Márquez stories exemplify how magic realism works: 'A Very Old Man with Enormous Wings: A Tale for Children' (1972) and 'The Handsomest Drowned Man in the World' (1968) (anthologised in *Leafstorm and Other Stories*, 1979 (1972)). In both tales, a supernatural 'stranger' comes to town: an angel and a corpse respectively. When we think of an angel, we think fantasy. But what would an angel be like in real life? How would it fly? Would it be gendered? Would it age? Here is García Márquez's angel:

> He was dressed like a ragpicker. There were only a few faded hairs left on his bald skull and very few teeth in his mouth, and his pitiful condition of a drenched great-grandfather took away any sense of grandeur he might have had. His huge buzzard wings, dirty and half-plucked were forever entangled in the mud (García Márquez, 2005 (1972), p. 105).

The angel is abused on his arrival, stoned, imprisoned, and mocked until he finally manages to escape.

In the second story, children find a dead body on the beach and play with it, until the women of the village find it, fall in love with it, dress it up and give it a personality. In the first story, the being is dehumanised; in the second, brought to life:

> They thought that if that magnificent man had lived in the village, his house would have had the widest doors, the tallest roof and the firmest floor, and the frame of his bed would have been made of giant timbers with iron bolts, and his wife would have been the happiest. They thought that he would have had such authority that he could have taken the fish from the sea by only calling them by name, and he would have put such effort in his work that he would have brought forth springs from between the driest rocks and would have been able to sow flowers on the cliffs. They compared him in secret to their own men, thinking that they would not be able to do in a lifetime what that man was capable of in a single night, and they ended up repudiating them in the depths of their hearts as the most squalid and paltry beings in the earth (García Márquez, 1979, p. 100).

This reads like Realism until we step back and say, 'Hang on, they're talking about a rotting corpse here!'

A.S. Byatt

Contemporary Magic Realism often slips into otherwise realist novels as a narrative technique, the way we slip into sleep or daydream. A.S. Byatt's Magic Realism is vivid and visceral and interwoven in her otherwise Victorian Realist style. For example, in her story 'A Stone Woman' (2003a, 2003b), a woman discovers an illness in her body and, as she slowly succumbs to it, realises that she is turning to stone – and not just any stone – she is growing into precious stones and becoming a work of art.

> One day, she found a cluster of greenish-white crystals sprouting in her armpit. These she tried to prize away, and failed. They were attached deep within; she felt their stony roots stirring under the skin surface, pulling at her muscles. Jagged flakes of silica and nodes of basalt pushed her breasts upward and flourished under the fall of flesh, making her clothes

> crackle and rustle. Slowly, slowly, day by quick day, her torso was wrapped in a stony encrustation, like a corselet. She could feel that under the stones her compressed inwards were still fluid and soft, responsive to pain and pressure (Byatt, 2003a, 2003b, p. 139).

Note how the details are meticulously researched. Unlike the description of fawns turning to stone in C.S. Lewis's *The Lion, the Witch and the Wardrobe* (1950), this is what it is *really* like to turn to stone.

'MAGICAL REALISM' EXERCISE

1. Find a fantasy story (either your own or a well-known, published story), locate a passage that is pure fantasy, and rewrite it realistically.
2. Find a realist story (either your own or a well-known, published story), locate a passage that is pure realism, and insert a magical element into it.

Byatt's 'The Thing in the Forest' (2003b) tells the story of two girls who find a 'loathly worm', a dragon-like creature in the English countryside woods. But it is no fantasy dragon. It is real, more real perhaps than even they are:

> The rest of its very large body appeared to be glued together, like still-wet papier-mâché, or the carapace of stones and straws and twigs worn by caddis-flies underwater. It had a tubular shape, as a turd has a tubular shape, a provisional amalgam. It was made of rank meat, and decaying vegetation, but it also trailed veils and prostheses of man-made materials, bits of wire-netting, foul dishcloths, wire-wool full of panscrubbings, rusty nuts and bolts. It had feeble stubs and stumps of very slender legs, growing out of it at all angles, wavering and rippling like the suckered feet of a caterpillar or the squirming fringe of a centipede (Byatt, 2003a, p. 16).

The experience of witnessing this 'thing' traumatises the girls for life, scarring their childhood and damaging their adulthoods. What Byatt does so marvellously is not allow us to turn this 'thing' into a symbol or a representation of something else (although critics have likened it to a phallus, the war, child abuse, patriarchy, and so on). The detailed realistic description of the impossible 'thing' does not allow the reader to short-circuit the magic. One of the protagonists concludes that there are things 'more real' than the material world.

> I think there are things that are real – more real than we are – but mostly we don't cross their paths, or they don't cross ours. Maybe at very bad times we get into their world, or notice what they are doing in ours (Byatt, 2003a, p. 28).

This does sound like fantasy, but the visceral description prevents us from a glib dualistic fantasy story. The consideration is a philosophic one, not a consideration we would ask of Harry Potter. (Is there *really* a Diagon Alley hidden behind the material streets of London?)

The real

'The Thing in the Forest' raises the issue central to Magic Realism, that of the 'Real'. We are in the territory of Alain Badiou's unnameable, Paul de Man's blindness, Jean-François Lyotard's inexpressible, Samuel Beckett's ineffable, Freud's uncanny, Conrad's secret, Wittgenstein's 'what lies beyond the limits of language', Emmanuel Kant's *noumenon*, the unknowable reality underlying all things – Jacques Lacan's 'Real'.

> The Reality of [the thing's] formless excremental remnant exemplifies perfectly the disintegration of reality into the ghostlike, substanceless appearance on an interface and the raw stuff of the remainder of the Real – the obsession with this remainder is the price we have to pay for the suspension of the paternal Prohibition/Law that sustains and guarantees our access to reality. We are parlêtres ('beings of language'), and find ourselves in this horrifying in-between state (Žižek, 2005, pp. 155–6).

Or as Lacan expresses it:

> Our reality consists of symbols and the process of signification. What we call 'reality' is associated with the symbolic order or

'social reality'. The real is the unknown that exists at the limit of this socio-symbolic universe and is in constant tension with it. The real is also a very paradoxical concept; it supports our social reality – the social world cannot exist without it – but it also undermines that reality (cited in Homer, 2005, p. 81).

Magic Realism asks us to participate in the essential human experience of the numinous, what is outside our realist construction of the world, and enter into an exhilarating and sometimes terrifying but mind-expanding embrace of a larger 'reality'.

References

Breton, André. 1971 (1924). *Manifestoes of Surrealism*. Trans. Richard Seaver and Helen R Lane. Ann Arbor: University of Michigan Press.

Breton, André and Philippe Soupault. 1920. *Les Champs megnétiques*. France: Éditions Gallimard.

Burroughs, William and Brion Gysin. 1977. *The Third Mind*. New York: Viking.

Byatt, A.S. 2003a. A Stone Woman. In *The Little Black Book of Stories*. London: Vintage.

Byatt, A.S. 2003b. The Thing in the Forest. In *The Little Black Book of Stories*. London: Vintage.

Elbow, Peter. 1998 (1973). *Writing Without Teachers*. New York: Oxford University Press.

Homer, Sean. 2005. *Jacques Lacan*. New York: Routledge.

Kafka, Franz. 2015 (1915). *The Metamorphosis*. Sweden: Wisehouse.

Márquez, Gabriel García. 1982. *The Solitude of Latin America*. www.nobelprize.org/nobel_prizes/literature/laureates/1982/marquez-lecture.html. Accessed 18 August 2018.

Márquez, Gabriel García. 2005 (1972). *Leafstorm and Other Stories*. New York: Harper Perennial.

Melehy, Hassan. 2017. *Kerouac: Language, Poetics and Territory*. London: Bloomsbury.

Rushdie, Salman. 2010. *Magical Realism is Still Realism*. https://bigthink.com/videos/magical-realism-is-still-realism. Accessed 18 August 2018.

Žižek, Slavoj. 2005. *Interrogating the Real* [online]. London: Continuum International Publishing Group. www.scribd.com/document/361769863/Interrogating-the-Real-Slavoj-Zizek#. Accessed 18 August 2018.

6 POSTMODERNISM: [DE]CONSTRUCTING 'REALITY'

Postmodernism presents writers with a kaleidoscopic array of practices, encourages innovation and experimentation, and has produced a dazzling smorgasbord of creative works, expanding the genre of the novel and pushing its boundaries. But postmodernism is a problematic term that has been loosely applied, appropriated, even disparaged and denounced. What exactly is postmodernism?

1. Postmodernism is impossible to define because a definition of postmodernism is that it has no definition. No definite terms. No boundaries. No absolute truth.
2. Postmodernism: 'a late 20th-century movement characterized by broad scepticism, subjectivism, or relativism; a general suspicion of reason; and an acute sensitivity to the role of ideology in asserting and maintaining political and economic power' (Encyclopaedia Britannica).
3. The name Postmodernism implies that it is another pendulum swing against the unfashionable tenets of Modernism. John Barth claimed that, by the 1960s, Modernism had become 'The Literature of Exhaustion' (1967) and argued for 'The Literature of Replenishment' (1980), a new era of postmodern abundance:

> My ideal Postmodernist author neither merely repudiates nor merely imitates either his 20th-century Modernist parents or his 19th-century premodernist grandparents. He has the first half of our century under his belt, but not on his back. Without lapsing into moral or artistic simplism, shoddy craftsmanship, Madison Avenue venality, or either false or real naiveté, he nevertheless aspires to a fiction more democratic in its appeal than such late-Modernist marvels as Beckett's Texts for Nothing… The ideal Postmodernist novel will somehow rise

above the quarrel between realism and irrealism, formalism and "contentism," pure and committed literature, coterie fiction and junk fiction (Barth, 1980, p. 48).

4. Jean-François Lyotard coined the word Postmodernism in his seminal essay 'The Post Modern Condition' (1979) and defined this destabilising amalgam of practices as 'incredulity towards metanarratives'. Postmodernism undermines Certainty and Meaning and reveals our loss of faith in the Big Lies we told ourselves, such as Religion, Science, Marxism, Liberalism… even Modernism. Even Postmodernism ('postmodernisms'?). Anything with a capital letter.
5. Fredric Jameson (ironically a Marxist metanarrativist himself) describes postmodernism as 'the cultural logic of late capitalism' (by which he means post-industrial, multi-national consumer capitalism). In his 1982 essay 'Postmodernism and Consumer Society', Jameson notes that the main characteristics of this new movement were the abolition of History (a central tenet in Marxist ideology) and a fixation on the perpetual present.

J.M. Coetzee, railing against the tyranny of History (capital H, not under erasure or even put in quotes), argues that the novel is a subversive postmodern space that deconstructs even history itself:

> In times of intense ideological pressure like the present, [1987 Apartheid South Africa] when the space in which the novel and history normally coexist like two cows on the same pasture, each minding its own business, is squeezed to almost nothing, the novel, it seems to me, has only two options: supplementarity or rivalry. [Rivalry] would lead to a novel that operates in terms of its own procedures and issues in its own conclusions, not one that operates in terms of the procedures of history and eventuates in conclusions that are checkable by history (as a child's schoolwork is checked by a schoolmistress). In particular I mean a novel that evolves its own paradigms and myths, in the process (and here is the point at which true rivalry, even enmity, perhaps enters the picture) perhaps going so far as to show up the mythic status of history … for example, a novel that is prepared to work itself out outside the terms of class conflict, race conflict, gender conflict or any of the other oppositions out of which history and the historical disciplines erect themselves (cited in Atwell, 1990, p. 286).

6. 'Reality' is always in quotes. In fact, most words are in quotes. 'All "language", to be sure, is in quotes'. Author of the postmodern crime thriller *The Name of the Rose* (1980), Umberto Eco explains postmodernism as an ironic and simultaneous rejection and acceptance of our flawed language:

> [P]ostmodernism ... [is] a Kunstwollen, a way of operating. ... I think of the postmodern attitude as that of a man who loves a very cultivated woman and knows that he cannot say to her "I love you madly", because he knows that she knows (and that she knows he knows) that these words have already been written by Barbara Cartland. Still there is a solution. He can say "As Barbara Cartland would put it, I love you madly". At this point, having avoided false innocence, having said clearly it is no longer possible to talk innocently, he will nevertheless say what he wanted to say to the woman: that he loves her in an age of lost innocence (Eco, 2014 (1980), p. 570).

7. A Postmodernist writer (to parody Salman Rushdie) holds up a mirror to nature and writes about the mirror.[1] Richard Rorty debunks the realist myth that language refers to and represents a reality outside itself, a 'mirror of nature'. In his seminal text *Philosophy and the Mirror of Nature* (1979), he argues that we need to cultivate 'ironism', the awareness of our contingent position in history. We need distance and scepticism to stand back from the cultural spider webs we think of as 'normal'. Following this thread, de Saussure claims that language is semantically self-contained or self-referential, not referential to a world outside, but creates that world outside. The meaning of words is not static and thus meanings are constantly 'deferred'. Signifiers are words that point to meaning and to the thing or 'referent' but are arbitrary.
8. Alfred Tennyson's poem 'The Lady of Shallott' (1833) describes the Realist relation of art to reality. The artist, a woman constructing a tapestry, copies reality outside and recreates it in her tapestry. The medium used to relay the information is a mirror which sharply divides the two realms of reality and art, so when the woman turns to look directly at reality, she breaks the sharp line of the distinction and hence her artwork is destroyed.

---

1 Salman Rushdie's blurb on the back of Italo Calvino's *If on a Winter Night a Traveller* (1979) reads: 'Calvino holds up a mirror to nature and writes about the mirror'.

A postmodernist correction of this view of art and reality is given by Thomas Pynchon in *The Crying of Lot 49* (1965) where Oedipa Maas describes a painting of a number of girls in a tower,

> Embroidering a kind of tapestry which spilled out of the slit windows and into a void, seeking hopelessly to fill the void: for all the other buildings and creatures, all the waves, ships and forests of the earth were contained in this tapestry, and the tapestry was the world (Pynchon, 1966, pp. 11–12).

Pynchon's view of art is that reality is a void and art is a construction that fills the void. Rather than serving as a reflection of reality, art itself becomes the reality that exists: 'Fiction cannot be a representation of reality, or an imitation, or even a recreation of reality, it can only be a reality' (Federman, 2011, p. 147).

9. 'There is no outside-text'. You cannot say Postmodernism without deferring to Jacques Derrida (1930–2004), the originator and leading practitioner of deconstruction. Deconstruction is that severing of the apparent relationship of text and meaning. Deconstruction asks us to read a text counter to the intended meaning or its structural unity in order to expose the notion that language is 'irreducibly complex, unstable, or impossible' (Zainab and Moinuddin, 2017, p. 13). In the early 1990s, I once visited University of California, Irvine, where Derrida was 'apparently' (a good Postmodernist word) lecturing (there was a signifier on his door), and I met some students in his class. What is he like? I asked in awe. We don't know, we haven't ever seen him, they replied.

10. The notion of being 'under erasure' or 'sous rature' originated with Heidegger (1889–1976), whereby a word in a text is crossed out (the strike-through key in Word a̶b̶c̶ performs a similar function) but is still visible, so we know it has been crossed out. Why? In order to demonstrate that the word is not up to its job but that it's all we've got. It is, in Derrida's words, 'inadequate yet necessary'. Sigh. Our imperfect language cannot give us anything better than this. By erasing a word, Derrida is indicating its paradoxical or undecidable nature. Its meaning is derived from difference, not by reference to a pre-existing notion.

For example, if I write 'God', I am naively subscribing to all the accumulated baggage that comes with such a loaded word. So I write G̶o̶d̶. God is an inadequate word yet necessary. Similarly, if I write 'erasure', I am naively subscribing to all the accumulated baggage that comes with such a loaded word. So I write ~~erasure~~. The word 'erasure' is inadequate yet necessary.

11. Imagine a cave. In this cave, men (where are the women?) are chained to face the back wall upon which images and shadows are projected by puppeteers behind them on a raised parapet. The only 'reality' these men have seen since birth are these shadows, so naturally this is what they think 'reality' is like. There is a one-to-one correspondence of signs and referents, of words to objects of the so-called real word they see.

The Modernist moment arises when one of the men (a writer) dares to turn around and see how his 'reality' has been constructed. He sees the mechanism of production. He sees he is in a cave. He breaks his chains and escapes into the light of day, marvelling at the real world outside the cave. We have constructed a web of language, and the sooner we as writers expose this the better. No point writing any longer and imitating the shadows on the walls. He writes about how the real world has been constructed.

The postmodernist moment arrives when the writer looks for an outside of the cave and realises that there is no outside, that reality has been constructed by the puppeteers, so he cannot escape its web except by exposing its flaws, pointing out that it is an illusion.

12. Postmodernism is bad news for authors who still believe they have agency and control over their text, who believe in the myth that authors actually write their own books and have ~~God~~-like control of meaning and words. Roland Barthes (1915–1980), in 'Death of the Author' (1967), argues that the intention and biographical context of an author is irrelevant to a text, as these words belong to the culture, and the author is a mere unconscious (or dead) conduit. Writing and creator are unrelated.

By the time John Fowles had written up to Chapter 13 of his novel *The French Lieutenant's Woman* (1969), he had given up all pretensions about being a ~~God~~-like author. He has lost control of his characters, has no idea where they are, and has to plunge into the story himself in order to work things out:

> I do not know. This story I am telling is all imagination. These characters I create never existed outside my own mind. If I have pretended until now to know my characters' minds and innermost thoughts, it is because I am writing in (just as I have assumed some of the vocabulary and "voice" of) a convention universally accepted at the time of my story: that the novelist

stands next to God. He may not know all, yet he tries to pretend that he does. But I live in the age of Alain Robbe-Grillet and Roland Barthes; if this is a novel, it cannot be a novel in the modern sense of the word (Fowles, 1969, p. 14).

13. ~~Don't forget to put it on your resumé. In quotes of course: 'I am a postmodernist'. Undermine the certainty of the assertion by adding 'I am not a postmodernist' or, better still, put the whole phrase under erasure as well: 'I am a postmodernist'. Debate long and hard whether to put the quotation marks themselves under erasure as well. A Postmodernist can hold two contradictory beliefs at once, deconstruct whatever system enslaves us, live in the present, feed off the tension of 'difference' between the sign and the referent, always defer meaning, and live life in quotes, ironically. A postmodernist wears clothes that are parodies of other clothes and lays bare the construction or process. For example, a postmodernist will wear his underpants on the outside of his pants or wear her bra on top of her T-shirt. A postmodernist begins every sentence with 'In a post modernist world, however,' or 'post structurally,' or 'As Derrida/Barthes/de Saussure intuits…'~~
13. O thin fathers of postmodernism, the question lingers: Do you not see how the blackbird walks around the feet of the women about you? Is Postmodernism a pastiche of dead white heteronormative males? A parody of patriarchy? Are the women under erasure? Can we not deconstruct deconstruction or is that a Grand Narrative too?

Characteristics of postmodernist literature

So now that we know what Postmodernism is (but we cannot define it unless we put the definition under erasure), what do writers do with this information? Postmodernism (and its underlying post-structuralist theoretical underpinning) is a way of reading the world, not writing about it. Authors are dispatched.

But don't despair.

Postmodernism has everything to do with writers. Postmodernism focuses on the nature of the 'Text': the world is a text, written the way we put words together; postmodernism is the way we construct reality; it draws attention to the process of meaning-making. The gift of postmodernism is that, as far as writing is concerned, it allows us to play. If the world is a text and there is no outside of the text, writers are the petit-heroes of the modern age.

The 'author/narrator' in John Fowles *Mantissa* (1982) has some 'tongue in cheek' advice for postmodernist writers:

> At the creative level there is in any case no connection whatever between author and text. They are two entirely separate things. Nothing, but nothing, is to be inferred or deduced from one to the other, and in either direction. The deconstructivists have proved that beyond a shadow of doubt. The author's role is purely fortuitous and agential. He has no more significant a status than the bookshop assistant or the librarian who hands the text qua object to the reader (Fowles, 1982, p. 117).

Thirteen ways to play

Postmodern writing is playful, parodic, ironic and humorous. It is less about 'objective reality' and more and more about its own creative processes. This is a relief. Writers can now play with innovative forms and styles, such as the following:

1. Metafiction (which undermines the text's authority or authenticity – see next chapter, where we will look at this in depth)
2. Magic Realism (see previous chapter)
3. Poioumena
4. Irony
5. Juxtaposition
6. Parody/pastiche
7. Collage
8. Intertextuality
9. Palimpsest
10. Fragmentation
11. Disruption
12. Erasure
13. Deconstruction

Postmodernist writing is fun. Prepare to enter the funhouse, wander the labyrinths of language and self-reflect in the hall of mirrors.

Poioumena

Alastair Fowler coined the term 'Poioumenon' (plural: poioumena) to describe self-conscious metafiction and specifically the process of creating fiction that questions the borderlines of fiction and its referents (Fowler, 1989). Here are two examples of this type of 'hall of mirrors' writing.

Tim O'Brien presents a 'story' in his composite novel *The Things They Carried* (1990), whose theme is how war stories are constructed.

> You can tell a true war story by the questions you ask. Somebody tells a story, let's say, and afterward you ask, "Is it true?" and if the answer matters, you've got your answer. For example, we've all heard this one. Four guys go down a trail. A grenade sails out. One guy jumps on it and takes the blast and saves his three buddies. Is it true? The answer matters. You'd feel cheated if it never happened. Without the grounding reality, it's just a trite bit of puffery, pure Hollywood, untrue in the way all such stories are untrue. Yet even if it did happen – and maybe it did, anything's possible – even then you know it can't be true, because a true war story does not depend upon that kind of truth. Happeningness is irrelevant. A thing may happen and be a total lie; another thing may not happen and be truer than the truth. For example: Four guys go down a trail. A grenade sails out. One guy jumps on it and takes the blast, but it's a killer grenade and everybody dies anyway. Before they die, though, one of the dead guys says, "What you do that for?" and the jumper says, "Story of my life, man," and the other guy starts to smile but he's dead. That's a true story that never happened (O'Brien, 1990, p. 64).

'Borges and I' (1960) is a fiction in which Jorge Luis Borges the man and Jorge Luis Borges the author break the boundaries between fiction and real life:

> The other one, the one called Borges, is the one things happen to. I walk through the streets of Buenos Aires and stop for a moment, perhaps mechanically now, to look at the arch of an entrance hall and the grillwork on the gate; I know of Borges from the mail and see his name on a list of professors or in a biographical dictionary. I like hourglasses, maps, eighteenth-century typography, the taste

of coffee and the prose of Stevenson; he shares these preferences, but in a vain way that turns them into the attributes of an actor. It would be an exaggeration to say that ours is a hostile relationship; I live, let myself go on living, so that Borges may contrive his literature, and this literature justifies me [...].
I do not know which of us has written this page (Borges, 2007 (1962), p. 246)

> **POIOUMENA EXERCISE**
>
> 1. Write the beginning of a story that is about writing a story, that exposes or questions the false dichotomies between fiction and 'reality'.
>
> 2. Write a story in which the author is a character or the character is the author.

Irony

> "I think the climax of the book will be the execution of poor old Edgar Derby," I said. "The irony is so great. A whole city gets burned down, and thousands and thousands of people are killed. And then this one American foot soldier is arrested in the ruins for taking a teapot. And he's given a regular trial, and then he's shot by a firing squad" (Vonnegut, 1991 (1969), p. 19).

Irony is difficult to pin down because it is contextual and cultural and depends on the reader's knowing more than the words spoken. Irony is a joke at the expense of the surface reality. The O'Brien passage above is saturated with irony. Irony undermines the seriousness of a surface pronouncement or situation and juxtaposes two 'realities'. Umberto Eco, reflecting on using irony in his novel *The Name of the Rose*, suggests that 'the postmodern reply to the modern consists of recognising that the past, since it cannot really be destroyed, because its destruction leads to silence, must be revisited: but with irony, not innocently' (Eco, 1985, p. 7).

Irony is nothing new, but in postmodern writings, irony becomes a method to deconstruct grand narratives and unexamined concepts.

Rorty's 'ironism', the awareness of our contingent position in history, is useful here if we as writers are to find the appropriate ironic distance in voice, style and tone to stand back from the cultural spider webs we think of as 'normal'.

 **IRONISM EXERCISE**

Write a 300-word ironic passage such as the Kurt Vonnegut or O'Brien one above, in which two meanings are possible and which is post-modernist in its subversion of reality. Use Rorty's 'ironism' and demonstrate an awareness of the construction of realities and of the limits of grand narratives.

Juxtaposition

Juxtaposition is the placing of incongruous elements next to each other without explaining the connection, if any. Postmodernist writing plays with contradictory elements, thrives on paradox and delights in contradicting itself. Brian McHale, in *Postmodernist Fiction* (1987), says:

> The space of a fictional world is a construct, just as the characters and objects that occupy it are, or the actions that unfold within it. Typically, in realist and modernist writing, this spatial construct is organized around a perceiving subject, either a character or the viewing position adopted by a disembodied narrator. The heterotopian zone of postmodernist writing cannot be organized in this way, however. Space here is less constructed than deconstructed by the text, or rather constructed and deconstructed at the same time. Postmodernist fiction draws upon a number of strategies for constructing/deconstructing space, among them juxtaposition, interpolation, superimposition, and misattribution (McHale, 2001 (1987), p. 45).

JUXTAPOSITION EXERCISE

Either: take two seemingly contradictory elements (statements, characters, styles, formats or situations) and juxtapose them in a 300-word narrative that intentionally clashes
Or: create a verbal/textual collage of incompatible source material and create a bricolage of reconstituted elements, a discordant polyphony of material.

Parody and pastiche

Postmodernism is a reaction to and sometimes a rewriting of Modernism, so postmodern writers will imitate and parody older forms of writing to expose them. A postmodern writer is often a *bricoleur*, borrowing forms, styles and even words and phrases to patch into their work. Derrida (1982 cited in Freshwater and Rolfe, 2004) claims that all work is derivative:

> All texts take their meaning only in relation to other texts; more than that, all texts are other texts, are nothing but a series of (literal and figurative) quotations; the text is a tissue of quotations drawn from the innumerable centres of culture ... the writer can only imitate a gesture that is always anterior, never original. His only power is to mix writings (2004, p. 11).

Marcus Zusak's *The Book Thief* (2005) plays literally with pastiche. In the middle of the book is a section of illustrations and story drawn over the washed out pages of Hitler's *Mein Kampf* (1925). David Lodge's *The British Museum Is Falling Down* (1965) parodies ten novelists' styles. Vladimir Nabokov's *Pale Fire* (1962), which consists of a poem and its exposition in footnotes, is a pastiche, a parody of a critical work that begins to bleed into a story between Shade (the poet) and Kinbote (the critic).

'CUT AND PASTE' EXERCISE

William Burroughs advocates for a cut-and-paste approach to writing. 'All writing is in fact cut ups', he claims, echoing Derrida.

> 'The method is simple. Here is one way to do it. Take a page. Like this page. Now cut down the middle and cross the middle. You have four sections: 1 2 3 4 ... one two three four. Now rearrange the sections, placing section four with section one and section two with section three. And you have a new page. Sometimes it says much the same thing. Sometimes something quite different–(cutting up political speeches is an interesting exercise)–in any case you will find that it says something and something quite definite. Take any poet or

> writer you fancy. Heresay, or poems you have read over many times. The words have lost meaning and life through years of repetition. Now take the poem and type out selected passages. Fill a page with excerpts. Now cut the page. You have a new poem. As many poems as you like' (Burroughs, 1963, n.p.).
>
> You can do this literally (cutting pictures and words and paragraphs from newspapers and magazines and pasting them into a hard copy of your story) or electronically cut and paste images and sections of text form other sources, genres and styles into your work. The effect?

Collage

To find examples of collage, we need look no further than John Ashbury's poem, 'They Knew What They Wanted' (2018), composed of movie titles. Here is the first stanza:

> They all kissed the bride.
> They all laughed.
> They came from beyond space.
> They came by night (Ashbury, 2018).

Collage, if you haven't already tried it, is subversive fun. It enacts the chaotic, random, postmodern experience of demonstrating that (1) all is text, (2) the author is dead, and (3) the connection between sign and signifier is arbitrary. A collage uses material from other sources and rearranges this material in order to allow new meanings to emerge. Here are the first two stanzas of Wendy Cope's 'Lonely Hearts' (2014), collaged from a dating site:

> Can someone make my simple wish come true?
> Male biker seeks female for touring fun.
> Do you live in North London? Is it you?
> Gay vegetarian whose friends are few,
> I'm into music, Shakespeare and the sun.
> Can someone make my simple wish come true? (Cope, 2010, p. 14).

POSTMODERNISM: [DE] CONSTRUCTING 'REALITY'

> ✏️ **COLLAGE EXERCISE**
>
> Using 'Lonely Hearts' as an exemplar, write a poem in which you cut and paste messages from dating sites or movie or song titles, paste them onto your blank page, and rearrange them to form a poem.

Intertextuality and palimpsest

> The best ideas are borrowed from other Poets, though possibly you are unconscious of the theft yourself (Lewis, 2008, p. xxvii).

The notion of the palimpsest put forward by Thomas De Quincey (1845) suggests that even though medieval scholars scraped their vellum clean in order to write on top of it, their chemistry was imperfect and so allowed future readers to 'make the traces of the elder manuscript' (2006 (1845), n.p.) visible. In this way, we can read through present work into the layers of the past. In the 1960s, the word palimpsest began to serve as a metaphor for the way language writes the author and to undermine the notion of the 'author' as originator or creator of the text. For Julia Kristeva (1986, p. 37), 'any text is constructed of a mosaic of quotations; any text is the absorption and transformation of another'. Barthes similarly argues that:

> Any text is a new tissue of past citations. Bits of code, formulae, rhythmic models, fragments of social languages, etc., pass into the text and are redistributed within it, for there is always language before and around the text. Intertextuality, the condition of any text whatsoever, cannot, of course, be reduced to a problem of sources or influences; the intertext is a general field of anonymous formulae whose origin can scarcely ever be located; of unconscious or automatic quotations, given without quotation marks (Barthes, 1981, p. 39).

The notion of the palimpsest foregrounds the fact that all writing takes place in the presence of other writings. The notion further subverts the concept of the author as the sole originator or source of his or her work.

And as readers, we always read 'through' texts:

> We aim to balance elements in a story which do not seem to tally at first, by means of a detour which leads to the "encyclopaedia of literature". ... Intertextuality "happens" inside the reader's head; there, too, is a network of previously read texts on the basis of which readers ascribe meaning to what they read (Mertens, 1990, p. 21).

To illustrate this, here are the first lines of three fictional autobiographies. The beginning of Charles Dickens's *David Copperfield* (1850) relies on a reader's ability to read 'through' the text:

> Whether I shall turn out to be the hero of my own life, or whether that station will be held by anybody else, these pages must show. To begin my life with the beginning of my life, I record that I was born (as I have been informed and believe) on a Friday, at twelve o'clock at night. It was remarked that the clock began to strike, and I began to cry, simultaneously (Dickens, 2005 (1850), p. 3).

The reader is asked to consider the question whether the protagonist is part of the tradition of hero literature or whether this novel is a departure from that tradition, ironically suggesting that it is possible for a protagonist of a fictional autobiography not to be the 'hero of one's life'. Later in this passage, the narrator reveals that he was born with a caul and invites the reader to brood over the implications and associations of being born on Friday, at midnight, and with such a mark.

J.D. Salinger's *The Catcher in the Rye* (1951) can be seen as a palimpsest of the previous work:

> If you really want to hear about it, the first thing you'll probably want to know is where I was born, and what my lousy childhood was like, and how my parents were occupied and all before they had me, and all that David Copperfield kind of crap, but I don't feel like going into it, if you want to know the truth. In the first place, that stuff bores me, and in the second place, my parents would have about two hemorrhages apiece if I told anything pretty personal about them (Salinger, 1991 (1951), p. 3).

The Dickens reference is deliberately provocative: the narrator wants to shock the reader and reject the tradition of fictional autobiography but at the same time link himself to it and bind the reader to the 'encyclopaedia of literature' by consciously referring to the novel's predecessor. It becomes clear that this is a palimpsest of *David Copperfield* when the reader notes that not only does Salinger's protagonist wear a symbolic caul throughout the novel but his name (Holden Caulfield) is a hybrid of the words 'caul' and 'Copperfield' and further is 'beholden' to this earlier work. *The Catcher in the Rye* is a consciously constructed palimpsest of *David Copperfield* and invites us to read 'through' it to previously 'absorbed' texts.

Salman Rushdie's *Midnight's Children* (1981) begins in a similar way:

> I was born in the city of Bombay...once upon a time. No, that won't do, there's no getting away from the date: I was born in Doctor Narlikar's nursing home on August 15th 1947. And the time? The time matters, too. Well then: at night. No, it's important to be more... On the stroke of midnight as a matter of fact. Clock hands joined palms in respectful greeting as I came. Oh, spell it out, spell it out: at the precise instant of India's arrival at independence, I tumbled forth into the world. There were gasps (Rushdie, 2006 (1981), p. 3).

It is difficult to read this extract without the texts it is written on showing through. The prevaricating tone reveals an uncertainty as to what genre the writer wants this novel to be, in much the same way that Dickens's narrator hovers over the hero genre. Is *Midnight's Children* a fairy tale? ('Once upon a time. No, that won't do'.) The reluctant narrator finally reveals that this is going to be both a political allegory (his birthday is parallel to the birth of an independent India) and a palimpsest (he shares David Copperfield's birthday and time, a Friday at midnight).

What is notable here is that this construction of 'a mosaic of quotations', this textual 'tissue of past citations', is a deliberate game played by self-conscious authors from three different generations. This is not an unconscious transmission of textual tissue by a 'scriptor' (Barthes's term for the emasculated author who helplessly transmits language codes and culture from a 'general field of anonymous formulae whose origin can scarcely ever be located', Barthes, 1981, p. 39) but rather a deliberate act of textual borrowing where each writer acknowledges the process of intertextuality and consciously constructed palimpsests in order to connect their readers to a literary field. It is a game that writers are playing.

A contemporary example of a writer whose work cannot be read without layers of other literary works extruding from its deceptively simple surface is J.M. Coetzee. His intertexts are written intentionally and self-consciously, pilfered 'without quotation marks' from a myriad of other sources:

> One of the teasing characteristics of novels soused in literariness, like J.M. Coetzee's, is their tendency to leak, to bleed, into vast inchoate terrains of intertextuality. Trails of significance proliferate seemingly without end. The reader is constantly challenged to measure and assess their implications within or against the frail containing form of the story (Wright, 2013, n.p.).

Disgrace (1999), for example, echoes with borrowed phrases and plagiarised ideas, scenes, characters and tropes: readers can find traces of Hawthorne, Dostoevsky, Flaubert, Nabokov (*Lolita* (1955) and *Despair* (1937)), Kafka, Byron, Wordsworth and Blake, to mention only a few. One example will suffice: at the end of the novel, the protagonist, disgraced in many ways, and having to dispose of euthanised dogs as part of his personal ignominy, contemplates that his own demise, like his daughter Lucy's after she has been raped, will be 'like a dog'.

> [I]t is humiliating. But perhaps that is a good point to start from again. Perhaps this is what I must learn to accept. To start at ground level. With nothing. Not with nothing but. With nothing. No cards, no weapons, no property, no rights, no dignity. Like a dog. Yes, like a dog (Coetzee, 1999, p. 114).

Kafka's *The Trial* (1925) ends with this exact phrase after the protagonist's ignominious descent into disgrace following a trial where he has been falsely accused: '"Like a dog!" he said, it was as if the shame of it should outlive him' (Kafka, 2015 (1925), n.p.).

For Kristeva and Barthes, intertextuality is not deliberate. It is how language operates unconsciously through 'scriptors' who are no longer authors of their works but passive conduits. But as writers we can consciously pilfer and overtly play the game of intertextuality, creating palimpsests as a central narrative technique.

> ✏️ **'INTERTEXTUAL PALIMPSEST' EXERCISE**
>
> Write a 300-word palimpsest (where you parody or imitate or refer to another story – write on top of another story where the reader can see the scraped-away previous work underneath yours). Use intertextuality: refer to, sample, allude to and directly quote text from other works consciously and deliberately.

Fragmentation

Fragmentation in Modernist writing seeks to demonstrate how we create reality through our various lenses. But a final objective reality is never in doubt. In postmodernist fragmentary novels, however, fracturing the narrative shows a form of deconstruction that demonstrates that this is how 'reality' has been constructed.

For example, Robert Coover's 'The Babysitter' from *Pricksongs & Descants* (2014 (1969)) presents us with a number of contradictory fragments of story. Modernist writing presents us with a jigsaw puzzle and it is up to us to put together the picture. But unlike Modernist writer Faulkner's *As I Lay Dying* (1930), for example, in which all differing jigsaw pieces fit together and coalesce to give us the whole picture, Coover's story disintegrates. None of the narratives is true or all of them are.

Vonnegut's *Slaughterhouse-Five* similarly presents the reader with 'spastic in time' fragments of stories that slide into each other with the premise that this is how time is seen by the aliens who form part of the narrative of the novel. Because of this time fragmentation, 'There isn't any particular relationship between the messages, except that the author has chosen them carefully … There is no beginning, no middle, no end, no suspense, no moral, no causes, no effects' (Vonnegut, 1991 (1969), p. 64). Vonnegut's narrator excuses his fragmentation in *Slaughterhouse-Five* thus: '[The novel] is so short and jumbled and jangled because there is nothing intelligent to say about a massacre' (ibid).

Postmodern writers play with fragmentation to show that this all we have – the shards of a lost 'reality'. In Coetzee's *Waiting for the Barbarians* (1980), the main protagonist is a Magistrate of an outlying colony of Empire who finds shards of a lost Barbarian civilisation (he calls these pieces 'slips'). He tries in vain to capture the meaning and ends up, the reader suspects, making meaning up:

> Now let us see what the next one says. See, there is only a single character. It is the barbarian character war, but it has other senses too. It can stand for **vengeance**, and, if you turn it upside down like this, it can be made to read *justice*. There is no knowing which sense is intended (Coetzee, 1980, p. 109; emphasis original).

In Chapter 12, we will return to fragmentation, this time in how modern media uses fragments to tell its message. Dislocation is an accepted method of delivery.

FRAGMENTATION EXERCISE

1. Read Coover's 'The Babysitter' and write a story in similar fragments that do not necessarily jigsaw together to make a whole picture.
2. Read Wallace Stevens's 'Thirteen Ways of Looking at a Blackbird' and write your own poem, imitating his structure. Replace 'blackbird' with your own subject and experiment with fragmentary forms.

Disruption

Disruption, by contrast, presents the reader with a whole story, a reality, but then breaks the illusion, either metafictionally or by indicating to the reader through pastiche or parody that the story is not to be taken seriously. John Barth, for example, gets his readers lost in the funhouse of language:

> For whom is the funhouse fun? Perhaps for lovers. For Ambrose *it is a place of fear and confusion.* He has come to the seashore with his family for the holiday, *the occasion of their visit is Independence Day, the most important secular holiday of the United States of America.* A single straight underline is the manuscript mark for italic type, which in turn is the printed equivalent to oral emphasis of words and phrases as well as the customary type for titles of complete works, not to mention. Italics are also employed, in fiction stories especially, for

"outside," intrusive, or artificial voices, such as radio announcements, the texts of telegrams and newspaper articles, et cetera. They should be used *sparingly*. If passages originally in roman type are italicized by someone repeating them, it's customary to acknowledge the fact. *Italics mine* (Barth, 1968, p. 1).

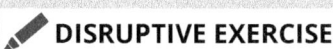
DISRUPTIVE EXERCISE
Using Barth's *Lost in the Funhouse* as an example, write a 300-word beginning of a story and disrupt it with interventions from (a) an intrusive narrator, (b) the author or (c) another discourse.

Erasure

An example of a text with words under erasure is *The Color Purple* (1982), in which the protagonist begins a letter to God in the following way:

> Dear God
> I am fourteen years old. ~~I am~~ I have always been a good girl (Walker, 1982, p.1).

In fiction, there are not many instances of words under erasure since it disrupts the narrative too much and looks like a marked-up edited proof. Nevertheless, it might be interesting to experiment this way with text.

Another technique of erasure is the practice of using a found text and selectively erasing words to produce a new work. For example, here is a found text (my story 'The Secret Bookshop') before erasure and the poem after erasure:

> ~~The book~~ he ~~presented to me~~ was in the shape of ~~a large pencil with a point at one end and an eraser at the other. 'Your book.'~~ He zipped it open down the middle and ~~inside were loose thin pages, like so many pencil shavings. 'Begin anywhere.'~~
> ~~I held the book, and leafed through the shavings. They looked as if they would crumble at~~ the ~~slightest touch.~~
> ~~A~~ young girl ~~looked up at me, smiled and then bowed her head down again over a large book. She blew hard~~ and ~~the dust rose and fell off it, like~~ a flock of birds ~~on a field. She held up the~~

~~book~~ with ~~her~~ tiny hands ~~and blew again. This time, what looked like words tore off and~~ danced into the air.
he was in the shape of the young girl
and a flock of birds with tiny hands danced into the air (Williams, 2019, p. 171).

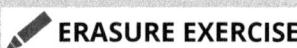 **ERASURE EXERCISE**

As in the above example, take a story or poem you have written and delete words to make another story or poem.

Deconstruction

In 'Structure, Sign and Play in the Discourse of the Human Sciences' (1966), Derrida describes the practice of deconstruction as 'simply a question of being alert to the implications, to the historical sedimentation of the language which we use' (Derrida, p. 271). We can apply this to not only the reading of a text but the writing of a text. The aim in postmodernist writing is to take apart, dismantle, expose the workings of, disrupt, fragment… to deconstruct.

Conclusion

1.01   When writing, look for the assumptions you are making about grand narratives.

1.02   Examine your position as an 'author' and your control over the meaning of the text you are creating.

1.03   Look at your mistakes and Freudian slips and see these as important as your 'darlings'.

1.04   Embrace ambiguity, contradictions, juxtaposition and paradox.

1.05   Let the text write you, instead of the other way around.

1.06   Play, make jokes and puns, use irony, and find the *jouissance* of the text that you are writing.

1.07   Disrupt convention.

1.08   Be aware of binaries and subvert them when you can.

1.09   Defer meaning.

1.10   Dissect the myths of our time.

1.11   Borrow, pastiche, collage, sample and be unoriginal.

1.12   Decentre, fragment, disrupt and erase.

1.13   Souse your writing in other texts.

References

Ashbury, John. 2018. *They Knew What They Wanted: Poems and Collages*. Ed. Mark Polizzotti. New York: Rizzoli Electa.

Attwell, David. 1990. The Problem of History in the Fiction of J.M. Coetzee. *Poetics Today* 11.3: 579–615.

Barth, John. 1968. *Lost in the Funhouse*. New York: Doubleday.

Barth, John. 1980. The Literature of Replenishment. In *The Friday Book: Essays and Other Non-Fiction*. London: The Johns Hopkins University Press, 1984

Barthes, Roland. 1981. Theory of the Text. In *Untying the Text*, ed. R. Young, 31–47. London: Routledge.

Borges, Jorge. 2007 (1962). *Labyrinths*. New York: New Directions.

Burroughs, William. 1963. The Cut Up Method in Leroi Jones, ed., *The Moderns: An Anthology of New Writing in America* (New York: Corinth Books, quoted in www.writing.upenn.edu/~afilreis/88v/burroughs-cutup.html. Accessed 20 October 2018.

Coetzee, J.M. 1980. *Waiting for the Barbarians*. London: Penguin.

Coetzee, J.M. 1999. *Disgrace*. New York: Viking.

Cope, Wendy. 2010. *Making Cocoa for Kingsley Amis*. London: Faber.

De Quincey, Thomas. 2006 (1845). The Palimpsest of the Human Brain. In *Quotidiana* [online] ed. Patrick Madden. http://essays.quotidiana.org/dequincey/palimpsest_of_the_human_brain. Accessed 18 August 2018.

Dickens, Charles. 2005 (1850). *David Copperfield*. London: Dover Publications.

Eco, Umberto. 1985. Reflections on the Name of the Rose. In *Encounter*, Volume LXiV, 7–19.

Eco, Umberto. 2014 (1980). *The Name of the Rose*. New York: Mariner Books.

Encyclopaedia Britannica [online]. www.britannica.com/topic/postmodernism-philosophy. Accessed 18 August 2018.

Federman, Raymond. 2011. *Federman's Fictions: Innovation, Theory, and the Holocaust*. Ed. Jeffrey R. Di Leo. New York: State University of New York Press.

Fowler, Alistair. 1989. The Future of Genre Theory: Function and Constructional Types. In *The Future of Literary Theory*, ed. Ralph Cohen. New York: Routledge.

Fowles, John. 1969. *The French Lieutenant's Woman*. London: Signet Press.

Fowles, John. 1982. *Mantissa*. London: Signet.
Freshwater, Dawn and Gary Rolfe. 2004. *Deconstructing Evidence-Based Practice*. New York: Routledge.
Jameson, Fredric. 1982. Postmodernism and Consumer Society. http://art.ucsc.edu/sites/default/files/Jameson_Postmodernism_and_Consumer_Society.pdf. Accessed 20 October 2018.
Kafka, Franz. 2015 (1925). *The Trial*. https://ebooks.adelaide.edu.au/k/kafka/franz/trial/chapter10.html.
Kristeva, Julia. 1986. Word, Dialogue, and Novel. In *The Kristeva Reader*, ed. Toril Moi. New York: Columbia University Press.
Lewis, Matthew 2008 (1796) *The Monk*, Oxford: Oxford University Press.
Lyotard, Jean-François. 1984 (1979). The Post Modern Condition: A Report on Knowledge. Manchester: Manchester University Press.
McHale, Brian. 2001 (1987). *Postmodernist Fiction*. London: Routledge.
Mertens, Anthony. 1990. Intertekstualiteit. In *Intertekstualiteit in theorie en praktijk*, eds. A. Mertens and K. Beekman. Dordrecht: Walter de Gruyter.
O'Brien, Tim. 1990. How to tell a True War Story. In *The Things They Carried*. New York: Mariner Books.
Pynchon, Thomas. 1966. *The Crying of Lot 49*. New York: J. B. Lippincott & Co.
Rorty, Richard. 1979. *Philosophy and the Mirror of Nature*. Princeton: Princeton University Press.
Rushdie, Salman. 2006 (1981). *Midnight's Children*. New York: Random House.
Salinger, J.D. 1991 (1951). *Catcher in the Rye*. New York: Little, Brown and Company.
Vonnegut, Kurt. 1991 (1969). *Slaughterhouse-Five*. London: Vintage.
Walker, Alice. 1982. *The Color Purple*. New York: Harcourt.
Williams, Paul. 2019. *The Art of Losing*. London: Bridge House.
Wright, Laurence. 2013. David Lurie's learning and the meaning of J.M. Coetzee's *Disgrace*. In *J.M. Coetzee's Austerities*, eds. Michael Neill and Graham Bradshaw. Ashgate: Amazon Digital.
Zainab, Mohammed and Khaja Moinuddin. 2017. A Systematic Theoretical Matrix for a Deconstruction of Metaphysics in the Critical Work of Jacques Derrida's 'Writing and Difference'. *IOSR Journal of Humanities And Social Science* 22.4: 13–17.

7 METAFICTION: WRITING ABOUT THE MIRROR

He slumps over his desk, staring at the words he has typed: Chapter 7: Metafiction: Writing about the Mirror. *The rest of the screen is blank. Should he plunge straight in with a definition, or should he invent some frame tale to cleverly show, rather than tell, how metafiction works?*

'It's six o'clock,' calls his partner from the other room, 'don't forget we're going to that launch tonight in Maleny. We need to leave now.'

'What launch?' He stretches. His back aches. He really shouldn't hunch over the keyboard like that for so long.

'Richard Flanagan, don't you remember?' she says. 'Richard Flanagan's launching his new novel First Person. *It's about a writer who is commissioned to write some criminal's memoirs and finds himself embroiled in the story that begins writing him.'*

He groans. 'Not another of those self-reflexive novels about a writer writing a novel about a writer writing a novel?'

'He won the Man Booker prize. He's a brilliant writer. If anyone can pull it off, he can.'

She's right. The event is inspirational. Richard Flanagan reads from his novel, and sure enough, it is about a writer caught between the demands of the subject (the criminal), his publisher who doesn't really believe in literature, and his own integrity. It is not crude metafiction but does all that metafiction should do without beating you over the head with its gimmickry.

Now he knows what he should do with his chapter: start with his memoir Soldier Blue *and how he tried to write it realistically but couldn't. Try to counter the students in his class who believe metafiction is frivolous and silly. 'A big wank,' one student said.*

As soon as they arrive home, he begins writing the chapter.

When I decided to write my memoir…

No. He deletes the phrase. He has to find a better way to start. Maybe:

He sits slumped over his desk…

Narcissism

Many students are sceptical when I present them with metafiction as a narrative technique. They regard it as an indulgence, a narcissistic attempt to photo-bomb the story or crowd the scene with selfies when all we really we want to see is the landscape behind. Look at me! (as Vonnegut does in *Slaughterhouse-Five*: 'That was I. That was me. That was the author of this book' (1991, p. 125)). Or else they see it as a gimmick that we could do without. Just get out of the way and get on with the story, they want to tell the author.

Linda Hutcheon's term for metafiction is *Narcissistic Narrative* (the title of her 1980 book). She alludes to the Ancient Greek myth of Narcissus, who fell in love with his reflection in a pool and could not pull himself away. Self-conscious narrative, Hutcheon says, is similar: we are trapped in the reflection of our linguistic constructions and cannot escape to the real world.

John Fowles uses his 1982 novel *Mantissa* to explore this narcissistic intrusion of author into the text. In this extract, the 'author' is lecturing his muse Erato, who naively believes that fiction reflects reality:

> 'The reflective novel is sixty years dead, Erato. What do you think modernism was about? Let alone post-modernism. Even the dumbest students know it's a *reflexive* medium now, not a reflective one.... Serious modern fiction has only one subject: the difficulty of writing serious modern fiction. First, it has fully accepted that it is only fiction, can only be fiction, will never be anything but fiction, and therefore has no business at all tampering with real life or reality. Right?' (Fowles, 1982, pp. 116–7).

The prison house of language: Definitions of metafiction

The movement of Literary Realism suggests that a novel 'holds a mirror up to nature' and reflects a faithful copy of the world just as a photograph captures the world 'as it is'. But we know this is not true. Nothing is unmediated. Even realistic photographs frame their subjects, and realistic novels reflect their authors' cultural and subjective biases about the 'reality' they depict. Increasingly, we have come to discover that it is through language that we create our realities, and if we want the novel to reflect 'a full and authentic report of human experience' (Watt, 1963, p. 32), then we need to take into account that the novel tells us more about the language we use to create reality than so-called 'reality' itself. Instead of mirroring reality, the novel holds up a mirror to itself. This is what metafiction is – a self-reflecting focus on how we create this 'reality'. Salman Rushdie's review of Italo Calvino's *If on a Winter's Night a Traveller* (1998) describes it beautifully: 'Calvino holds up a mirror to nature and writes about the mirror' (back cover blurb).

Add 'meta' to any discipline and we get the study of what is behind or above that discipline. Metafiction is the awareness of how fiction works, a self-conscious look at its mediation through language of the world. Metafiction simply is 'fiction about fiction' (Hutcheon, 1980, p. 1). The term was used for the first time in 1970 by the American novelist/critic William Gass in his essay 'Fiction and the Figures of Life'. Gass described metafiction as 'fictional writing which self-consciously and systematically draws attention to its status as an artifact in order to pose questions about the relationship between fiction and reality' (Waugh, 1984, p. 2).

'The Literature of Exhaustion', a seminal 1967 essay by John Barth, tells us that literary realism is all 'used up' and 'exhausted' and we need smarter and more self-aware fiction, 'novels which imitate the form of a novel, by an author who imitates the role of Author' (Barth, 1967, p. 79).

Barth's own fiction does just that: *Lost in the Funhouse* (1968) presents the reader with fictions that show off their fictionality and do not allow the reader to maintain a suspension of disbelief. In the title story, about a boy going to visit a funhouse, the narrator constantly interrupts the narrative with commentary on various narrative devices employed in the writing of the story:

> En route to Ocean City he sat in the back seat of the family car with his brother Peter, age fifteen, and Magda G____, age fourteen, a pretty girl and exquisite young lady, who lived not far from them on B____ Street in the town of D___, Maryland. Initials, blanks, or both were often substituted for proper names in nineteenth-century fiction to enhance the illusion of reality. It is as if the author felt it necessary to delete the names for reasons of tact or legal liability. Interestingly, as with other aspects of realism it is an illusion that is being enhanced, by purely artificial means (Barth, 1988, p. 72).

By drawing our attention to the way the story is written, Barth reveals how artificial and arbitrary 'realist' narrative is. The story ends with the boy lost in a hall of mirrors, unable to tell the 'real' from the reflected.

> **'NARCISSISTIC NARRATIVE' EXERCISE**
>
> Using Barth's piece as an example, write a realist passage describing a short car journey (150 words) and then overwrite it or interject it with comments on how/why it was written. Make reference to one or more of your chosen narrative elements.

What's wrong with realism?

When I decided to write my memoir, *Soldier Blue* (2008), I chose conventional literary realism:

> They [my parents] arrived in Rhodesia with a pram full of saucepans, a few shillings jangling in their pockets, and an optimistic trust in a benevolent universe, that things would somehow work out.... My first memories are of the white bars of my cot and a square, mauve wallpapered room. Every morning, I waved goodbye to my mother as she guiltily drove off to work... I remember from about the age of four onward (Williams, 2007).

I wanted to tell the truth as accurately and as realistically as possible. But as I read over what I had written, I discovered I was not being honest. This was not necessarily how it happened: this was what I *thought* happened. I was not actually sure whether these were my first memories. And that story of my parents' arrival sounded suspiciously like a rags-to-riches fairy tale they repeatedly told me over the years. How accurate were my memories? How accurate was my hold on reality? I rewrote the passage, this time admitting to myself that my 'reality' had been linguistically constructed:

> They [my parents] arrived in Rhodesia, *the story goes*, with a pram full of saucepans, a few shillings jangling in their pockets, and an optimistic trust in a benevolent universe, that things would somehow work out. That's how they tell it, anyhow....

> My first memory *apparently is a stark image of* the white bars of my cot, a square, mauve wallpapered room.... *I am also told that* I waved goodbye to my mother every morning as she guiltily drove off to work... *But I really only remember* from about the age of four onward (Williams, 2008, p. 6, 11; emphasis added).

What this does to the story is make it a truer account of my life, a more honest admission that the truth is told, not given. This is important because the memoir, *Soldier Blue*, is about how I grew up in a bubble of propaganda and how my reality was constructed by the media and people around me and I was deceived into seeing the world a certain way and conned into fighting for an illegal, racist regime.

But writing this way also destabilises the authority of my story. You can no longer trust that what I am telling you is a one-to-one relation to reality. Not 'this is what happened', but 'this is what people say what happened'. By implication then, I am saying, 'reality' is always linguistically constructed.

The basic dilemma for me was that by setting out to represent the world, I realised that the world could not be represented. I could, to use postmodern lingo, represent only the discourses of that world. And the more I tried to find language that actually represented my experiences of the world, the more I discovered that language was a hall of mirrors and only referred back to itself. The more I tried to escape this prison house of language to get outside to the 'real' world, the more entangled I became. Try looking up the meaning of a word that purportedly refers to a 'real' thing, like *mirror*. All it can give you are other words: *a surface, glass coated with a metal amalgam, which reflects a clear image.* Look up those words and it will give you others – or the first word again: image = *reflection in a mirror; glass: mirror.*

Welcome to the hall of mirrors called metafiction.

'HALL OF MIRRORS' EXERCISE

(a) Write a 200-word account of your first memory. Try to find words that accurately describe that experience.

(b) Now see whether there is a gap between the experience and the words used. Using a dictionary or thesaurus if necessary and referring to the *Soldier Blue* extract as an example, rewrite the piece, reflecting on the nature of that recall with as much honesty as you can.

Unmasking the wizard of Oz

In Chapter 2, I argued that it was absolutely necessary to maintain suspension of disbelief and to maintain verisimilitude so that readers could experience stories and characters as if they were real.

This is how we read novels. And write them. We construct other worlds which are plausible, characters who are rounded, and plots that resonate with the ring of truth. We want our readers to plunge into the virtual realities we create and enjoy them as if they were real.

But postmodernist writers ask us to question the very structure of the reality we are imitating. Postmodernism, as we saw in the previous chapter, is concerned with the nature of the 'text', the way we put words together, and the way we construct reality and draws attention to the process of meaning-making. 'Reality' is not a given.

If we, as writers, are to honestly reflect our experience of living in the world, we need to expose the fiction that the world is fixed, solid and unmediated.

That is why many postmodern authors write metafiction, which is an attempt to make the reader aware of the fictionality of fiction and expose the presence of the fictioneer, the person constructing reality. Think of L. Frank Baum's *The Wonderful Wizard of Oz* (1900), in which the illusion has been created of a wizard with God-like powers. 'Pay no attention to the man behind the curtain!' says Oz. The metafictional moment comes when Dorothy runs behind the screen and finds a small man (the author of this smoke-and-mirrors wizard) operating the controls. The novel unmasks the illusion of reality created by a con man.

A common human experience is that of being caught in a lie of someone else's making when you have been deceived about the nature of reality, as Dorothy was in *The Wonderful Wizard of Oz*. Think of *The Truman Show* (1998). All his life, Truman believed he was living his truth only to discover that his entire existence was a construct, that he was the star of a reality TV show where every moment of his day was scripted, and that every member of his family was an actor. His life-script was written for him. Think of all those people pranked by some *Candid Camera*–type set up. This is how metafiction works.

METAFICTION: WRITING ABOUT THE MIRROR

> ### ✏️ 'UNMASKING THE WIZARD' EXERCISE
>
> (a) Write a 200-word piece about a lie or illusion you have been deceived by. Do not reveal it is a lie. Keep the reader inside the bubble of propaganda/illusion.
>
> (b) Now 'unmask' the lie/illusion by showing us how it was constructed.

Lost in the funhouse

Despite its serious intent, metafiction is light-hearted and humorous in its delivery and absurdly playful and entertaining. Metafiction can also be disarmingly self-mocking and self-deprecating. Perhaps this is because metafictional writers are thumbing their noses at the seriousness of realism and flouting rules. The situational irony in such texts (where self-effacing authors and bewildered characters roam labyrinths of language) is liberating. Barth calls this place a 'funhouse'. Ryan O'Neill's story *The Weight of a Human Heart* (2012), about a typewriter which has a defective key, is an excellent example of funhouse fun. Not only does this expose the fictionality of the story and how it is constructed, but it is gleeful and inventive.

> When Da came downstairs this morning, he was happyy because of the greyy skyy. Da is Scottish, which is whyy I call him Da and not Dad, but Mum was alwayys Mum and not Ma.
> 'Amyy, what are yyou doin with yyour mother's tyypewriter?' he asked me.
> 'It's not a tyypewriter, it's a word processor,' I said.
> 'Be careful with it. It's old.'
> 'It's alreadyy broken. The yy keyy doesn't work properlyy. When yyou press it once, it tyypes twice. Whyy is that?'
> 'Because yyour mother was like yyou. She was alwayys askin whyy. I think she wore it out' (O'Neill, 2012, p. 202).

Metafictional techniques

What follows are some metafictional techniques that help break the illusion of a given reality and expose the little man behind the giant voice of Oz.

Author intrusion

In Victorian novels, readers were accustomed to the authors' addressing them as 'Gentle reader' in order to facilitate the flow of the narrative. But in postmodern fiction, when an 'author' directly exposes him or herself, this stops the show and destroys the flow of narrative. Authorial intrusion is a disruption and may come as a shock, especially when he (in Barth's case below) is aggressive and angry.

> The reader! You, dogged, uninsultable, print-oriented bastard, it's you I'm addressing, who else, from inside this monstrous fiction. You've read me this far, then? Even this far? For what discreditable motive? How is it you don't go to a movie, watch TV, stare at a wall, play tennis with a friend, make amorous advances to the person who comes to your mind when I speak of amorous advances? Can nothing surfeit, saturate you, turn you off? Where's your shame? (Barth, 1988, p. 123).

One stunning example of authorial intervention in an otherwise smoothly realist fiction is John Fowles's *The French Lieutenant's Woman* (1969). For the first third of the novel, we readers are lulled into a reality that is as Victorian as a George Eliot novel, but just as we have suspended our disbeliefs, the author breaks the illusion and speaks directly to us:

> I do not know. This story I am telling is all imagination. These characters I create never existed outside my own mind. If I have pretended until now to know my characters' minds and innermost thoughts, it is because I am writing in (just as I have assumed some of the vocabulary and "voice" of) a convention universally accepted at the time of my story: that the novelist stands next to God. He may not know all, yet he tries to pretend that he does. But I live in the age of Alain Robbe-Grillet and Roland Barthes; if this is a novel, it cannot be a novel in the modern sense of the word (Fowles, 1969, p. 85).

By intruding, the author is exposing the puppetry of his role. *Here are the strings I pull to make this work*, Fowles is saying. *Here is how the magical illusion works.*

I grew up watching the old Gerry Anderson *Thunderbirds* TV series. Most of the time, I was mesmerised by the realistic characters, but every now and then the lighting would reveal a gleaming puppet string tied to Penelope's wrist or Brains's head and the illusion would be broken.

> **'PULLING THE STRINGS' EXERCISE**
>
> (a) Write a 200-word exchange between two characters, describing them and fleshing them out as 'real', rounded characters. Create verisimilitude and credibility. Suspend our disbelief.
>
> (b) Now bring on the 'author', who interrupts and breaks this illusion of a 'real' world by explaining how he or she pulls the strings of these characters. This 'author' can explain his or her relation to the characters ('this character is really me disguised' or 'I have no idea what to do with this character: he just does NOT do what I tell him to do!')

Breaking the fourth wall

Breaking the illusion of a 'real' scene in theatre by actors' stepping off the stage is a distancing effect known as *Verfremdungseffekt*, a concept coined by playwright Bertolt Brecht. The stage (normally a proscenium arch) is akin to a TV box or cinema screen, a cube of reality we are watching from the outside. We are watching the action through a one-way mirror or 'fourth wall', which, by consensual agreement, is unacknowledged. The actors pretend there is no audience sitting outside this fourth wall, and the audience does not interfere with the acting. But if the fourth wall is opened and allows characters to wander off-stage and interact directly with the audience, then this illusion is broken. Brecht uses this device in order to combat the escapist realism of what he regards as 'bourgeois' theatre of his time. He argues that the suspension of disbelief relies on emotional manipulation of the audience and their emotional identification with the main character. The realist devices used to create this illusion – realistic sets, the fourth wall, and theatre technology such as lighting and special effects – cause emotional manipulation, and he works in his plays to jolt his audience out of what he describes as a 'narcotic spell' (Brecht, 1949, p. 179). He does this by exposing the mechanics of the realistic effect produced, such as showing how the lighting is manipulated or having make-up artists rush on stage to apply tears to an actor's face. The effect is comic but also jarring as it causes audiences to distance themselves from the action and see it for what it is – a manipulation of theatrical devices designed to deceive. In the most notable early break-frame scene, Groucho Marx faces the camera (fourth wall) and says: 'I've got to stay here, but there's no reason you folks shouldn't go out into the lobby till this thing blows over' (1932). The 1986 movie *Ferris Bueller's Day Off* begins with Ferris addressing the camera ('They bought it!') and uses this technique by including the audience as an accomplice to Ferris's playing hooky. He even lets us in on the tricks he uses (Hughes, 1986).

How does this work in fiction? Characters cannot step outside the pages of a novel, so this has to be simulated. A character can address the reader, pull the reader into the narrative, or expose the illusion of reality/fictionality of the text by stating that he or she is a character.

> ✏ ***VERFREMDUNGSEFFEKT*** **EXERCISE**
>
> Take the realist interchange of characters from the previous exercise and, instead of having the 'author' disrupt the scene, have one or two of the characters 'break the fourth wall' and address the reader directly or refer to the way he or she is being written into the story.

Authors as characters

An author cannot literally step into a novel but an 'author' can. An 'author' is a simulation of the real person writing the novel and becomes a character. Stephen King plays with this idea in *The Dark Tower* series when his character goes to consult the author 'Stephen King', a character in the novel. Kurt Vonnegut begins his novel *Slaughterhouse-Five* with the author visiting a friend and worrying about how he will write the novel *Slaughterhouse-Five*. John Fowles employs this method in many of his novels, most notably *The French Lieutenant's Woman* and *Mantissa*. The reader is aware that the main character of *The French Lieutenant's Woman*,

Charles, is being stared at by another passenger on a train. This character has a large red beard and looks very much like the author John Fowles we know from the photograph on the inside jacket cover of the novel. It is John Fowles!

> I take my purse from the pocket of my frock coat, I extract a florin, I rest it on my right thumbnail, I flick it, spinning, two feet into the air and catch it in my left hand. So be it. And I am suddenly aware that Charles has opened his eyes and is looking at me. There is something more than disapproval in his eyes now; he perceives I am either a gambler or mentally deranged. I return his disapproval, and my florin to my purse. He picks up his hat, brushes some invisible speck of dirt (a surrogate for myself) from its nap and places it on his head. We draw under one of the great cast-iron beams that support the roof of Paddington station. We arrive, he steps down to the platform, beckoning to a porter. In a few moments, having given his instructions, he turns. The bearded man has disappeared in the throng (Fowles, 1969, p. 318).

What is disconcerting here is that the author seems to have lost control of the plot and does not even know where his main protagonist is. Instead of being the God-like omniscient presence of Victorian fiction who has total control, this author admits that 'in the age of Alain Robbe-Grillet and Roland Barthes', the author is a minor character in the production of a novel:

> Now the question I am asking, as I stare at Charles, is not quite the same as the two above. But rather, what the devil am I going to do with you? I have already thought of ending Charles's career here and now; of leaving him for eternity on his way to London. But the conventions of Victorian fiction allow, allowed no place for the open, the inconclusive ending; and I preached earlier of the freedom characters must be given. My problem is simple – what Charles wants is clear? It is indeed. But what the protagonist wants is not so clear; and I am not at all sure where she is at the moment (Fowles, 1969, p. 317).

> ✏ **'HI, I'M YOUR AUTHOR' EXERCISE**
>
> Write a scene (150 words) in which you (the 'author') arrive at a scene (train, party or park) to either observe or interact with your characters up close. The other characters can be either aware of or oblivious to your identity.

Beginnings

If you have ever agonised over the beginning of your story or novel, you are not alone. The difficulty is to suck a reader into a world that does not exist. Once your reader is safely in, you can relax. But if you are a metafictional postmodernist writer (and we all are by virtue of the age we live in and the knowledge we now have), writing a beginning is an opportunity to expose the fictional connivance of reality. J.M. Coetzee begins his novel *Elizabeth Costello* (2003) with these lines (in a chapter ironically entitled 'Realism'):

> There is first of all the problem of the opening, namely, how to get us from where we are, which is, as yet, nowhere, to the far bank. It is a simple bridging problem, a problem of knocking together a bridge. People solve such problems every day. They solve them, and having solved them push on. Let us assume that, however it may have been done, it is done. Let us take it that the bridge is built and crossed, that we can put it out of our mind. We have left behind the territory in which we were. We are in the far territory; where we want to be.
> Elizabeth Costello is a writer, born in 1928, which makes her sixty-six years old, going on sixty-seven. She has written nine novels, two books of poems, a book on bird life, and a body of journalism. By birth she is Australian. She was born in Melbourne and still lives there, though she spent the years 1951 to 1963 abroad, in England and France. She has been married twice. She has two children, one by each marriage (Coetzee, 2003, p. 1).

The narrator/author tells us how hard it is to write a beginning. We are daunted with the blank page. But it should be easy, he says nonchalantly, like knocking together a bridge. How does Coetzee write the beginning of *Elizabeth Costello*? The bridge he makes is constructed of metafictional material – the difficulty of writing a beginning. Done. He can then enter the 'realist' world of his main protagonist. But having exposed the trick of beginning a realist novel, we are more likely to see the rest of the novel as a device too, another bridge. Sure enough, the details of her life are listed as a resumé to give the semblance of a real character.

Calvino knocks up a bridge to each of his beginnings to *If on a Winter's Night a Traveller* in a similar way. The novel is a series of beginnings to novels that the reader can never manage to finish, but Calvino will not allow his reader to plunge into a 'real' world. We can only skate on the surface of the words that signify a real world but are all self-referential:

> The novel begins in a railway station, a locomotive huffs, steam from a piston covers the opening chapter, a cloud of smoke hides part of the first paragraph. In the odor of the station there is a passing whiff of station café odor. There is someone looking through the befogged glass, he opens the glass door of the bar, everything is misty, inside, too, as if seen by near sighted eyes, or eyes irritated by coal dust. The pages of the book are clouded like the windows of an old train, the cloud of smoke rests on the sentences. It is a rainy evening; the man enters the bar; he unbuttons his damp overcoat; a cloud of steam enfolds him; a whistle dies away along tracks that are glistening with rain, as far as the eye can see' (Calvino, 1998, p. 10).

Australian writer Murray Bail does the same: aware that he could begin his novel *Eucalyptus* (1998) many ways, he chooses to self-consciously play with the fairy tale beginning and immediately becomes defensive about his own choice:

> Once upon a time there was a man--what's wrong with that? Not the most original way to begin, but certainly tried and proven over time, which suggests something of value, some deep impulse beginning to be answered, a range of possibilities about to be set down.
> There was once a man on a property outside a one-horse town, in New South Wales, who couldn't come to a decision about his

daughter. He then made an unexpected decision. Incredible! For a while people talked and dreamed about little else until they realised it was entirely in keeping with him; they shouldn't have been surprised. To this day it's still talked about, its effects still felt in the town and surrounding districts (Bail, 1998, p. 1).

The authorial intrusions and address to the reader ('what's wrong with that?'; 'Incredible!') distance us from any emotional involvement with the story and instead show us that this story is being constructed.

> **'KNOCKING TOGETHER A BRIDGE' EXERCISE**
>
> (a) Write the beginning of a story that occurs on a train platform and describe exactly how the story is being written and read, including the difficulties of writing the beginning.
>
> (b) Begin a story using a convention (such as in medias res or 'Once upon a time') and then justify that convention or show that you are aware of its fictionality.

The sense of an ending

Endings are as tricky as beginnings. If you have reached the end of your novel, congratulations. If you have reached the end of your novel and thought 'Hmm, that's not quite right, let me write another ending' and then cannot decide which is right, you are also not alone. The 'sense of an ending', as discussed in Chapter 2, is the tying up of all loose ends of plot, character and theme and reaching catharsis.

But postmodernist novelists often present readers with multiple endings or no ending at all. *The French Lieutenant's Woman* ends two ways, equally weighted: the happy and the tragic (Chapters 60 and 61) ending. Earlier in the novel (Chapter 44), a third, deterministic ending is proposed as well. These endings are contradictory but are not a 'choose-your-own-adventure' ending. They reflect the ambiguity and destabilising of the 'realities' that bifurcate from the consequences of relinquishing God-like authorial control.

Richard Brautigan takes this to extremes in his first novel, *A Confederate General from Big Sur* (1964). One satisfying ending is given, the reader sighs, turns the page for THE END, but instead finds...

A SECOND ENDING
A seagull flew over us. We got dressed and went back to Lee Mellon and Elizabeth. They were just as we had left them…
A THIRD ENDING
A seagull flew over us, its voice running with the light, its voice passing historically through
songs of gentle color. We closed our eyes and the bird's shadow was in our ears…
A FOURTH ENDING
A seagull flew over us. We got dressed and went back to Lee Mellon and Elizabeth. Roy Earle was there with them. It was good that I was not surprised…
A FIFTH ENDING
A seagull flew over us. I reached up and ran my hand along his beautiful soft white feathers, feeling the arch and rhythm of his flight. He slipped off my fingers away into the sky…
186,000 ENDINGS PER SECOND
Then there are more and more endings: the sixth, the 53rd, the 131st, the 9,435th ending, endings going faster and faster, more and more endings, faster and faster until this book is having 186,000 endings per second (Brautigan, 1964, p. 116).

Providing multiple endings does not allow the reader the emotional satisfaction of closure and points to the arbitrariness of ending a novel in any way at all.

In *Soldier Blue*, I attempted to deal with the artificial nature of endings by using the Coetzee trick of building a metafictional bridge made of the artifice of writing an ending to get me there.

> So here I am, back on the banks of Lake Kariba, staring out at the dead water, listening to the roar of another plane I missed. If this were a novel, there would be a crescendo of action, the crunch point where the protagonist's ultimate resolve is tested and he wins. Then would come the swift denouement to the satisfying ending, where all antagonists are vanquished. If it were a movie, it would follow Vreitag's [sic] triangle, or the steps of Joseph Campbell's Hero of a Thousand Faces. If it were an autobiography, there would at least be some moral lesson

to be learned from the struggle and triumph or defeat of the hero. But it is none of these. So herewith the anti-climax (Williams, 2008, p. 385).

>  **'A SEAGULL FLEW OVER US' EXERCISE**
>
> Write three endings that contradict each other in order to disrupt the 'sense of an ending'.

The frame story

Also known as a frame tale or frame narrative or a *roman à tiroirs* (a novel with drawers), this device breaks the illusion of a realist narrative by contextualising it as a story told by a teller. Frame tales are as old as the *Arabian Nights* (1701), in which Scheherazade had to continue to tell stories to her husband every night and never finish them to prevent her execution in the morning. Chaucer's *The Canterbury Tales* (1387) and Boccaccio's *The Decameron* (1353) are collections of stories told by pilgrims or cloistered people and serve to show that the story in its frame is not real but part of a larger context.

How is this metafictional? In conventional frame tales, the frame serves simply to contextualise the story, not destabilise its verisimilitude, but modern frame tales are used as a device to expose the fictionality of such stories. William Goldman's 1973 novel *The Princess Bride* is framed in this way: the story is read by a father to his son, and they comment on the story throughout, constantly pulling readers out of their reading pleasure.

> But take the title words- 'true love and high adventure'- I believed that once. I thought my life was going to follow that path. Prayed that it would. Obviously it didn't, but I don't think there's high adventure left anymore. Nobody takes out a sword nowadays and cries, 'Hello. My name is Inigo Montoya. You killed my father; prepare to die!' (Goldman, 1973, p. 27).

Such a frame destabilises the story and much in the way that Brecht desires us to stand outside our emotional attachment to the story, this novel asks us to question the nature of storytelling through its frame.

Calvino's *If on a Winter's Night a Traveller* has already been mentioned as a metafictional novel in the way it refers to its own processes. But it is also a frame narrative, a collection of beginnings of novels, held together by the frame story of a reader who wishes to read Italo Calvino's *If on a Winter's Night a Traveller* but is constantly foiled in his attempts. Each time the reader tries to enter into a realist story world and suspends his (and later her and their) disbelief, the frame breaks and the story is cut off, disrupting the illusion of the narrative and demonstrating that this is just a story and this is how stories are made, printed, bound and translated.

Conclusion

Should YOU write metafiction?

> YES: it demonstrates a sophisticated awareness of our contemporary postmodern condition and deconstructs 'reality' and the myths of our time.
> NO: it is pretentious self-obsession. A writer's writing about writing is narcissistic. Just get out of the way and tell the story. And even if you attempt it, it is difficult to pull off well and will look like a gratuitous piece of gimmickry.
> MAYBE YOU HAVE NO CHOICE: The bad news is that now you know about it, it will be impossible to naively write realistically again. You can run from the artificial nature of your fiction, but you cannot hide from metafictional truth.

He read over what he had written. He was tired: he had written through the night, blocked out the whole chapter, and still was not satisfied with it. Especially the ending. He couldn't end the chapter like that. Had he proven that metafiction was not 'a big wank'? Should he even use the words 'big wank' in a creative writing textbook? He might have to cut that out at the editing stage or see what the editor suggests.

Or maybe he should end the chapter with a list of recommended books that he loves, metafictional novels that shift the world a little, that dislodge the complacent reality people cling too so tightly, that do what real art should do?

'Reader?' He turned toward the invisible fourth wall and tapped on its thick glass. 'What do you think?'

You the reader, surprised that you could be seen from inside the text, pointed to your chest. 'Me?'

'What do you think? How should I end this chapter? Multiple contradictory endings that disrupt the time continuum of your universe?'

You shook your head. 'You think you're so smart, so pretentious, too clever by half. By adding yourself and now me in your metafictional chapter about metafiction – now that really is a big wank.'

'I'm sorry. I thought… it would help.'

'Perhaps just cut out the whole self-reflexive frame tale altogether. Readers just want the chapter.'

'If you say so.' He sighed, and deleted the entire section in italics he had just written.

References

Bail, Murray. 1998. *Eucalyptus*. Melbourne: Text Publishing.
Barth, John. 1967. The Literature of Exhaustion. In *The Novel Today: Contemporary Writers on Modern Fiction*, ed. Malcolm Bradbury. 1977. UK: Manchester University Press.
Barth, John. 1988. *Lost in the Funhouse*. New York: Anchor Books.
Brautigan, Richard. 1964. *A Confederate General from Big Sur*. New York: Grove Press.
Brecht, Bertolt. 1949. A Short Organum for the Theatre. In *Brecht on Theatre: The Development of an Aesthetic*, ed. and trans. John Willett, 1964: 179–205. London: Methuen.
Calvino, Italo. 1998. *If on a winter's night a traveller*. Great Britain: Vintage.
Coetzee, J.M. 2003. *Elizabeth Costello*. New York: Penguin.
Fowles, John. 1969. *The French Lieutenant's Woman*. London: Jonathan Cape.
Fowles, John. 1982. *Mantissa*. London: Jonathan Cape.
Goldman, William. 1973. *The Princess Bride*. New York: Harcourt Brace Jovanovich.
Hughes, John (dir.). 1986. *Ferris Bueller's Day Off*. Paramount Pictures.
Hutcheon, Linda. 1980. *Narcissistic Narrative: The Metafictional Paradox*. Ontario: Wilfrid Laurier University Press.
O'Neill, Ryan. 2012. *The Weight of a Human Heart*. Carlton, Victoria: Black Inc.
Vonnegut, Kurt. 1991. *Slaughterhouse*-5. New York: Dell Publishing.
Watt, Ian. 1963. *The Rise of the Novel: Studies in Defoe, Richardson and Fielding*. Penguin: Harmondsworth.
Waugh, Patricia. 1984. *Metafiction: The Theory and Practice of Self-Conscious Fiction*. London and New York: Methuen.
Williams, Paul. 2007. Soldier Blue unpublished draft.
Williams, Paul. 2008. *Soldier Blue*. Cape Town: David Philip Publishers.

8 THE TRANSGRESSIVE NOVEL: WRITING WITH DARK INK

In the science fiction movie *Planet of the Apes* (1968), earth space travellers find themselves on a strange planet which contains a Forbidden Zone no one dares enter: to transgress this border means madness and sure death. The Forbidden Zone holds secrets that should never be revealed because knowledge of this will destroy civilisation. But these travellers from earth cross the line and discover something about themselves that is shocking. This self-revelation unmasks the lies of this planet's civilisation and reveals a naked truth.

It's the 'serpent in Eden' myth rewritten. You can eat of any tree except this one, for if you do you shall surely die. But Eve transgresses and eats of the fruit and discovers… death, yes, but also knowledge and self-awareness.

This chapter invites you to transgress, step across the line into the Forbidden Zone, eat the fruit, unmask the lies of civilisation and discover that truth.

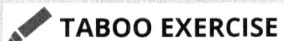

TABOO EXERCISE

Freewrite for three minutes on taboos. What is a taboo? List some taboos in your society. Why are they taboos?

Part I: Transgressive fiction

Transgressive fiction is a revolt against the norms of society, a descent into the darker nature of ourselves or, as Allon White claims, the 'the act of breaking the rules' (White, 1982, p. 51). Transgression literally means trespassing or crossing a line into a forbidden zone. But what is this line and what is 'forbidden'? Is it a moral line? Cultural? Is it a relative line, depending on our subjective tolerance for things? Transgressive fiction delights in perversion, taboo and the illicit and in destabilising social forms, disrupting, and crossing the line we have made between civilised and savage.

Disgust

Michel Foucault coined the phrase in his essay 'A Preface to Transgression' (1963) and cites Georges Bataille's 1928 novella *Story of the Eye* (*L'histoire de l'oeil*) as a prime example of transgressive literature because it crosses many lines society has put up. *Story of the Eye* is an exploration of sexuality between teenagers and involves rape, fetishisation, necrophilia, coprophilia and more:

> she so bluntly craved any upheaval that the faintest call from the senses gave her a look directly suggestive of all things linked to deep sexuality, such as blood, suffocation, sudden terror, crime; things indefinitely destroying human bliss and honesty (Bataille, 2001 (1928), p. 11).

To many people, these topics will elicit disgust and revulsion, a primal emotional response, and a moral distaste for what is outside the norms or conventions of our society. Faeces, rotten food and bad smells cause disgust, as do what are deemed immoral acts – sex with children and incest – in what is argued to be an evolutionary protection device. Or is this socially conditioned behaviour?

Consider Sade's *The 120 Days of Sodom* (1904), *or the School of Libertinage* (1785), 'the most impure tale that has ever been told since our world began' (Sade cited in Sciolino, 2013, n.p.), a primal transgressive text that subjects its readers to extreme sexual activities: sexual abuse, torture and slaughter.

Or Burroughs's *Naked Lunch* (1959), which some would consider a brutal, obscene and disgusting book. The novel follows the story of a junkie and includes scenes of paedophilia, child murder and explicit graphic sexuality: 'Naked Mr. America, burning frantic with self bone love, screams out: "My asshole confounds the Louvre! I fart ambrosia and shit pure gold turds! My cock spurts soft diamonds in the morning sunlight!"' (Burroughs, 2004 (1959), p. 64).

What is the purpose of such writing? To simply shock? To elicit disgust? To expose the sham and hypocrisy of conventional society and reveal the raw reality underneath? Is it akin to a flasher's exposing him or herself at a respectable dinner party? Is it saying: *All is not well in the world. Don't get comfortable. People do vomit and shit and piss. Why not write about that too?*

Jonathan Swift's *Gulliver's Travels* (1726) is a transgressive text in that its primary function appears to be to demonstrate that the physical body is revolting, society is a festering cesspit of hypocrisy, and 'mankind' is a revolting scourge of the earth. Swift's view is scatological and misanthropic. All humans are filthy disgusting Yahoos. In this novel, perhaps we get a clue to understand transgressive fiction: its motive is to expose, dissect myths, deconstruct and disrupt.

Consider Justine Ettler's *The River Ophelia* (1995), in which the protagonist describes in detail the bodily fluids that exude from every orifice – diarrhoea, menstruation, vomit and sexual fluids. Objectively, of course, there is nothing disgusting about our bodily functions – unless we are Puritans/prudes who see our animal nature as abhorrent. But Ettler's novel is a palimpsest, written on top of both *Story of an Eye* and *The 120 Days of Sodom*, the two main male characters in the novel being Bataille and Sade. Ettler says that she wrote this book 'from below' to explore what it would be like to be 'a female character in Brett Easton Ellis' *American Psycho*':

> The thing is ... the thing about all this pain (women) go through, all this love that just hurts all the time, the thing about all this pain is that it's really exquisite. It's exquisite pain. That's what makes us keep going back for more (Thompson, 2018, n.p.).

✏️ DISGUST EXERCISE

1. Freewrite for three minutes on 'disgust'. What is disgusting to you? How does it feel to be disgusted? Why do you feel this way?

2. Write about bodily functions graphically and unsparingly as Swift does. What effect does this writing have?

3. Write a scene set at a respectable dinner party where someone transgresses the rules and norms.

Oscar Wilde's writing was 'obscene', according to his critics at the time, and he was jailed not only for his 'crime' of homosexuality but for his transgressive writing which was banned, reviled and called immoral. What was most objectionable apparently was the idea of 'free sex', sex between people of the same gender. But as Wilde himself reminded us in *The Picture of Dorian Gray* (1890), 'The books that the world calls immoral are books that show the world its own shame' (Wilde, 2001 (1890), p. 168).

This sex business

Writing about sex has always been problematic for writers. Whereas many modern writers feel they have to include graphic sex to render the narrative authentic, Victorian writers avoided it. (The dry aged academic scholar Casaubon, who marries the young and vibrant Dorothea, discovers on his wedding night that 'the poets had much exaggerated the force of masculine passion' (Eliot, 2018 (1871), p. 63).) By contrast, medieval writers revelled in it. In his 'bawdy' *The Canterbury Tales* (1387), Chaucer describes acts of penetration, debauchery, lust and adultery with glee. But sex (to be Freudian here) is central to the drive of most narratives, whether sublimated or overt.

The Victorian era made writing about sex a taboo, so when D.H. Lawrence transgressed this taboo in 1928 with his novel *Lady Chatterley's Lover*, the establishment erupted in disgust at the subject matter and the use of four-letter graphic words. Nowadays, we would not find such a novel transgressive. But in 1928, it was banned and, where it was allowed to be published, was restricted to the 'top shelf' of the bookstore and only a limited number of copies were allowed to be printed. What was also scandalous was that graphic sex portrayed in this novel was between a working-class servant and his aristocratic lady. Even more scandalous was the author's suggestion that women could enjoy sex autonomously, perhaps as recreation. Lawrence begins the novel upfront with the literary transgression he is about to commit:

> A woman could yield to a man without yielding her inner, free self. That the poets and talkers about sex did not seem to have taken sufficiently into account. A woman could take a man without really giving herself away. Certainly she could take him without giving herself into his power. Rather she could use this

sex thing to have power over him. For she only had to hold herself back in sexual intercourse, and let him finish and expend himself without herself coming to the crisis: and then she could prolong the connexion and achieve her orgasm and her crisis while he was merely her tool (Lawrence, 2007, p. 3).

Henry Miller's *Tropic of Cancer* (1934) suffered a similar fate to *Lady Chatterley's Lover* in that his novel was banned, and both books were the centre of obscenity trials. Both were acquitted of their crime and thus their transgressive 'filth' was allowed to be spilled out into the world. But whereas Lawrence was transgressive only in so far as he focused on sexuality as a positive force in its own right, Miller actively sought to streak across the metaphorical dinner party table, flaunting his avant-garde artistic rage: 'I start tomorrow on the Paris book. First person, uncensored, formless – fuck everything!' (cited in Nazaryan, 2013). Miller's novels are a curious blend of rampant sexual adventure, philosophic reflection, and an attack on whatever is conventional.

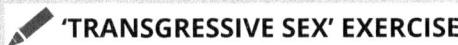

'TRANSGRESSIVE SEX' EXERCISE

Locate and read some descriptions of sex in Miller, Lawrence, Ettner, Sade and Bataille. What is transgressive about them? What narrative techniques do they use to trespass into forbidden territory? Write a sex scene (300 words) in which a character transgresses the norms.

Strangely, fifty years after the taboo on writing graphically about sex has been lifted, a novel is smuggled into readers' lives, read in private and talked about in hushed tones: a transgressive popular novel called *Fifty Shades of Grey* (2011). Bondage and S&M are nothing new, but somehow in the popular mainstream, they are. *Fifty Shades of Grey*, however, turns out to be a conventional romance, and the obstacle to the happily-ever-after ending is that the male object of desire is a sexual pervert, someone who has a bondage room full of forbidden pleasures. The female protagonist therefore has to be initiated into this deviance, but she resists and reinforces the mainstream view that what he really needs is love and monogamy, and she is the one who will break through his cold heart and teach him. The transgressive is played with but then rejected for the norm.

The explicit sex is there but is so badly written it could be mistaken for parody. For example: 'I had no idea giving pleasure could be such a turn-on, watching him writhe subtly with carnal longing. My inner goddess is doing the merengue with some salsa moves' (James, 2011, p. 43). Or: 'His voice is warm and husky like dark melted chocolate fudge caramel… or something' (ibid, p. 29). Or: 'Now I know what all the fuss is about. Two orgasms… coming apart at the seams, like the spin cycle on a washing machine, wow' (ibid).

Vladimir Nabokov's *Lolita* (1955) is a transgressive text that has no descriptions of graphic sex or four-letter words. It has a fancy style ('You can always count on a murderer for a fancy prose style' (Nabokov, 1989 (1955), p. 9), boasts the paedophile protagonist), and avoids cliché ('In pornographic novels, action has to be limited to the copulation of clichés', ibid, p. 313). So how is it transgressive? Because he takes the most transgressive topic possible, runs with it, and seduces the readers into seeing the world from a paedophile's point of view. As Nabokov explains in his afterword:

> Certain techniques in the beginning of Lolita (Humbert's Journal, for example) misled some of my first readers into assuming that this was going to be a lewd book. They expected the rising succession of erotic scenes; when these stopped, the readers stopped, too, and felt bored and let down. This, I suspect, is one of the reasons why not all the four firms read the typescript to the end. Whether they found it pornographic or not did not interest me. Their refusal to buy the book was based not on my treatment of the theme but on the theme itself, for there are at least three themes which are utterly taboo as far as most American publishers are concerned. The two others are: a Negro-White marriage which is a complete and glorious success resulting in lots of children and grandchildren; and the total atheist who lives a happy and useful life, and dies in his sleep at the age of 106 (ibid, p. 315).

How did Nabokov do it? By using poetry and humour. David Lodge (2014, n.p.) argues that the secret of Nabokov's sexual style is that 'elegant variation and metaphorical figures of speech were applied lavishly to sexual parts and acts':

> How to defamiliarise the limited repertoire of sexual acts was never a problem for him, because of his extraordinary stylistic virtuosity, his metaphorical inventiveness and mastery of an entire thesaurus of other rhetorical devices, which make other novelists (this one anyway) gape in admiration and feel inadequate, whatever his subject (ibid).

For example, this is the scene in which Lolita sits on Humbert's lap: 'my moaning mouth, gentlemen of the jury, almost reached her bare neck, while I crushed out against her left buttock the last throb of the longest ecstasy man or monster had ever known' (Nabokov, 1989 (1955), p. 61).

Poetry and humour temper this otherwise transgressive taboo scene into something else. It jars and the form and content subvert each other, creating a discordance, a transgression of the narrative itself.

> ✎ **'WRITING TABOOS' EXERCISE**
>
> **Go back to the list of taboos you made at the beginning of this chapter and write about one of them, using humour and poetry to create discordance between form and content.**

Paedophilia is not the exclusive domain of the transgressive male writer. As a counterpoint to Nabokov's *Lolita*, Alissa Nutting's novel *Tampa* (2013) unashamedly documents a 26-year-old female schoolteacher's seduction of her 14-year-old male student. But unlike *Lolita*, *Tampa* graphically exposes the adult's (Celeste Price's) pathological and explicit lust:

> I spent the night before my first day of teaching in an excited loop of hushed masturbation on my side of the mattress, never falling asleep. To bed I'd worn, in secret, a silk chemise and sheer panties, beneath my robe of course, so that my husband, Ford, wouldn't pillage me (Nutting, 2013, p. 1).

The Beat poets of the late 1950s wrote transgressive manifestos to proclaim their rebellion against society:

> The only people for me are the mad ones, the ones who are mad to live, mad to talk, mad to be saved, desirous of

everything at the same time, the ones who never yawn or say a commonplace thing, but burn, burn, burn, like fabulous yellow roman candles exploding like spiders across the stars and in the middle you see the blue centerlight pop and everybody goes "Awww!" (Kerouac, 1999 (1957), p. 5).
Bukowski, you are so fucked up and you still survive. I decided not to kill myself.... So in a way I save people.... Not that I want to save them: I have no desire to save anybody.... So these are my readers, you see? They buy my books – the defeated, the demented and the damned – and I am proud of it (Kirsch, 2005, n.p.).

Whereas most of the transgressive literature was written by men, Sylvia Plath's *The Bell Jar* stands out as a 'female counterpart' to male alienation and transgression against mainstream society. The protagonist, Esther Greenwood, documents her experience of being a woman in an oppressive male society and her descent into madness and suicide:

I saw my life branching out before me like the green fig tree in the story. From the tip of every branch, like a fat purple fig, a wonderful future beckoned and winked. One fig was a husband and a happy home and children, and another fig was a famous poet and another fig was a brilliant professor, and another fig was Ee Gee, the amazing editor, and another fig was Europe and Africa and South America.... I wanted each and every one of them, but choosing one meant losing all the rest (Plath, 2006 (1966), p.73).

Esther's rebellion echoes the transgressive voices in J.D. Salinger's *The Catcher in the Rye*, Ralph Ellison's *Invisible Man* (1952), and Jack Kerouac's *On the Road* (1957), yet she demarcates a particular focus on female experience, alienation and disgust with mainstream patriarchal society.

Grunge literature

In the 1990s, a new wave of transgressive fiction flowered darkly in such novels as Chuck Palahniuk's *Fight Club*. Palahniuk's 1996 novel transgressed society norms in many ways. Superficially, it celebrated an anarchic secret society of men who fought each other in undisclosed venues, spat in the food they served to customers, and asserted themselves in existentialist acts of meaning-making in a nihilistic, absurd world. Here is the protagonist's manifesto:

> You are not special. You're not a beautiful and unique snowflake. You're the same decaying organic matter as everything else. We're all part of the same compost heap. We're the all-singing, all-dancing crap of the world (Palahniuk, 1996, p. 134).

Palahniuk's schizophrenic protagonist advocates a secret society of transgressive subversives to rage against the machine.

James Frey's 'memoir' *A Thousand Little Pieces* (2003) – I put this in postmodernist quotes because Oprah publicly exposed the book as full of lies – boasts of a transgressive life of drugs, sex, crime, debauchery and low life:

> I wake up to the drone of an airplane engine and the feeling of something warm dripping down my chin. I lift my hand to feel my face. My front four teeth are gone, I have a hole in my cheek, my nose is broken and my eyes are swollen nearly shut. I open them and I look around and I'm in the back of a plane and there's no one near me. I look at my clothes and my clothes are covered with a colorful mixture of spit, snot, urine, vomit and blood. I reach for the call button and I find it and I push it and I wait and thirty seconds later an Attendant arrives (Frey, 2003, p. 1).

Andrew McGahan's *Praise* and Ettler's *The River Ophelia* both revel in vomit, diarrhoea, drug use, sexual abuse and general depravity. Such transgressive novels are popular. Why? Is the appeal to write about things we shouldn't, to go where others are afraid to go, that taboos are fascinating, that the forbidden holds an irresistible attraction? Perhaps the *jouissance* of it, the thrill of transgression itself, of freedom from boundaries, the exhilaration of breaking rules, or being brutally honest? Transgressive fiction is not merely gratuitous: it exposes the absurdity of life, the phoniness of people and the lies of 'sivilisation'; it disrupts and deconstructs: 'What begins as a cathartic exercise in beating the hell out of someone turns, by an easy but twisted logic, into an impotent attack on the social order' (Jourdan, 2012, n.p.).

In the next chapter, we will examine some transgressive novels by women, such as Kathy Acker's *Blood and Guts in High School* (1984) and Ettler's *The River Ophelia*, which use transgression to deconstruct patriarchy.

Part II: J.M. Coetzee
Writing from the dark side

J.M. Coetzee, 2003 Nobel laureate, writes transgressive fiction, and it is worth examining his narrative techniques in detail. In *Boyhood* (1997), his fictional autobiography, the young writer confesses his literary ambitions and outlines his transgressive manifesto:

> What he would write if he could...would be something darker, something that, once it began to flow from his pen, would spread across the page out of control, like spilt ink. Like spilt ink, like shadows racing across the face of still water, like lightning crackling across the sky (Coetzee, 1998 (1997), p. 140).

A great book cannot come from a trivial concept. To be truly transgressive, we need to write about something deep, profoundly disturbing, and rich. We need to be honest. Undermine surface. As stated earlier, 'some works', Coetzee says, 'reinforce the myths of our culture, others dissect these myths. In our time and place, it is the latter kind of work that seems to me more urgent' (Olsen, 1985, p. 47). Are we going to perpetuate the status quo and lull our readers into complacent acceptance of their received notions of culture, or are we going to dissect these myths and disturb the deep waters of our culture? For our writing to have *gravitas*, we must wrestle with the dark shadows of our civilisation. This can be achieved by a technique Coetzee articulates: engaging with the countervoices of our culture, of our dark selves, and of our literary history.

Countervoices

Disgrace is Coetzee's 1999 Booker prize–winning novel in which a university professor, David Lurie, gives in to his darker desires and 'solves the problem of sex' (as he calls it) by having languid sex first with a prostitute and then with a young student he seduces/rapes. It may be tempting to observe that Lurie and his creator, Coetzee, at the time of writing *Disgrace*, are both professors of literature at the University of Cape Town, both in their early fifties, both white, and both highly literate, steeped in Romantic poetry, and both divorced. This may simply be a question of writing what you know, but in a much earlier interview, Coetzee gives us a clue as to why he parallels his own life to create such a 'monster':

> To write is to awaken counter-voices within oneself, and to dare enter into dialogue with them. As consciousnesses trapped in bodies, communicating with the imperfect tool of language, we often use stories to convey information – to reach toward some sort of truth – and yet because we have no objective access to other consciousnesses, what we are left communicating are stories about ourselves. We are all one self full of countervoices telling stories and seeking truths (cited in Attwell, 1992, p. 65).

Lurie is a countervoice, a parallel Coetzee in a parallel fictional universe, a test tube case where problems of male sexuality are posed, hypotheses tested, and counter selves allowed to roam freely and explore their dark sides. Herein lies the liberation for writers: in fiction, we are given licence to explore countervoices:

> Writers are used to being in control of the text and don't resign it easily. But my resistance is not only a matter of protecting a phantasmatic omnipotence. Writing is not free expression. There is a true sense in which writing is dialogic: a matter of awakening the countervoices in oneself and embarking upon speech with them. It is some measure of a writer's seriousness whether he does evoke/invoke those countervoices in himself, that is, step down from the position of what Lacan calls "the subject supposed to know" (cited in Attwell, 1992, p. 65).

✏️ COUNTERVOICE EXERCISE

Write a 300-word paragraph from the point of view of a character who is a 'counter self' to you. Perhaps take on the voice of a character who has the opposite values to you and whose moral world view is diametrically opposite to yours.

Nerve points

For a dentist, touching a nerve is a bad thing, but apparently for a novelist, it is a good thing. Nadine Gordimer says of Coetzee's *Waiting for the Barbarians* (1980): 'J.M. Coetzee's vision goes to the nerve-centre of being. What he finds there is more than most people will ever know about themselves' (Gordimer, 1980, back cover). Surprisingly, Coetzee's novel *Disgrace* was not well received in his home country. Reactions to *Disgrace* show how close to the bone (another surgical metaphor) its subject matter is. It deals with (amongst other things) intellectual emasculation, old age, animal rights, land repossession, gang rape, and male sexuality. You do not write about gang rape by blacks on whites in a country where such racial stereotyping is provocative and where rape is statistically the highest in the world. You do not write about farm invasions and land repossession in a country next to one that has recently collapsed economically because of land repossession. If you do, you should expect this type of response:

> the African National Congress accused Coetzee of representing "as brutally as he can the white people's perception of the post-apartheid black man," and of implying that in the new regime whites would "lose their cards, their weapons, their property, their rights, their dignity," while "the white women will have to sleep with the barbaric black men." [...] some interpreted a subplot [...] as a sign that the novelist cared more about animal rights than human rights (Donadio, 2007, n.p.).

'NERVE POINT' EXERCISE

Using the Coetzee example above, write a 300-word passage about a nerve point in your culture. Stir the surface of political waters. Write something that will cause outrage, something that will disturb the complacent truths of society. Challenge preconceptions and touch nerves. Deconstruct and demystify subjects and challenge assumed positions and received opinions. In this way, writing can crackle across the sky like forked lightning.

Out-language

It may be that the dark side is better left unsaid. As in all good minimalist prose, what is left out is more powerful than what is stated. Absence of language becomes a narrative technique itself.

Geoffroy Alain (1994) coins the term 'out-language' when discussing Coetzee's work, suggesting that when it comes to subjects like pain, death, deprivation and terror, language cannot suffice to capture the 'ineffable realness of the world' and words become 'quick-silver between fingers':

> Coetzee outlines a theory of writing which links together the fictional discourse and the hole(s) of the real it both conceals and fills up. According to him, writing is an attempt to make the silent world speak, a world which is "out-language," as one says "out-law," a world which throws Magda into a panic when she is suddenly deprived of the powers of speech, and "from [her] throat comes something which is not a cry, not a groan, not a voice, but a wind that blows from the stars and over the polar wastes and through [her]. The wind is white, the wind is black, it says nothing." [Coetzee, 1977, p. 55] That very same breath, come from a realm in which neither symbols nor language reign, escapes from Friday's mouth like "the roar of the waves in a seashell; and over that, as if once or twice a violin-string were touched, the whine of the wind and the cry of a bird" [Coetzee, 1986, p. 154] (Alain, 1994).

If we wish to get to the dark space of the novel and the dark matter of our own writing, then perhaps we need to acknowledge the absences, the holes, the inadequacies of language and reason in the very discourse or medium we are using to communicate. We need to explore our counter selves and, despite the inadequacy of our language, we need to encircle the dark centre of being and allow dark spaces in our text through the cracks of an out-language.

References

Alain, Geoffroy. 1994. The Quest for Identity in Multicultural Society: South Africa. In *Alizés N° 9, Proceedings of International Seminar*. Université de La Réunion, December: 201–212.

Attwell, David. 1992. Doubling the Point: Essays and Interviews. Cambridge, MA: Harvard University Press.
Bataille, Georges. 2001 (1928). *Story of the Eye*. London: Penguin.
Burroughs, William. 2004 (1959). *Naked Lunch*. New York: Grove Press.
Coetzee J.M. 1977. *In the Heart of the Country*. South Africa: Ravan Press.
Coetzee J.M. 1986. *Foe*. New York: Viking.
Coetzee, J.M. 1998 (1997). *Boyhood*. London: Vintage.
Coetzee J.M. 1999. *Disgrace*. London: Vintage.
Donadio, Rachel. 2007. Out of South Africa. *The New York Times*, December 16. www.nytimes.com/2007/12/16/books/review/Donadio-t.html?pagewanted=all. Accessed 1 September 2018.
Eliot, George. 2000 (1871). *Middlemarch*. Hertfordshire: Wordsworth.
Ettler, Justine. 1995. *The River Ophelia*. London: Picador.
Foucault, Michel. 1963. A Preface to Transgression. In *Michel Foucault, Language, Counter-Memory, Practice: Selected Essays and Interviews*, ed. Donald Bouchard, 1977: 29–52. Ithaca: Cornell UP. https://monoskop.org/images/a/a3/Foucault_Michel_1963_1977_A_Preface_to_Transgression.pdf. Accessed 1 September 2018.
Frey, James. 2003. *A Thousand Little Pieces*. Great Britain: John Murray Publishers.
Gordimer, Nadine. 1980. Back cover blurb on JM Coetzee's *Waiting for the Barbarians*. New York: Penguin.
James, E.L. 2011. *Fifty Shades of Grey*. London: Vintage.
Jourdan, Phil. 2012. Transgression in Theory: The Idea of a Fight Club. *Lit Reactor*, February 29. https://litreactor.com/columns/transgression-in-theory-the-idea-of-a-fight-club. Accessed 1 September 2018.
Kerouac, Jack. 1999 (1957). *On the Road*. New York: Penguin.
Kirsch, Adam. 2005. Smashed: The pulp poetry of Charles Bukowski. *The New Yorker*, March 14. www.newyorker.com/magazine/2005/03/14/smashed. Accessed 1 September 2018.
Lawrence, D.H. 2007 (1928). *Lady Chatterley's Lover*. Hertfordshire: Wordsworth.
Lodge, David. 2014. The secret of Nabokov's sexual style. *The Guardian*, June 7. www.theguardian.com/books/2014/jun/07/nabokov-lolita-writing-sex-triumph-style. Accessed 1 September 2018.
Miller, Henry. 2005 (1934). *Tropic of Cancer*. London: Harper Perennial.
Nabokov, Vladimir. 1989 (1955). *Lolita*. New York: Vintage Books.
Nazaryan, Alexander. 2013. 'Henry Miller, Brooklyn Hater'. *The New Yorker*, May 10. www.newyorker.com/books/page-turner/henry-miller-brooklyn-hater. Accessed 1 September 2018.
Nutting, Alissa. 2013. *Tampa*. New York: Ecco Books.
Olsen, Lance. 1985. The Presence of Absence: Coetzee's *Waiting for the Barbarians*. *Ariel: A Review of International English Literature* 16, 2: 47–56. http://ariel.synergiesprairies.ca/ariel/index.php/ariel/article/view/1887. Accessed 4 June 2013.

Palahniuk, Chuck. 1996. *Fight Club*. New York: W.W. Norton.
Plath, Sylvia. *The Bell Jar*. 2006 (1966). New York: HarperCollins.
Sade, Marquis de. 2015 (1904). *The 120 Days of Sodom*. London: Penguin.
Sciolino, Elaine. 2013. It's a Sadistic Story, and France Wants It. *The New York Times*, January 22. www.nytimes.com/2013/01/22/books/frances-national-library-hopes-to-buy-sades-120-days.html. Accessed 1 September 2018.
Thompson, Jay Daniel. 2018. Rereading The River Ophelia in the era of #MeToo. *Overland* January 18. https://overland.org.au/2018/01/rereading-the-river-ophelia-in-the-era-of-metoo/. Accessed 1 September 2018.
White, Allon. 1982. Pigs and Pierrots: The Politics of Transgression in Modern Fiction. *Raritan* 2: 51-70.
Wilde, Oscar. 2001 (1890). *The Picture of Dorian Gray*. Hertfordshire: Wordsworth.

9 ECRITURE FEMININE: WRITING THE BODY

The first thing you might ask is this: who am I, Paul Williams, to be writing a chapter on *l'ecriture feminine*? It's a question that must be asked because it raises the issue of whether other genders and sexes have different ways of writing, how other genders experience and write the world differently, and even more importantly, how white, cis-gendered, able-bodied men's voices have dominated literary discourse, women's and 'other' voices have been silenced, and men tend to speak over women and others, appropriating their voices.

I do not identify as a woman and have not experienced the total living conditions of women's experience of the world, let alone of their bodies. Therefore, I cannot speak for them or use any authoritative personal experience to speak on how women should write. But I can acknowledge that, up to now, the discourse in this book has been very male-centred; the majority of the 'Great Writers' cited are male and there is a bias towards a 'masculine' prose and a heterosexual, white, able-bodied, cis-gendered, Western way of thinking. I also acknowledge that I can speak only from my limited point of view and defer to the writings of others to choose to reveal what *l'ecriture feminine* is and let the book unfold that way.

Yet I think it is crucial that we all (men included) understand *l'ecriture feminine*, inhabit it as a technique and question the essentialisms that divide 'women' from 'men' and binarise/privilege these two genders. It is also crucial that we do not accept writing as neutral, or patriarchy and male discourse as 'natural' or invisible, as they appear to many people. If both gender and sex are social constructs, and we need to be aware of how gendered writing is and what to do as creative writers so as not to write into phallocentric traps, like the one I am falling into by even writing this disclaimer!

Binaries

We think in binaries. Our language is structured in binaries such as good/bad and day/night, and our digital world operates in a binary system of opposites: 0s and 1s. Importantly, male/female is perceived as an opposite distinct category, in which sexuality matches gender and behaviours associated with these cis-gender binaries are reinforced perpetually by society, the media and (some would argue) our biology.

The problem with binaries, as Jacques Derrida points out, is that there is an underlying binary system that positions and places a 'violent' hierarchy of one over the other – white/black, male/*fe*male, man/*wo*man, phallus/vagina – where the first is present and the second connotes absence of the first. This dichotomy enforces a power structure favouring the former over the latter. As writers, we can either reinforce or dissect/deconstruct such binaries in our writing.

Plato was perhaps the first to set up such strict binaries by opposing what he called the 'real' world or the Forms (the spiritual world) and copies or reflections of the real world (the material world). This does seem upside-down, but his reasoning was that the abstract was more 'pure' than the manifestation. For example, a perfect circle exists in theory (a round plane figure whose circumference consists of points equidistant from the centre), but try drawing a perfect circle and you will come up with a bad copy of that idea. There is no way you will be able to draw a circle where all points are equidistant from the centre. Even the thickness of the very line you draw disqualifies your circle from being perfect.

Neoplatonists and medieval Christians reinforced this binary by seeing the mortal 'flesh' as inferior to the immortal 'soul'. This binary was perpetuated by René Descartes (1637), who 'proved' that the mind ('res inextensa') was more real than the body ('res extensa') with his famed 'I think therefore I am' experiment (Descartes, 2006 (1637), p. 28). You could be a mind imagining you had a body (as you do when you are dreaming), but you can never disprove you have a mind, because even when doubting you have a mind, you are thinking with one. So, he reasoned, the body is somehow inferior to or lower than the mind/spirit/soul. Reason is superior to emotion or impulses of the body. This 'rational' train of thought has dominated Western thinking for centuries and is associated mostly with 'masculine' thinking.

Essentialism

Essentialism posits that there are innate, essential differences between men and women and that we are born with certain traits that match our sex. Men are inherently hard, rational, unfeeling and strong; women are inherently soft, intuitive, emotional and caring. This perpetuates the binary that, at worst, women are inferior to men or, at best, women are different from men. Simone de Beauvoir, in her book *The Second Sex* (1949), argues that gender is socially constructed.

But Gayatri Chakravorty Spivak (1987) advocates what she calls a strategic essentialism, arguing that sometimes it is necessary to identify with essentialism in order to highlight the binary powers at work, to create a 'temporary solidarity amongst women for the purpose of social action' (cited in Crimmins, 2014, p. 175). Luce Irigaray (1977) too seeks to alter the exclusion of the feminine by repeating or reiterating naturalising discourses about female bodies.

Many writers have struggled with binaries in depicting characters and using language. The most obvious is the use of the pronouns 'he' and 'she'. In English, there is no way to break the binary. Various strategies have been used but they are all clumsy: 'they' used as a singular pronoun (as in 'a writer can decide their own future as they see fit') rather than the binary ('a writer can decide his/her own future as he or she sees fit') or the equally clumsy 's/he'.

So too with writing stereotypes. Writing about people ('men' and 'women'), we cannot help but fall into binary descriptions based on appearance. How do we deconstruct these in our writing?

BINARY EXERCISE

In your own writing (stories and novel chapters), examine one of your male or female characters and see whether you have reinforced stereotypical gender-essentialist binaries. Rewrite this character to break this stereotype by giving them an atypical characteristic.

L'ecriture feminine

'Feminine writing' appears to be a deliberate strategic essentialist narrative technique. Hélène Cixous outlines strategies for women writers in her manifesto *The Laugh of the Medusa* (1976):

> Woman must write her self: must write about women and bring women to writing, from which they have been driven away as violently as from their bodies-for the same reasons, by the same law, with the same fatal goal. Woman must put herself into the text-as into the world and into history-by her own movement (Cixous, 1976, p. 875).

Writing is, for Cixous, not writing from the mind but from the body:

> By writing her self, woman will return to the body which has been more than confiscated from her […] Write your self. Your body must be heard. Only then will the immense resources of the unconscious spring forth (ibid, p. 880).

How does one write from one's body? Cixous uses the metaphor of white ink or breast milk. Kathy Acker claims to write from her vaginal juices in the throes of orgasm. But writing from the body does not have to be about sex. It's about speaking from the truth of the body, which includes sexuality but subverts the power binary of mind/body and male/female by acknowledging what has been denied. It's about celebrating the female body.

In *Manly Writing: Gender, Rhetoric and the Rise of Composition*, Miriam Brody suggests that what we have associated with standards of 'good' writing are virtues that are manly, 'writing that is plain, forceful, cogent, and true' (Brody, 1993, p. 1). And 'bad' writing has often been characterised as effeminate, vague, unorganised, ornate and deceitful. Examining writing as gendered enables us to break the false binaries of so-called 'good' and 'bad' writing and allow a more fluent style of prose.

> To write well in western culture is to write like a man. Advising boys, and more recently, girls too, how to write, men have for centuries imposed images of their best selves on descriptions of good writing: selves that are productive, coherent, virtuous, and heroic; writing that is plain, forceful and true. On their

worst writing they have imagined themselves beset by uncertainty, vagueness, and timidity, by a writing that is ornate, unconvincing, and sometimes deceitful. In the long tradition of writing about writing, these best selves have been called manly writers, and the worst effeminate (ibid).

Minimalism can be used as a method, a remedy for lazy and sloppy writing, but so then can Cixous's concept of *l'ecriture feminine*, which exposes a masculinist agenda in writing and allows writers to connect to a more visceral and sensual experience of writing. For Cixous, writing, like public speaking, is performative:

> She doesn't 'speak', she throws her trembling body forward; she lets go of herself, she flies; all of her passes into her voice, and it's with her body that she vitally supports the 'logic' of her speech. Her flesh speaks true. She lays herself bare. In fact, she physically materialises what she's thinking; she signifies it with her body. In a certain way, she inscribes what she's saying, because she doesn't deny her drives the intractable and impassioned part they have in speaking (Banting, 1992, p. 227).

For Cixous, writing should tap into the 'immense resources of the unconscious' through the body. But how exactly do writers invigorate their writing in a way that will '"realise" the decensored relation of woman to her sexuality, to her womanly being, giving her access to her native strength' (Cixous, 1976, p. 880).

L'ecriture feminine provides techniques that help us write passionate and fluid prose that is neither derivative nor banal and unblocks the false binaries of 'bad' (spontaneous) and 'good' (minimalist) writing.

Shakespeare's sister and the feminine sentence

Virginia Woolf, in *A Room of One's Own* (1929), maps out the space and resources women need to be writers: money and a room of her own. She also shows how little space women have had to be writers:

> Let me imagine, since facts are hard to come by, what would have happened if Shakespeare had a wonderfully gifted

> sister, called Judith. ...any woman born with a great gift in the 16th century would certainly have gone crazed, shot herself, or ended her days in some lonely cottage outside the village, half-witch, half-wizard, feared and mocked at... (Woolf, 2012 (1929), p. 60).

Furthermore, she maintains that *l'ecriture feminine* would have grammar, style and syntax rules different from those of masculine writing. She suggests that 'the feminine sentence, a more elastic fibre than the old, capable of stretching to the extreme, of suspending the frailest particles, of enveloping the vaguest shape' (Woolf, 1965, p. 191) because a sentence made by men 'does not fit her' (ibid, 124–125).

What does such a sentence look like? Maybe:

> Did it matter then, she asked herself, did it matter that she must inevitably cease completely; all this must go on without her; did she resent it; or did it not become consoling to believe that death ended absolutely? but that somehow in the streets of London, on the ebb and flow of things, here, there, she survived, Peter survived, lived in each other, she being part, she was positive, of the trees at home; of the house there, ugly, rambling all to bits and pieces as it was; part of people she had never met; being laid out like a mist between the people she knew best, who lifted her on their branches as she had seen the trees lift the mist, but it spread ever so far, her life, herself (Woolf, 2000 (1925), p. 5).

We are used to 'masculine' sentences, those with a recognisable subject-verb-object structure. But here we have a sentence that hovers emotionally, that swims through people's minds, interior to exterior.

According to Erich Auerbach, Woolf attempts 'to render the flow and the play of consciousness adrift in the current of changing impressions' (2013 (1946), p. 535). She has subverted the binaries of interior and narrative events, in which the former has always been subordinate to the latter and in which inner thoughts comment on or prepare the ground for the movement of plot. But, in Virginia Woolf's case, the external events have lost their hegemony, they serve to release and interpret inner events. Auerbach comments: 'we are given not merely one person whose consciousness ... is rendered, but many persons, with frequent shifts from one to the other' (ibid, p. 536). Shifts can occur even mid-sentence.

How though is this a 'feminine' sentence? What makes it feminine? Just our essentialist notions of femininity? (Flowing, emotional, meandering, intuitive and non-linear?) Woolf said that words have a 'need of change [...] because the truth they try to catch is many-sided, and they convey it by being themselves many-sided, flashing this way, then that' (Woolf, 1937, p. 131).

Irigaray explains 'masculine' sentences (phallocentric discourse) as this: 'I am a unified, coherent being, and what is significant in the world reflects my male image' (1977, p. 64). By contrast:

> Woman has sex organs more or less everywhere. She finds pleasure almost anywhere [...] The geography of her pleasure is much more diversified, more multiple in its differences, more complex, more subtle, than is commonly imagined-in an imaginary [system] rather to narrowly focused on sameness (Irigaray, 1985 (1977), p. 28).
> "She" is indefinitely other in herself. This is doubtless why she is said to be whimsical, incomprehensible, agitated, capricious ... not to mention her language, in which "she" sets off in all directions [...] Hers are contradictory words [...] inaudible for whoever listens to them with ready-made grids, with a fully elaborated code in hand (ibid, pp. 28–29).

For Woolf, this 'geography of pleasure' manifests as a stream of consciousness:

> Examine for a moment an ordinary mind on an ordinary day. The mind receives a myriad impressions – trivial, fantastic, evanescent, or engraved with the sharpness of steel. From all sides they come, an incessant shower of innumerable atoms; and as they fall, as they shape themselves into the life of Monday or Tuesday, the accent falls differently from of old (Woolf, 2002 (1925), p. 148).

> ✏️ **'GEOGRAPHY OF PLEASURE' EXERCISE**
>
> Using the idea of the feminine sentence, freewrite for five minutes in order to capture as best as you can a moment in time with all its myriad sense impressions, its bifurcating thoughts and meandering word and image associations, creating 'feminine sentences' and streams of consciousness.

Dismantling patriarchal language: Monique Wittig

Monique Wittig, an early seventies '*Féministé révolutionnaire*', wrote *ecriture feminine* in two novels – the tribal sisterhood of *Les Guérillères* (1969) and *Le Corps lesbien* [*The Lesbian Body*] (1973) – both of which explore a post-phallocentric social order. Her aim:

> to define what we call oppression in materialist terms, to make it evident that women are a class, which is to say that the category "woman," as well as "man," are political and economic categories, not eternal ones […] Our first task, it seems, is to always thoroughly dissociate "women" (the class within which we fight) and "woman," the myth. For "woman" does not exist for us: it is only an imaginary formation, while "women" is the product of a social relationship (1993, p. 106).

How does Wittig write the female body? Literally:

> The women say that in the feminary the glans of the clitoris and the body of the clitoris are described as hooded. It is stated that the prepuce at the base of the glans can travel the length of the organ exciting a keen sensation of pleasure. They say that the clitoris is an erectile organ. It is stated that it bifurcates to right and left, that it is angled, extending as two erectile bodies applied to the pubic bones. These two bodies are not visible. The whole constitutes an intensely erogenous zone that excites the entire genital, making it an

organ impatient for pleasure. They compare it to mercury also called quick- silver because of its readiness to expand, to spread, to change shape (2007 (1969), p. 14).

They say that it has been written that vulvas are traps vices pincers. They say that the clitoris has been compared to the prow of a boat to its stem to the comb of a shellfish. They say that vulvas have been compared to apricots pomegranates figs roses pinks peonies marguerites. They say these comparisons may be recited like a litany (ibid, p. 19).

The Lesbian Body too writes the body, uses 'feminine sentences' and has little punctuation and no plot (although this may be a masculine judgement that a novel should have a hard linear 'plot' and be punctuated tightly). Here, the protagonist dissects, dismantles and thus demystifies her lesbian lover's body in her attempt to love every part of her. This deconstructs the masculine notion of the female body as mystery, as other, and the narrative literally tears skin from limbs and writes each sinew, ligament and tendon, dismantling patriarchal language and creating a new feminine discourse.

> I discover that your skin can be lifted layer by layer, I pull, it lifts off, it coils above your knees, I pull starting at the labia, it slides the length of the belly, fine to extreme transparency, I pull starting at the loins, the skin uncovers the round muscles and trapezii of the back, it peels off up to the nape of the neck, I arrive under your hair, m/y fingers traverse its thickness, I touch your skull, I grasp it with all m/y fingers, I press it, I gather the skin over the whole of the cranial vault, I tear off the skin brutally beneath the hair, I reveal the beauty of the shining bone traversed by blood-vessels, m/y two hands crush the vault and the occiput behind, now m/y fingers bury themselves in the cerebral convolutions, the meninges are traversed by cerebrospinal fluid flowing from all quarters, m/y hands are plunged in the soft hemispheres, I seek the medulla and the cerebellum tucked in somewhere beneath, now I hold all of you silent immobilized every cry blocked in your throat your last thoughts behind your eyes caught in m/y hands, the daylight is no purer than the depths of m/y heart m/y dearest one (1975 (1973), p. 17).

ECRITURE FEMININE: WRITING THE BODY

> ✏️ 'WRITING THE BODY' EXERCISE
>
> Using the examples of Wittig above, in 300 words, 'write the body' by focusing on specific aspects of body function or pure description (not necessarily sexual). Celebrate and affirm an aspect of the female body.

Margaret Atwood

Another way of deconstructing patriarchal phallocentric notions of the female body is what Margaret Atwood does in her novels *Alias Grace* (1996) and *The Handmaid's Tale* (1985) and in this short story called 'The Female Body':

> The Female Body has many uses. It's been used as a doorknocker, a bottle-opener, as a clock with a ticking belly, as something to hold up lampshades, as a nutcracker, just squeeze the brass legs together and out comes your nut. It bears torches, lifts victorious wreaths, grows copper wings and raises aloft a ring of neon stars; whole buildings rest on its marble heads (Atwood, 1990, pp. 491–492).

> ✏️ 'CONSTRUCTING AND DECONSTRUCTING THE FEMALE BODY' EXERCISE
>
> Write a 200-word paragraph in the style of Margaret Atwood's 'The Female Body', listing some images of the female body you have experienced and encountered in the media or in conversation. Then use this list to make a poem or a short story about how the female body has been constructed in patriarchal society. Use 'feminine' discourse, à la Irigaray, Wittig or Woolf.

Terribly feminist books: A.S. Byatt

A.S. Byatt describes herself as a postmodernist Gothic Victorian writer. She combines a heavy realism with playful postmodern techniques such as magic realism and metafiction. The writing style in her novels (*Possession*, 1990) and in her short story collections is *l'ecriture feminine:* 'All my books are about the woman artist – in that sense, they're terribly feminist books – and they're about what language is…the problem of female vision, female art and thought' (cited in Tredell, 1991).

I'd like to focus on two stories from her 2003 collection, the *Little Black Book of Stories*, which writes the female body in surprising ways. 'Body Art' tells the story of Daisy, a homeless, self-neglecting, self-doubting woman artist who works at a local hospital. She is noticed by one of the male doctors, Damian, who thinks he is the main protagonist of the story. A controlling, self-assured agent who decides to 'take her in hand', he gives her the task of cataloguing a 'collection' of past gynaecological instruments which have been kept in the basement, bequeathed to the hospital by its founder. This 'horror chamber' of what look like torture instruments reveals the nature of the history of modern medicine's abuse of women's bodies in the name of (male) science. Daisy uses this collection, however, to create a transgressive work of art, a woman's body made of all these instruments that have been used to humiliate and dominate women, transformed into the powerful goddess of creative destruction, Kali.

Damian is outraged that she has used ('stolen' is his word) medical equipment this way. But she has enacted an *ecriture feminine* in her art. This is a pastiche, a collage of women's bodies, composed of what men have done to them.

> It was a representation of the goddess Kali, who was constructed like an Arcimboldo portrait out of many elements. She was enthroned in what resembled – what was – a seventeen-century birthing chair, below which, under the hole into which the baby would drop, was a transparent plastic box full of a jumble of plaster Infants and plaster Mothers from creches old and new (Byatt, 2004 (2003), p. 103).

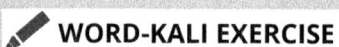
WORD-KALI EXERCISE

Find a similar collection of abuses against women – for example, popular misogynist songs about women (the Eagles' *Witchy Woman* and Cliff Richard's *Devil Woman* come to mind) or advertising slogans – and put these in a 300-word collage or pastiche as Atwood and Byatt have done to make a word-Kali of your own.

Transgressive *ecriture feminine*

In a sense, all *ecriture feminine* is transgressive and aims to subvert phallocentric patriarchal masculine discourse, but some women writers empower women's bodies in the very act of degrading them.

Kathy Acker, an experimental novelist, punk poet, playwright, essayist, postmodernist and sex-positive feminist writer, writes the female body using porn, violence, self-styled illustrations, plagiarised texts and a lack of any discernible plot. She describes feminine writing in this way:

> Writing is basically about time and rhythm. Like with jazz. You have your basic melody and then you just riff off of it. And the riffs are about timing. And about sex […] So writing was really associated with body pleasure -- it was the same thing (cited in Sirius, 1994, n.p.).

Acker aims for what she calls 'schlock' writing as a way of subverting the binaries of good and bad writing and of undermining 'good' (read masculine) literature:

> [t]here were two kinds of writing…: good literature and schlock. Novels which won literary prizes were good literature; science fiction and horror novels, pornography were schlock. […] Schlock's content was sex horror violence and other aspects of human existence abhorrent to all but the lowest of the low, the socially and morally unacceptable (Acker, 1990, n.p.).
> I'm looking for what might be called a body language. One thing I do is stick a vibrator up my cunt and start writing – writing from the point of orgasm and losing control of the language and seeing what that's like… I have become interested in languages which I cannot make up, which I cannot create or even create in: I have become interested in languages which I can only come up upon (as I disappear), a pirate upon buried treasure. The dreamer, the dreaming, the dream. I call these languages, languages of the body (cited in Sirius, 1994, n.p.).

Corporeal feminism

Just as Wittig does, Justine Ettler dismantles and demystifies the female body. *The River Ophelia* (1995) is full of vomit, piss, diarrhoea, menstruation, bleeding, illness, drug use, and sexual abuse – the lived experience of a real female body, not a constructed male fantasy, but a self, viscerally depicted. The act of empowerment is in the writing of such a disempowered body. Elisabeth Grosz, in *Volatile Bodies: Toward a Corporeal Feminism* (1994), focuses on (as we saw above) corporeality, the female body as a site of struggle, and the subjective phenomenological experience of sexual difference. The power of Ettler's novel is in the laying bare and the 'unselfing' of the main protagonist, Justine, through violent sexual acts and pain.

> I hadn't even managed to lock the front door behind us when Sade grabbed me and started tearing all my clothes off. He kissed me hard and I tasted blood in my mouth. He dragged me to my bed and ripping my underpants in half pushed me down on the bed and fucked me, plunging right in up to the hilt so that it hurt (Ettler, 1995, p. 11).
> 'The thing is,' Ophelia said ominously, making (Justine) turn around, 'the thing about all this pain (women) go through, all this love that just hurts all the time, the thing about all this pain is that it's really exquisite. It's exquisite pain. That's what makes us keep going back for more' (ibid, p. 134).

What about the 'men'?

I have assumed that those reading this and doing the exercises are 'women' writers. But what about the 'men'? Can 'men' write *ecriture feminine*?

Yes, says Cixous. Anyone, she argues, can occupy the marginalised position of 'woman' and can write from that position as well.

L'ecriture feminine is strategically essentialist, and once the binaries that imprison us as 'men' and 'women' have been deconstructed, we can write outside of these essentialisms. If the feminine is socially constructed, as is the masculine, we can overcome such constructions first by acknowledging them, as Byatt and Atwood do (collecting the broken images and making them into art), and then by writing beyond these binaries.

Queer writing

If *l'ecriture feminine* advocates for more fluid genders and identities, then Queer writing goes further and advocates for a 'dynamic collectivity of possible sexualities… that may vary at different points during one's life' (Tyson, 2006: 335).

'Queer' is in the process of formation. Queer theory attempts to resist definition and also rejects heterosexuality as a norm or base from which other sexualities grow. Queer theory tries to demonstrate the impossibility of 'natural' sexuality and calls into question categories such as 'man' and 'woman'. If our gender and sexual identities are not determined by biological sex and if writing is (as we have seen) about the representation of self or selves, we can 'queer' writing to help us rethink, challenge, deconstruct, dissect and re-make notions of identity.

Two classic novels that play with gender fluidity and dabble in transgender experimentation are Ursula K. Le Guin's *The Left Hand of Darkness* (1969) and Virginia Woolf's *Orlando* (1922), the latter of which is regarded as the first English-language trans novel.

In Le Guin's fantasy novel, the inhabitants of Gethen can become either male or female at various times in their lives during a period called *kemmer*, which illustrates the idea that gender distinctions and binaries are products of heteronormativity. Imagine, Le Guin is saying, a world where there are no gender roles. Imagine how a visitor from earth (a permanently biologically male) is seen by these non-gendered inhabitants as a sexual deviant.

Woolf's *Orlando* is a similar study in gender fluidity, featuring a male who falls in love with both women and men and who, on a diplomatic mission to Constantinople, becomes a woman.

Such gender switching and fluidity are nothing new in literature. Ovid's *Metamorphoses* plays with shape-shifting to accommodate a protagonist's sexual needs. *The Arabian Nights* presents us with gender-switching plots and cross-dressing, as do Shakespeare's comedies, which feature women who are men who are really women, and on the stage, every female role was cross-gender, as women were not allowed to perform.

Judith Butler (1990) claims that the way to break down/disturb established normative ideologies and structures and create 'gender trouble' is to confuse and therefore subvert prevailing forms of 'identity'. She argues for a writing practice that performs a writer's subjectivities of gender and sexuality, denaturalises false binaries and undermines heteronormativity by exposing how sex and gender are constructed. By performing the self (seeing the self as an actor who can occupy a 'mutable discursive writing position' rather than a stable fixed self and identity), a writer can take on or occupy a variety of social, cultural and ideological positions and become fluid regarding performing the self.

Michel Foucault (1990), in *The History of Sexuality*, argues that sexual and gender identities are produced through discourse and, as a result, this discourse can be rewritten, disrupted and countered. Creative writing is an opportune place to recreate identity and experiment with non-normative representations of self or, in his words, to 'self-make'.

Foucault also suggests that our writing self can be seen as 'an ongoing assembly and disassembly of subjectivity that constitute[s] a kind of self-bricolage' (Rabinow, 1997). As we saw in the chapter on postmodern writing practices (Chapter 6), bricolage is a method that allows a writer (bricoleur) to assemble selves from whatever materials are at hand and use them in innovative ways. Bricolage can create new subjectivities, dismantle an apparently stable and unified self and perform in writing what Dallas J. Baker calls a 'Queer becoming' (Baker, 2013).

Examples of self-making novels are Rita Mae Brown's *Rubyfruit Jungle* (1973) and Alice Walker's *The Color Purple* (1982), both of which are explorations of fluid sexual relations using bricolage. The latter novel features epistolary fragments which piece together a woman's self-becoming.

'SELF-MAKING BRICOLAGE' EXERCISE

Assemble a bricolage of your possible subjective sexualities. Document in autobiographic fragments how you have intersected with, rebelled against or conformed to traditional notions of sexuality. You could use the following as prompts:

1. Write about sexual incidents that may have occurred (pleasurable or traumatic) that helped define or unsettle your perception of your sexuality.

2. Chronicle stages of development and insight (puberty, first sexual experiences with self or others or both, first awareness of your sexuality, and how you perceived your sexuality).

3. Document any coming-out or 'aha' moments about your sexuality, awareness of how your gender and sexuality have been constructed, awareness of any gender fluidity or leakages, and slippages in binary systems. Then, as a bricoleur, construct a subjective self (or selves!).

Queer form

Alanna Duncan (2018) observes that recent queer writing tends to favour a fragmented structure, the use of white space, the creation of gaps in time and narrative, and the fracturing of character identities. Duncan cites novels such as Maggie Nelson's memoir-in-fragments *Bluets* (2009), with its disjointed structure and indefinable genre; Anne Garréta's 2015 novel *Sphinx*, in which the narrative is segmented and jumps around in time; and Patti Yumi Cottrell's *Sorry to Disrupt the Peace* (2018), in which the introduction of a queer double helps destabilise an otherwise conventional narrative.

How is this different from conventional experimentation though? Queer writing, Duncan argues, performs what it is like to exist outside of the 'normal' traditional narrative:

> Much in the way that queer people have been forced to create spaces for themselves and codes of behavior when out in the world, queer authors have similarly carved out and utilized new forms for their work, perhaps not by choice, but out of necessity, in order to tell their stories and reflect worldviews that have been informed by their queerness (Duncan, 2018, n.p.).

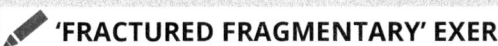 **'FRACTURED FRAGMENTARY' EXERCISE**

Experiment with form by fragmenting, using white space and creating gaps to create a narrative that performs a subjective 'queer' narrative by using examples inspired from the novels mentioned above.

Writing LGBTQI+ and gender-diverse characters

The hazards of straight or cis-gender writers writing LGBTQI+ characters are tokenism, stereotyping and appropriation. It is easy to stereotype, oversimplify or unintentionally denigrate people who identify as LGBTQI+. Jeffrey Eugenides's *Middlesex* (2002) won the Pulitzer Prize for his coming-of-age story of an intersex protagonist and did much for queer visibility, but the author does not identify as intersex and did not consult with intersex people before writing the novel and so has come under some criticism from the intersex community for his portrayal of LGBTQI+ characters. If you do not identify as Queer but write LGBTQI+ and also diverse gender presentations such as trans or non-binary- or non-gender-conforming characters into your novel, it is wise to make use of sensitivity readers. Find an LGBQTI+ friend who identifies in the same way as your character to read your work, read Queer fiction to see how other authors write about LGBTQI+ characters, and watch movies with Queer characters. Remember too that your first response in sketching character is likely to be the cliché and the best way to remedy this – if you wish to create complex characters that have sexual orientations different from yours (and you should!) – is to do some research on sexual orientation and differentiations in sexualities. To write realistic and meaningful Queer characters, there is a delicate balance: sexuality needs to be foregrounded but not in a way that it is the defining feature of that character or else an ornament or accessory to someone's identity. Avoiding LGBTQI+ characters altogether is also an issue. It makes the statement that you are perpetuating their marginalisation and invisibility.

Writers who identify as LGBTQI+ can encourage and support others who write Queer by writing true-to-life LGBTQI+ characters based on personal experience, putting them into the mainstream, showcasing them in writers' workshops and in traditional avenues of publishing, and exposing assumptions of heteronormality wherever they are found.

LGBTQI+ EXERCISE

If you do not identity as LGBTQI+, write a short scene involving an LGBTQI+ character based on your present knowledge and then show this scene to an LGBTQI+ friend and ask for a critique. Then rewrite the scene according to their suggestions. If you do identify as LGBTQI+, write a short scene that demonstrates Queer writing.

References

Acker, Kathy. 1990. Dead Doll Humility. *Postmodern Culture* 1, 1. http://pmc.iath.virginia.edu/text-only/issue.990/acker.990. Accessed 1 October 2018.

Atwood, Margaret. 1990. The Female Body. *The Michigan Review* 29: 490–493. https://web.stanford.edu/~jonahw/AOE-SM10/Readings/Atwood-FemaleBody.pdf. Accessed 1 October 2018.

Auerbach, Erich. 2013 (1946). *Mimesis: The Representation of Reality in Western Thought*. Princeton: Princeton University Press.

Baker, Dallas J. 2013. 'Creative writing praxis as queer becoming', *New Writing: The International Journal for the Practice and Theory of Creative Writing*, vol. 10, no. 3, pp. 359–377.

Banting, Pamela. 1992. The Body as Pictogram: Rethinking Helene Cixous's ecriture feminine. *Textual Practice* 6, 2: 225–246.

Brody, Miriam. 1993. *Manly Writing: Gender, Rhetoric and the Rise of Composition*. Carbondale: Southern Illinois University Press.

Butler, Judith. 1990. *Gender Trouble: Feminism and the Subversion of Identity*. Routledge: London

Byatt, A.S. 2004 (2003). *The Little Black Book of Stories*. London: Vintage.

Cixous, Hélène. 1976. *The Laugh of the Medusa*. Trans. Keith Cohen and Paula Cohen. *Signs* 1, 4: 875–893. https://artandobjecthood.files.wordpress.com/2012/06/cixous_the_laugh_of_the_medusa.pdf. Accessed 1 October 2018.

Crimmins, Gail. 2014. An Arts-Informed Narrative Inquiry into the Lived Experience of Women Casual Academics. PhD Thesis. University of the Sunshine Coast.

Descartes, René. 2006 (1637). *Discourse on the Method of Rightly Conducting the Reason, and Seeking Truth in the Sciences*. Trans. Ian Maclean. Oxford: Oxford University Press. www.rlwclarke.net/Theory/SourcesPrimary/DescartesDiscourseonMethod.pdf. Accessed 24 October 2018.

Duncan, Alanna. 2018. 'How Queer Writers Are Creating Queer Genres.' *Electric Lit*. June 18. https://electricliterature.com/how-queer-writers-are-creating-queer-genres/. Accessed 29 June 2019.

Ettler, Justine. 1995. *The River Ophelia*. Picador: New South Wales.

Foucault, Michel. 1990. *The History of Sexuality: An Introduction*, Volume One. Vintage Books: New York.

Irigaray, Luce. 1977. Women's Exile. *Ideology and Consciousness* 1: 62–76. Reprinted in *The feminist critique of language: A reader*, ed. Deborah Cameron, (trans. Diana Adlam and Couze Venn). 1990. London: Routledge.

Irigaray, Luce. 1985 (1977). *This Sex Which Is Not One*. Trans. Catherine Porter. New York: Cornell University Press.

Rabinow, Paul. 1997. *Michel Foucault: Ethics, subjectivity and truth*. The New Press, New York.

Sirius, R. U. 1994. A Conversation with Kathy Acker. *io* 2. www.altx.com/io/acker.html. Accessed 6 March 2016.

Tredell, Nicolas. 1991. A.S Byatt in Conversation. *PN Review* 17, 3. www.pnreview.co.uk/cgi-bin/scribe?item_id=4354. Accessed 1 October 2018.

Tyson, Lois. 2006. *Critical Theory Today: A User-friendly Guide*. Routledge: New York.

Wittig, Monique. 1975 (1973). *The Lesbian Body*. Trans. Peter Owen. New York: William Morrow and Company.

Wittig, Monique. 1993. One is Not Born a Woman. In *The Lesbian and Gay Studies Reader*, eds Henry Abelove, Michele Aina Barale and David M. Halerin, 103–109. New York and London: Routledge.

Wittig, Monique. 2007 (1969). *Les Guérillères*. Trans. David Le Vay. University of Illinois Press.

Woolf, Virginia. 1937. Craftsmanship. *Listener* 5 May 1937: 868–869. Reprinted in *The Death of the Moth*. 1942. London: Hogarth.

Woolf, Virginia. 1965. *Contemporary Writers*. London: Hogarth Press.

Woolf, Virginia. 2000 (1925). *Mrs Dalloway*. London: Penguin.

Woolf, Virginia. 2002 (1925). *The Common Reader*. London: Maritime Books.

Woolf, Virginia. 2012 (1929). *A Room of One's Own*. Hertfordshire: Wordsworth.

10 POSTCOLONIALISM: WRITING BACK TO EMPIRE

During the final years of Apartheid in South Africa, I was teaching in the English department at the University of Zululand and moved to Johannesburg to teach in a newly formed breakaway department from the English department at Wits University (University of the Witwatersrand, Johannesburg), the department of African literature. Why the split? The English department, it was argued, was Eurocentric in its offerings, reflecting a colonial approach to literature and seeing Europe as the motherland and origin of culture and the South as the colony. The new department was Afrocentric, meaning that it focussed on local culture (Zulu and Xhosa and Tswana oral traditions, South African literature, both black and white, and then other African literature, then the diaspora, and finally European and American literature).

The African literature department was also the first to introduce creative writing to the university, staffed by African writers such as Ezekiel Mphahlele, Njabulo Ndebele, guest lectured by Nadine Gordimer and Ngũgĩ wa Thiong'o and allied to the Congress of South African Writers. The intention was to move from a colonial to a postcolonial approach to studying literature and writing.

Definitions

Postcolonialism is the study of how colonialism (European and American global domination and expansionism) has affected (materially, socially, politically and psychologically) the Indigenous people and cultures of those dominated and those who dominated them.

> We use the term 'post colonial' to cover all the culture affected by the imperial process from the moment of colonisation to the present day. This is because there is a continuity of

preoccupations throughout the historical process initiated by European imperial aggression (Ashcroft et al., 1989, p. 2).

Survey of colonial literature
1. Prospero and Caliban

> You taught me language, and my profit on't
> Is I know how to curse. The red plague rid you
> For learning me your language! (*The Tempest*, 1991 (1611), I.ii.366–368).

Shakespeare's *The Tempest* (1611) is in part a prefiguring of the colonial relationship of the colonised (the Indigenous Caliban) and the coloniser (Prospero the wizard). It is telling that the colonised Indigenous is portrayed as a savage monster and a would-be rapist with no moral restraint (whose name is anagrammatic of 'cannibal') whereas Prospero is a wise and powerful patriarch.

2. *Robinson Crusoe* (1719) and *Gulliver's Travels* (1726)

Daniel Defoe's *Robinson Crusoe* is regarded as the first colonial novel in that it demarcates the path that Imperialist Europe would follow – exploration of foreign lands, occupation, settlement, conquest and domination of its peoples. Robinson Crusoe colonises the island he finds himself on, reproduces 'civilisation' and subdues and enslaves the Indigenous person he finds there, renaming him Friday. His behaviour to Friday prefigures that of colonial powers towards its colonised subjects. He teaches 'Friday' English, discourages his native tongue and forces Christianity on him, discouraging his 'heathen cultural practices'.

> In a little time I began to speak to him, and teach him to speak to me; and, first, I let him know his name should be Friday, which was the day I saved his life; I called so for the memory of the time. I likewise taught him to say Master, and then let him know that was to be my name; I likewise taught him to say Yes and No, and to know the meaning of them (Defoe, 1719, p. 87).

In *Gulliver's Travels*, on the other hand, the protagonist responds very differently to the peoples he meets. He recognises first that these lands are already inhabited, not *terra nullius* (in contrast to Robinson Crusoe's island), and negotiates with the native peoples, learning their customs and sharing knowledge rather than imposing his own. He realises too that he is not always welcome and when he tries to show off the superiority of his British culture and history to the Brobdingnagians, he is mocked and disregarded. At the end, he suffers an identity crisis with the self-realisation that his race is a bunch of Yahoos. You could almost say that *Gulliver's Travels* is a postcolonial novel in that it deconstructs the entire colonial enterprise.

3. H. Rider Haggard and Enid Blyton

The colonial literature that followed *Gulliver's Travels* was not so self-reflective. H. Rider Haggard was an immensely popular adventure writer, setting his novels in a constructed African continent of savages and exotic wilderness to be exploited by the adventurer, or as Charles Larson says, 'Africa as a backdrop where white characters were permitted to work out their neuroses in rather stock patterns' (Larson, 1972, p. 278). *King Solomon's Mines* (1885), for example, pits the enterprising white hero against savage Zulu tribes in his quest to wrest the lost treasures of Solomon.

Colonial literature, like patriarchy, has been largely naturalised so that the reader accepts the assumptions made. I grew up reading Enid Blyton, and even though I was not British, I accepted the underlying Empire mentality of the books I read: British were best, foreigners quaint or stupid or immoral, and villains always dark-skinned.

> The black man appeared, his usual scowl even blacker. 'What you doing?' he demanded, his dark eyes rolling, and the whites showing plainly. 'That's my boat.'
> 'All right, all right,' said Jack impatiently. 'Can't I look at it?'
> 'No,' said Jo-Jo, and scowled again.
> 'Naughty boy,' said Kiki, and screeched at Jo-Jo, who looked as if he would like to wring the bird's neck.
> 'Well, you certainly are a pleasant fellow,' said Jack, stepping away from the boat, feeling suddenly afraid of the sullen black man (Blyton, 1944, p. 16).

4. The White Man's burden

Rudyard Kipling, author of the *Just So Stories* (1902) and *The Jungle Book* (1894), became the advocate for Empire in his poetry and novels and is best known for the poem below:

> Take up the White Man's burden –
> Send forth the best ye breed –
> Go send your sons to exile
> To serve your captives' need
> To wait in heavy harness
> On fluttered folk and wild –
> Your new-caught, sullen peoples,
> Half devil and half child (Kipling, 1899).

5. Tarzan

Edgar Rice Burroughs never set foot in Africa yet wrote the popular Tarzan series about a white man 'gone native' among the savage Africans, who were portrayed on a par with other wild animals he had to contend with.

The fascination and popularity were due in part to the idea of apes bringing up human beings, but an equal pull was the exotic jungle backdrop of Africa (the TV series curiously was filmed not in Africa but in Florida): Africa was constructed as exotic 'other', full of wild animals and dangerous tribes, and Tarzan was the conqueror of such wilderness, as his tree-hut plaque proclaims: 'This is the house of Tarzan, the killer of beasts and many black men' (Burroughs, 1973 (1912), p. 116).

Tarzan is a symbol of the white man's conquest of Africa during the heyday of European (especially British) colonialism. Tarzan is not just a man gone native, however. He is none other than Lord Greystoke, who has a seat on the House of Lords, and this 'civilised breeding' sets him above the animal-like savages in the jungle.

6. *Heart of Darkness* (1899)

Another white man gone native is Kurtz, the rogue coloniser who sets himself up as a god in the novella *Heart of Darkness*. To be fair, Joseph Conrad's novella is an anti-colonial critique of colonial horrors, Kurtz being a symbol of the limitless and insane power of the Imperialist, and the title of the novel is a reference not only to the darkness of the continent but to the heart of the coloniser himself.

> ✏️ **'IMAGE OF AFRICA' EXERCISE**
> Find what you consider to be a racist description of a character in a novel you have read and analyse how this character has been constructed. What narrative techniques have been used? What clichés or stereotypes? Melodramatic tropes? If you were to rewrite this character, how would you remedy this racist image?

The empire writes back

From the 1950s, African writers have been 'writing back' to the 'centre', writing black experience as a counter history (alternative narrative) to the master narratives of white history. For example, Chinua Achebe's *Things Fall Apart* (1958) writes back to Conrad's *Heart of Darkness* as he explains in 'An Image of Africa: Racism in Joseph Conrad's *Heart of Darkness*'): 'Joseph Conrad was a bloody (thoroughgoing) racist. That this simple truth is glossed over in criticisms of his work is due to the fact that white racism against Africa is such a normal way of thinking that its manifestations go completely unremarked' (Achebe, 1977, p. 257).

Heart of Darkness purports to be anti-colonial, but it is racist and portrays Africans as 'a burst of yells, a whirl of black limbs, a mass of hands clapping, of feet stamping, of bodies swaying, of eyes rolling under the droop of heavy and motionless foliage… incomprehensible frenzy… prehistoric man' (Conrad, 1999, p. 107).

Achebe points out that Conrad's narrator (and, by implication, Conrad himself) struggles to admit that Africans are even human:

> No they were not inhuman, Well, you know that was the worst of it – this suspicion of their not being inhuman. It would come slowly to one. They howled and leaped and spun and made horrid faces, but what thrilled you was just the thought of their humanity – like yours – the thought of your remote kinship with this wild and passionate uproar. Yes, it was ugly enough, but if you were man enough you would admit to yourself that there was in you just the faintest trace of a response to the terrible frankness of that noise, a dim suspicion of there being a meaning in it which you – you so remote from the night of first ages – could comprehend (ibid, p. 108).

'And the question', Achebe says, 'is whether a novel which celebrates this dehumanization, which depersonalizes a portion of the human race, can be called a great work of art. My answer is: No, it cannot' (1977, p. 257).

This is vitally important to writers. We cannot always write outside of our own prejudices and cultural assumptions, but Achebe's cautionary note is crucial: 'Literature is always badly served when an author's artistic insight yields to stereotype and malice. And it becomes doubly offensive when such a work is arrogantly proffered to you as your story' (ibid). Achebe then writes a counter narrative to show the humanity of those people Conrad dismisses as savages with no culture and who speak only in grunts ('Kill him and eat him' and 'Mista Kurtz he dead'). In *Things Fall Apart* then,

> Africans are people in the same way that Americans, Europeans, Asians, and others are people. Africans are not some strange beings with unpronounceable names and impenetrable minds. Although the action of ***Things Fall Apart*** takes place in a setting with which most Americans are unfamiliar, the characters are normal people and their events are real human events (Achebe, 1991, p. 22).

Things Fall Apart became 'one of the most important books of the twentieth century, a universally acknowledged starting point for postcolonial, indigenous African fiction' (Appiah, 2013, n.p.). Princeton scholar Kwame Anthony Appiah likened its influence on postcolonial writing to that of Shakespeare: 'It would be like asking how Shakespeare influenced English writers or Pushkin influenced Russians' (ibid).

The novel not only depicts 'real' complex African characters like Okonkwo, who breaks stereotypes and tries in vain to resist colonisation, but ironically displaces itself and places itself as a paragraph in the Grand Colonial Narrative:

> The Commissioner went away, taking three or four of the soldiers with him. In the many years in which he had toiled to bring civilization to different parts of Africa he had learned a number of things. One of them was that a District Commissioner should never attend to such undignified details as cutting a hanged man from a tree. Such attention would give the natives a poor opinion of him. In the book which he planned to write

he would stress that point. As he walked back to the court he thought about that book. Every day brought him some new material. The story of this man who had killed a messenger and hanged himself would make interesting reading. One could almost write a whole chapter on him. Perhaps not a whole chapter but a reasonable paragraph, at any rate. There was so much else to include, and one must be firm in cutting out details. He had already chosen the title of the book, after much thought: The Pacification of the Primitive Tribes of the Lower Niger (Achebe, 1994 (1958), p. 209).

Decolonising the mind

Decolonising the Mind: The Politics of Language in African Literature (Heinemann Educational, 1986) is Kenyan novelist Ngũgĩ wa Thiong'o's seminal text that argues how African and colonised cultures have been brainwashed into accepting their mental servitude and need to decolonise their thinking. In the words of Bob Marley, Ngũgĩ asks Africans to 'free yourselves from mental slavery; none but ourselves can free our minds' (Marley, 1980). How is this done? Ngũgĩ did this by first changing his name. Christened as James Ngugi, he discarded his Western name and took the name of his ancestors. Second, he threw off the English language ('the language of the coloniser') and wrote in his native African language, which was translated into English, an English now stripped of its cultural and Imperialist power.

I will never forget when Ngũgĩ wa Thiong'o came to speak at our university. At the time, Apartheid was coming to an end, Nelson Mandela was the chancellor of the university but had been in prison for the duration of his tenure, the Defiance Campaign meant that people in large numbers were deliberately disobeying Apartheid laws, and the university was a newly free non-racial space.

In the large auditorium, literary heavyweights Nadine Gordimer and Njabulo Ndebele sat up front, and a packed house of excited students waited for the Kenyan author to appear. The rumour was that Kenyan authorities had recently tried to arrest one of his fictional activist characters, Matigari, and that this novel had been written on toilet paper while Ngũgĩ himself had been imprisoned for activism. There was a spontaneous roar of the crowd as Ngũgĩ stepped up to the podium, a stamping of feet, ululating and a standing ovation.

Ngũgĩ began to speak – he had a considered paper to give – but with every breath he took, the crowd cheered. They wanted slogans. The celebrated author found it difficult to get through his paper, as the crowd kept applauding and calling out 'Decolonise our minds, Ngũgĩ!' and at one point broke into song. Ngũgĩ looked embarrassed, surprised at the reception he was getting, but flattered. At the end of his speech/paper, students rushed the stage and hoisted him up on their shoulders, parading him around campus as a hero of the struggle amidst chanting and singing and dancing.

Writers in Africa, particularly anti-colonial writers, a threat to the ruling conservative colonial or neo-colonial social order, have typically been viewed as heroes of the people by activists and enemies of the people by the State. Some have died for their words.

African literature has as its mission to write back to Empire, to decolonise itself, and to redress false images of Africa. So too are the many revisions of *The Tempest* and *Robinson Crusoe*. In my novel *Cokcraco* (2013), a palimpsest of *The Tempest*, Caliban is a freedom fighter who resists the Imperialist Prospero. In Adrian Mitchell's play *Man Friday* (1973), Crusoe is silenced by Friday, who overrides his imperialist discourse and instead legitimates his own culture. In J.M. Coetzee's novel *Foe* (1986), the quest is to retrieve the voice of Friday, whose tongue slavers have cut out.

> ✏️ **'DECOLONISING THE MIND' EXERCISE**
>
> Write about an encounter between colonised and coloniser. Rewrite Prospero/Caliban or Crusoe/Friday or a scene from Tarzan, an Enid Blyton novel, *Heart of Darkness, King Solomon's Mines*, or another 'colonial' text.

Orientalism

Edward Said's 1978 seminal text *Orientalism* illustrates how the east ('the Orient') is seen and depicted in literatures by the West. Orientalism creates a binary between West and East, in which the former is superior and projects clichéd stereotypes onto the latter. Although Said's work began as an academic exploration of how the East is portrayed in literature, it represents a world view that determines a political attitude to – and often an Imperialist domination of – the Orient.

The images projected onto the Orient, particularly the Middle East, are typically that Arab-Islamic people are:

> primitive, irrational, violent, despotic, fanatic, and essentially inferior to the westerner or native informant, and hence, "enlightenment" can only occur when "traditional" and "reactionary" values are replaced by "contemporary" and "progressive" ideas that are either western or western-influenced (Marandi and Pirnajmuddin, 2009, p. 24).

ORIENTALIST EXERCISE

(a) What stereotypes of Middle Eastern peoples are prevalent in the media – movies, news and literature. How are these characters and people portrayed?

(b) Take an Orientalist character you have named and rewrite them with a view to dismantle the stereotype. What narrative techniques and strategies do you use to do so?

Women postcolonial writers

Most postcolonial theorists have been male, and until recently women's voices have been silenced even in this arena. Gayatri Chakravorty Spivak, one woman postcolonial theorist to challenge this patriarchal bias, coined the term *subaltern*, meaning the 'oppressed other' (particularly female) victim of cultural imperialism. She also made use of the terms 'essentialism' to illustrate how subalterns or oppressed peoples can be easily stereotyped and oversimplified and 'strategic essentialism' as a conscious strategy for subalterns to fight back:

> the "Subaltern [woman] must always be caught in translation, never [allowed to be] truly expressing herself", because the colonial power's destruction of her culture pushed to the social margins her non–Western ways of perceiving, understanding, and knowing the world (Sharp, 2008).

bell hooks (1952–) is a postcolonial feminist who emphasises what she calls the 'intersectionality' of race, class and gender, which all conspire to perpetuate oppression: 'for contemporary critics to condemn the imperialism of the white colonizer without critiquing patriarchy is a tactic that seeks to minimize the particular ways gender determines the specific forms oppression may take within a specific group' (hooks, 1994, p. 203).

Recently, a plethora of postcolonial women writers have positioned themselves as postcolonial feminist writers, who correct what they see as a Western bias in feminist theory and who 'write the body' in award-winning and popular novels to give voice to how racism and colonialism have affected non-white, non-Western women.

Toni Morrison's *Beloved* (1987), for example, uses a stream-of-consciousness technique in portraying strong subaltern women characters who subvert patriarchy and racism. Jean Rhys's *Wide Sargasso Sea* (1966) 'writes back to Empire' by responding to Charlotte Brontë's *Jane Eyre* and deconstructing notions of 'civilisation' and 'rationality'. In her fiction and non-fiction, Egyptian feminist author Nawal El Saadawi attacks the oppression of religious fundamentalism (including female genital mutilation, veiling and public execution). Alice Walker's epistolary novel *The Color Purple* (1982) – quoted in Chapter 1 – chronicles the growth of a disempowered and sexually abused young woman to self-actualisation and independence. Arundhati Roy's *The God of Small Things* (1997) tackles social discrimination and misogyny in India. Such authors enliven the novel's possibilities as a force for social and political change.

J.M. Coetzee

How does a white male 'coloniser' such as the Nobel prize–winning J.M. Coetzee, for example, write about South Africa? Coetzee's first work, the double novella *Dusklands* (1974), presents the narratives of two colonisers: the first is a purported ancestor who cuts a swathe of destruction of the natural environment and Indigenous people wherever he goes; the second, an American Imperialist propaganda writer for the Vietnam War, is trying to win the 'hearts and minds' of the Vietnamese people. Coetzee does not protest or appropriate the voice of the colonised. Instead, he accepts his part in the colonising:

> The whites of South Africa participated, in various degrees, actively or passively, in an audacious and well-planned crime against Africa. Afrikaners as a self defining group distinguished themselves in the commission of that crime. Thereby they lent

their name to it. It will be a long time before they have the moral authority to withdraw that brandmark. [...] Is it in my power to withdraw from the gang? I think not.[...] More important, is it my heart's desire to be counted apart? Not really. Furthermore – and this is an afterthought – I would regard it as morally questionable to write something like the second part of *Dusklands* – a fiction, note – from a position that is not historically complicit (Attwell, 1992, pp. 342–343).

Similarly, in *Waiting for the Barbarians* (1980), the (white) protagonist, no matter how much he tries to distance himself from Empire, realises he is complicit in its Imperial penetration of the 'other'. In *Disgrace* (1999), David Lurie is 'stripped of all dignity [and] afflicted by his own shame and the complicity of history's disgrace' (Wastberg, 2003, n.p.).

 WHO AM I: 'WRITING A POSTCOLONIAL SELF' EXERCISE

Take fifteen minutes to answer the question 'Who are you?' in a journal freewrite. Construct your 'self' in connection to what you know about your ancestors, your race, gender, culture, group you belong to, your geography, and sense of belonging to the land you live in. Now stand back, read what you have written and examine this constructed self. Freewrite for another ten minutes on how cultural difference – race, religion, class, gender, sexual orientation, cultural beliefs, and customs – has combined to form your individual identity. How have you been 'enculturated' into what you consider to be 'natural' and how has this enculturation occurred?

Black skin, white masks

My mother once worked in a school library in Zimbabwe and the Shona librarian complained to her that the children would never take out any African books or read anything local. Instead they fed solely on Enid Blyton. Why, the librarian asked, did black children want to identify with snobbish middle-class English kids who looked down on foreigners and who fought 'bad guys' who were black?

W.E.B. Du Bois, in *The Souls of Black Folk* (1903), calls this 'double consciousness', the psychological state of seeing oneself through the eyes of the coloniser and measuring oneself against those 'white' values. This applies 'doubly' to women of colour who need to deal with double discrimination of race and gender in a society that expects them to measure themselves against patriarchal white culture.

Similarly, Franz Fanon, in *Black Skin, White Masks* (1952), documents the psychological confusion of a person who is both black (own culture) and white (the dominant culture). Whichever side of the scale you slide towards feels wrong. Reject white culture altogether? Assimilate and embrace it? Compromise?

The answer may lie in Homi Bhabha's concept of hybridity: the crossbreeding or cross-pollination of two species creating a 'third space'. Examples of hybridity in language illustrate this well: Pidgin English and Creole are hybrid forms in which local culture adapts English into its own culture. Mikhail Bakhtin sees this as a positive disruption of the monolithic linguistic domination of the coloniser where a carnivalesque linguistic style mocks the formal qualities of English language and makes it their own. For example, here is John chapter 1, verse 1 from a bible in Kriol, the language spoken in parts of the Northern Territory: *'Orait, longtaim bifo enijing bin jidan, det Wed bin jidan, en det Wed bin jidan garram God, en det Wed na im God'*. 'Translation': All right, long time before anything been made, that Word been made, and that Word been made by God, and that Word was God (Kriol Bible, 2018).

Things Fall Apart is a hybrid novel. It is written in English and bases its structure on Greek tragedy yet uses African oral devices such as a collective voice, the use of Igbo proverbs and a cyclical rhythmic backloop narrative technique. Oppressed groups often take back the language of oppression (the racial and sexist epithets) and use it as a weapon against the dominant culture.

> ✏️ **'DOUBLE CONSCIOUSNESS' EXERCISE**
>
> In a ten-minute freewrite, describe how you measure yourself and your values. How do you find yourself imitating the dominant culture's ideology (usually American). How would you write to resist this cultural domination? What is yours that is not taken on from a dominant culture? Or if your culture is the dominant culture, how do you resist this?

Cultural appropriation

At a Brisbane Writers Festival I attended a few years back, the keynote speaker, Lionel Shriver (wearing a Mexican hat), proclaimed her right to write about whatever subject she wanted to and from whatever point of view. Shriver had been criticised for depicting a black woman with Alzheimer's disease kept on a leash by her homeless white husband in the novel *The Mandibles* (2016). She argued that writers have the right to depict members of minority groups and other races and genders, 'otherwise, all I could write about would be smart-alecky 59-year-old 5-foot-2-inch white women from North Carolina' (Nordland, 2016, n.p.).

Counter to this is the argument that white writers need to be sensitive to appropriation of other cultures, especially voices that have been silenced and culture that is already dominated by white voices.

> [There is] no need to hear your voice, when I can talk about you better than you can speak about yourself. No need to hear your voice. Only tell me about your pain. I want to know your story. And then I will tell it back to you in a new way. Tell it back to you in such a way that it has become mine, my own. Re-writing you, I write myself anew. I am still author, authority. I am still [the] colonizer, the speaking subject, and you are now at the center of my talk (hooks, 1990, p. 241).

Writers who identify as white need to be aware of the issues involved in writing Indigenous characters or cultures. The history of Western literature, as we have seen, is fraught with cultural obliteration, stereotyping and appropriation. Yet Western writers still write about the 'other' in this way. In the country I live in, the Australian Council has set guidelines and protocols to help writers avoid such appropriation:

> Indigenous people and their cultures have been depicted widely in Australian literature. Some of what has been written about Indigenous people has served to develop stereotypes that do not adequately reflect the diversity of Indigenous people and their culture. Writers need to be aware of these issues about the use of Indigenous cultural and intellectual property within their works. Attention must be paid to the cultural

accuracy of using Indigenous knowledge, cultural protocols require thought when writing down Indigenous cultural information (Protocols, 2007, p. 6).

Appropriation, however, may be a strategy that colonised peoples can use in order to intervene in the dominant discourse.

> **APPROPRIATION EXERCISE**
>
> Write a paragraph about a character from another culture, race and gender. Now look carefully at this writing and decide whether you have culturally appropriated. How have you described this character/event? How would you rewrite this character/event in light of this chapter?

Conclusion

How do we write postcolonial rather than colonial novels? Writers need to ask these questions:

- How aware am I of 'othering' other cultures and people?
- How do I represent various aspects of colonial oppression?
- How do we write about postcolonial identity, including double consciousness and hybridity?
- What person(s) or groups do I write as 'other' or stranger? How do I describe and treat such persons/groups?
- How does my writing reinforce or resist colonialism?
- How does my writing respond to or comment upon the assumptions of past canonised (colonialist) works?
- Do I reinforce or undermine colonialist ideology through an absence of, or a silence about, colonised peoples?

References

Achebe, Chinua. 1977. An Image of Africa: Racism in Conrad's 'Heart of Darkness'. *Massachusetts Review* 18, 4: 782–794.

Achebe, Chinua. 1991. *Approaches to Teaching Achebe's Things Fall Apart*, ed. Bernth Lindfors. Approaches to Teaching World Literature Series 37. New York: Modern Language Association.

Achebe, Chinua. 1994 (1958). *Things Fall Apart*. London: Penguin Books.

Appiah, Kwame Anthony. 2013. In Celebrated Nigerian writer Chinua Achebe dies at 82. *CBS News*, March 22, 9:59 AM. www.cbsnews.com/news/celebrated-nigerian-writer-chinua-achebe-dies-at-82/. Accessed 27 August 2018.

Ashcroft, Bill, Gareth Griffiths, and Helen Tiffin. 1989. The Empire Writes Back: Theory and Practice in Post-Colonial Literatures. London: Routledge.

Attwell, David. 1992. Doubling the Point, Essays and Interviews. Cambridge, MA: Harvard University Press.

Blyton, Enid. 1944. The Island of Adventure. London: Macmillan.

Burroughs, Edgar Rice. 1973 (1912). *Tarzan of the Apes*. New York: Ballantine.

Conrad, Joseph. 1999 (1899). *Heart of Darkness*. Ontario: Broadview Press.

Defoe, Daniel. 1719. *The life and adventures of Robinson Crusoe, of York, mariner* [e-edition Google Books]. London: Knight and Son.

hooks, bell. 1990. Marginality as a site of resistance. In Out There: Marginalization and contemporary Cultures, eds R. Ferguson et al., 241–243. Cambridge, MA: MIT.

hooks, bell. 1994. Outlaw Culture. New York: Routledge.

Kipling, Rudyard. 1899. The White Man's Burden: The United States and the Philippine Islands. *McClure's Magazine* 12: 290–291.

Kriol Bible. 2018. http://aboriginalbibles.org.au/Kriol/Conc/root.htm. Accessed 27 August 2018.

Larson, Charles. 1972. *The Emergence of African Fiction*. Indianapolis: Indiana University Press.

Marandi, Seyed Mohammad and Hossein Pirnajmuddin. 2009. Constructing an Axis of Evil: Iranian Memoirs in the "Land of the Free". The American Journal of Islamic Social Sciences 26, 2: 23–47.

Marley, Bob. 1980. Redemption Song. *Uprising* [album].

Nordland, Rod. 2016. Lionel Shriver's Address on Cultural Appropriation Roils a Writers Festival. *The New York Times*, September 12. www.nytimes.com/2016/09/13/books/lionel-shriver-cultural-appropriation-brisbane-writers-festival.html. Accessed 27 August 2018.

Protocols. 2007. *Protocols for producing Indigenous Australian writing*. Australia Council for the Arts. www.australiacouncil.gov.au/symphony/extension/richtext_redactor/getfile/?name=fc8a5cc73467cb405e8943ae14975da7.pdf. Accessed 27 August 2018.

Shakespeare, William. 1991 (1611). The Tempest. In *William Shakespeare Complete Works*, ed. W.J. Craig, 1–22 (I.ii.366–368). Leicester: Oxford University Press.

Sharp, Joanne P. 2008. 'Can the Subaltern Speak?' *Geographies of Postcolonialism*. SAGE Publications.

Wästberg, Per. 2003. The Nobel Prize in Literature 2003, Presentation Speech. Stockholm Concert Hall. Nobel e-Museum. Swedish Academy, Nobel Foundation. www.nobel.se/literature/laureates/2003/presentation-speech.html. Accessed 27 August 2018.

11 THE GRAPHIC NOVEL AND ILLUSTRATED BOOKS

> Alice was beginning to get very tired of sitting by her sister on the bank and of having nothing to do: once or twice she had peeped into the book her sister was reading, but it had no pictures or conversations in it, "and what is the use of a book," thought Alice, "without pictures or conversations?" (Carroll, 1993 (1865), p. 1).

I grew up reading novels, yes, but also comics, those so-called trashy, garishly coloured narratives consisting of six or eight frames per page, speeches in balloons with too many exclamation marks, and caricatured superheroes doing impossible things. My teachers condemned this form of reading, contrasted it with 'real' books, and disparaged its blend of visual and textual art. We would get in trouble at school for reading comics, but not books with pictures, and I was not sure why. One teacher said that comics were 'lazy reading', the images given to us rather than created by our imaginations, and were another form of TV.

I was, however, introduced to the classics this way – *Moby-Dick* (1851), *The Scarlet Letter* (1850), *Two Years before the Mast* (1840), and so on – and comics fed my curiosity for 'serious' novels. But when I was a pre-teen, my literary diet consisted mainly of an escapist addiction to DC's Batman and Superman comics and occasionally a foray into enemy territory, Marvel, although I found those latter heroes too self-conscious and too full of self-doubt. As an eleven-year-old, I drew comics myself, creating a plethora of my own superheroes and selling these comics to friends, but secretly so that teachers would not find out.

What was this prejudice against the visual? Was it simply the superficial content of the comics, or was it the form itself that was not 'highbrow' enough for my teachers? Neil Postman explains:

> In learning to interpret the meaning of images, we do not require lessons in grammar or spelling or logic or vocabulary.

> We require no analogue to the McGuffey Reader, no preparation, no prerequisite training… [But] when one learns to read, one learns a peculiar way of behaving of which physical immobility is only one feature… Sentences, paragraphs, and pages unfold slowly, in sequence, and according to a logic that is far from intuitive. In reading, one must wait to get the answer, wait to reach the conclusion (Postman, 1994, p. 77).

Visual and graphic artists would disagree. We need to learn to read visually as well, and reading both text and visuals requires an even more complex skill.

Visual learning

If my eleven-year-old self were writing this chapter, it would be in the form of a comic (in frames and panels), my monologue would appear in speech bubbles coming from a caricatured and inked representation of me, and my lines would end in a string of exclamation marks. I was a visual learner, meaning that I preferred diagrams, maps and spatial ways of conceptualising knowledge. Rather than taking notes in conventional format, I would draw diagrams, or mind-maps, organising the information visually on the page. I would draw an image in the centre of a blank page and add words or images connected by lines branching out from the central idea. Is there perhaps also a visual writer? Do you, for example, tend to think of stories in visual scenes or movie sequences rather than words? If you were to plan a story, would you be more comfortable sketching out a storyboard rather than word narratives? Are the words less important than the ideas? Not that you have to choose one or the other, but visual learning and writing are often considered childish or not as 'good' as conceptual or word-based learning, and often the word has been prioritised over the picture.

✏ 'VISUAL LEARNING' EXERCISE

Plot a novel you are writing or planning to write by sketching or mapping your notes spatially, drawing pictures to illustrate the scenes rather than writing notes.

Graphic novels, comics and illustrated books are now regarded as 'respectable' literature, and innovative novels increasingly incorporate visual and graphic elements as part of their narrative form. The way text has been laid down in a conventional novel (merely as a means to communicate) has been challenged, and readers are being asked more and more to read visual texts.

For example, *The Book Thief* (2005) is a conventional text with a graphic section in the middle of the book, a palimpsest purportedly drawn by one of the book's characters on the bleached pages of *Mein Kampf* (1925).

The first comic written was a children's book I read as a child, and it scared me so much I still remember the terror of its graphic pictures. This was Heinrich Hoffman's *Der Struwwelpeter* (1845), a moral handbook for his three-year-old boy on how to behave – why you must not, for example, suck your thumb or be racist or shoot animals or rock on your chair at mealtimes or play with matches. The illustrations were not like those of other children's books. These were in panels, brightly coloured, with larger-than-life characters. The book graphically depicted Harriet burnt to death, Suck-a-Thumb's bleeding stumps where the scissor man had chopped off his thumbs, a wizard plunging little boys into a huge vat of black ink, and a rabbit shooting a hunter.

According to Eva-Maria Metcalfe, *Der Strewwelpeter* was 'the forerunner of comics and cartoons', was 'the beginning of modern design through the interplay of picture and text', and featured 'tableaux' (Metcalfe, 1996, p. 201).

In Japan, Manga as a comic art form began its appearance in the early 19th century. In the US, the first recognisable comics were *The Yellow Kid* (1895–1898) and in cartoons lampooning politicians and current events (*Punch*, 1841–1992). This new literary art form arose in parallel with the movie industry, the panelling and dialogue imitating the visual form of the storyboarding of movies.

By the 1930s, comics in both the UK and the US grew into a mass popular form, which included *The Funnies* (1929–1930), *The Dandy* (1937), *Superman* (1938), and *The Batman* (1939), three of which still publish in the same form nearly a hundred years later.

What does this form consist of? Each frame is a scene, and each page is a panel. Like any other form of storytelling, comics need a plot, a conflict, setting, characters, actions, and a style (Anime/Manga, American Superhero, Sprites/Clip art, Noir, Stick figures, and Sunday funnies, to name a few). Visual formatting is crucial, and you'll need to adhere to comic conventions, such as not too much text, dialogue in speech balloons, thoughts in speech bubbles, one scene per frame, and a logical sequence to frames (although this can be broken for effect as long as the reader knows where to go).

> 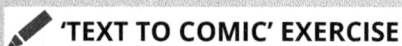 **'TEXT TO COMIC' EXERCISE**
>
> Create the beginning of a narrative/short story in comic format like the Classic Comics. Visualise the actions, and storyboard it on one page as if it were going to be a movie. Use one frame per scene and be creative with the panelling, text font, and actions portrayed in comic conventions. If you cannot draw well, use rough stick figures and place holders. (Often the writer of the comic is not also its artist.)

Illuminated manuscripts

Graphic novels were made long before comics. In the Middle Ages, books were illustrated (or visually 'illuminated') and the book business involved a parchment maker (pages or vellums were made from animal skin), a scribe (copier-writer), an illuminator (artist) and a bookbinder. Monks were employed to copy sacred texts like the Bible in scriptoriums. 'Manuscript' is derived from the Latin *manus* (hand) and *scriptus* (writing), and 'illuminated' (from the Latin 'to light up') describes the bright illustrations, often literally glowing in gold and silver. The illustrated scenes in these texts were called 'Miniatures', but Monks often 'doodled' with letters, embroidered the borders and edges of pages, and framed and panelled borders. 'Doodled' seems an inappropriate description of such fine art, but if you have ever doodled on your writing page or prettied up your writing with floral borders or embroidered letters, this is in essence what manuscript illumination is.

The effect is that the text becomes an artefact, not just a device to get to the meaning 'behind' the words. The text and the interactive illustrations are woven together to make a beautiful combined graphic text.

> ✏️ **'ILLUMINATED MANUSCRIPT' EXERCISE**
>
> Write a page of text – the beginning of a novel or short story – and 'illuminate' it by doodling around the edges, framing it, adding 'miniatures', and 'prettying up' the page. For inspiration, see Google examples of illuminated manuscripts from the Middle Ages.

Fonts, handwriting and calligraphy

The medieval European Christian monks created a series of what we now call fonts, or writing styles, which often are unnoticed or may become invisible if our aim as readers is to simply see through the words to the meaning. But if we are editors, publishers or graphic artists, the way words are shaped is also crucial to meaning-making. In the exercise on comics, what font did you use? Handwritten? Type?

Handwriting and calligraphy are increasingly becoming forgotten arts. At school, I was taught both and developed an individual writing style. There is a theory that writing by hand does something in our brain and enables a different kind of creative output or thinking as we form the words. When using a computer, we know we can always delete, so we are less careful with the words we choose as they are more provisional. Before word processing, writers had to write whole novels by hand or type on typewriters; a mistake sometimes meant redoing whole pages or sections of the novel.

Calligraphy is the visual art form using typography. It is a skill, an art form, and an expression of personality and an individual self. In other languages such as Chinese, which is pictorial, or Arabic, which requires great care and skill in forming and decorating each letter, the penmanship of forming the letters and words is a crucial skill to learn. But in most Western languages, in which the words have become functional and secondary to meaning, this art form is in decline. But whatever our language, we should find (or re-find) beauty in the shape of words and their visual appeal.

The point is to see the text as visual as well as a means to an end.

> **✏️ HANDWRITING EXERCISES**
>
> 1. Copy out by hand a favourite passage from a favourite author. What is different than if you simply cut and pasted this passage?
> 2. Write by hand in your journal (you may do this already unless you type in an eJournal). What is the difference in experience? For example, you might write slower by hand and be more aware and careful with the words. What is unique and individual about your handwriting style? How would you characterise it?
> 3. Use a different font when typing your next story or chapter. How does the narrative change? Are certain fonts better? What do different fonts do?
> 4. Experiment with different writing instruments: ink, pencil, pen, calligraphy pen and keyboard. Try an old-fashioned typewriter.
> 5. What letters are your favourite shape? Even if you have no skill in calligraphy, play with the shapes of these letters. Then go back to your illuminated manuscript exercise and re-form the words on that page you made and play with the font and the shapes of the words. Make the first letter on the page a work of art.

Illustrated books

> And you who wish to represent by words the form of man and all the aspects of his membrification, relinquish that idea. For the more minutely you describe the more you will confine the mind of the reader, and the more you will keep him from the knowledge of the thing described. And so it is necessary to draw and to describe (Bland, 1958, p. 15).

I used to think of illustrations in novels as just supplements. I thought the pictures were in the way of an authentic reading experience. They were something to be skipped if possible. For example, Enid Blyton's

The Adventure Series (1944–1955) was illustrated by Stuart Tressilin, and although I admired the pictures, I felt that my interpretation and visualisation of the narrative were better. The illustrations merely duplicated scenes from the novel. Most children's books were made this way, to aid the reader in literacy and to supplement meaning. Yet illustrations can function in many different ways and co-create meaning or even challenge the meaning of the text.

Edward Lear is a prime example. Who can read a Lear limerick without associating it with the illustration that goes with it? The absurdity of the text is complemented, even augmented, by the absurdity of the accompanying sketch, made by Lear himself. As Vivien Noakes argues, the text and illustration are inseparable:

> Part of Lear's achievement was in broadening the scope of traditional Nonsense and bringing it into the literary fold. Though now within the pages of a book, the element of performance is retained, created by the conjunction of words and pictures. The two are inseparable. Together they set the scene and tell the story (Noakes, 2006, p. 10).

Similarly, Lewis Carroll's *Alice's Adventures in Wonderland* was never a text-only book. An integral part of the reading experience of the novel is the phenomena of John Tenniel's spidery (and sometimes creepy) drawings of Alice. The drawings were so integral to the project that the first publication of *Alice* was delayed and a whole print run scrapped because of issues with illustration (Cohen and Wakeling, 2003, p. 5).

Similarly, when we think of a Roald Dahl story, we cannot separate it from Quentin Blake's wiry illustrations of the strange characters that are a hybrid creation of both Dahl and Blake.

And if we think of any Dr. Seuss book, a text-only edition with no characteristically strange creatures or lopsided, sagging houses would be inconceivable. The illustrations are the text as much as the words are.

Seuss's first 'novel', *And to Think That I Saw It on Mulberry Street* (1937), was rejected 27 times by publishers, not only because it had 'No moral or message' and 'Would not help transform children into good citizens' but it had 'cartoonlike, exaggerated pictures' (Cohen, 2004). Eventually, Dr. Seuss's subversive style of visual and textual absurdity caught on and some of his books became the best-selling children's books of all time, even though many of them contained only as few as 50 words (*Green Eggs and Ham* (1960)).

> Dr. Seuss accepted for a fact our own youthful artistic openness. Every page was a new and stimulating visual adventure with an endless variety of amusing creatures and expressionistic sets. Like his stories, his text illustrations were a poke in the eye of literary and artistic convention (Brezzo, 1986, p. 2).

The third space

An interesting case study in which illustrations forefront the text is Maurice Sendak's *Where the Wild Things Are* (1963), containing 338 words and having the honour of being banned in libraries and receiving negative reviews, selling 20 million copies worldwide, and winning the Caldecott Medal in 1964 for being the 'most distinguished American picture book for children', which 'usher[ed] in the modern age of picture books', 'perfectly crafted, perfectly illustrated ... simply the epitome of a picture book' (Randolph Caldecott Medal, 2013).

What made it work as an illustrated book? In Sendak's own words, the illustrations subverted the text. I will quote him at length as his positioning of illustrations is crucial to understanding their function:

> You must never illustrate exactly what is written. You must find a space in the text so that pictures can do the work. Then you must let the words take over where words do it best. It's a funny kind of juggling act, which takes a lot of technique and experience to keep the rhythm going... You have worked out a text so supple, that it stops and goes, stops and goes, with pictures shrewdly interspersed. The pictures too, become so supple that there's an interchangeability between them and the words; they each tell two stories at the same time. The peculiar gift of being an illustrator is that one has an odd affinity with words – it's natural to interpret them, like a composer who thinks music while reading poetry. The illustrator's first task is to comprehend deeply the nature of his text, then to give life to that comprehension in his own medium, the picture (cited in Lanes, 2003, p. 110).

If the text is the first story and the illustrations tell another story, then the juxtapositioning of these two stories tells a 'third' story.

Worth a thousand words

Finally, what if there is no text and only illustrations in a 'text'? How do we 'read' such a book? An example of this is Shaun Tan's wholly graphic fiction *The Arrival* (2013), which dispenses with the use of words entirely. To understand this, let us go back to Alice's words at the beginning of her story, this time the Walt Disney screenplay version:

Alice's Sister:	Alice. Will you kindly pay attention to your history lesson?
Alice:	I'm sorry, but how can one possibly pay attention to a book with no pictures in it?
Alice's Sister:	My dear child, there are a great many good books in this world without pictures.
Alice:	In this world, perhaps, but in my world, the books would be nothing but pictures. (Disney, 1951).

> ✏️ **'ILLUSTRATED BOOK' EXERCISE**
>
> Take a story you have written (or a favourite story of yours) and suggest illustrations for it (or illustrate it yourself). Choose whether you want to
>
> 1. duplicate the scenes or
> 2. complement them
> 3. subvert them and create a third story with your illustrations or
> 4. do away with text altogether and have the pictures speak a thousand words.

Graphic novels

I always used to associate the term 'graphic' novel (from the Latin 'graph', to draw) with something pornographic or unsavoury because of the way people always yoke the word 'graphic' with violence or sex. Ironically then, it was the use of the term 'graphic novel' that gave the comic book respectability, and books with cartoon caricatures, speech bubbles and exclamation marks became 'literature' in their own right. The first 'graphic' novel to bear that title was Will Eisner's *A Contract with God* (1978) after Richard Kyle invented the term in an essay he published in *Capa-Alpha*. Marvel later initiated a line of comic books called 'Graphic Novels' in 1982.

What's the difference between this and a 'comic'? A comic is associated with frivolous escapism, superheroes saving the world, or the 'Funnies'. A graphic novel deals with deep issues, and the art is not caricature or cartoonish. Art and text come together to make a hybrid work of art that has *gravitas*, that resonates, and that dissects the myths of society.

For example, Art Spiegelman's *Maus* (1980) describes an experience of the Nazi holocaust. Alan Moore and Dave Gibbons's *Watchmen* (1986) deconstructs the superhero and is regarded as one of the most significant works of 20th-century literature; its publication is described in a BBC review as 'The moment comic books grew up' (Barber, 2016, n.p.). Marjane Satrapi's *Persepolis* (2000) is a young woman's autobiography in Iran during the Islamic Revolution. All of these significantly changed the perception of what a comic book could do.

GRAPHIC EXERCISE

***Persepolis* is an autobiographic graphic novel. Using a significant memory from your own life, sketch two pages of this scene, visually mapping out the beginning of your own autobiographic graphic novel.**

Concrete novels

Concrete poetry plays with the visual element of poetry in which the words are used as concrete blocks to construct a visual image. For example, in *Alice's Adventures in Wonderland*, Alice listens to the 'sad and long tale' of a mouse and this 'tale' is presented in the shape of a mouse's tail:

> 'Mine is a long and a sad tale!' said the Mouse, turning to Alice, and sighing. 'It *is* a long tail, certainly,' said Alice, looking down with wonder at the Mouse's tail; 'but why do you call it sad?' (Carroll, 1993 (1865), p. 36).

Recently, novels that add a visual element in this way (which I call concrete novels) have been winning Pulitzer and Man Booker prizes and have been *New York Times* best-sellers. For example, Jonathan Foer's *Extremely*

Loud and Terribly Close (2005) plays with visual form in this way. At one point, the text becomes more and more dense and unreadable until it is a solid black rectangle. J.M. Coetzee's *Diary of a Bad Year* (2007) presents the reader with three blocks of text on each page, each telling a different but interrelated story. Richard Flanagan's *Gould's Book of Fish* (2001) is printed in different font colours for each chapter. Jennifer Egan's *A Visit from the Goon Squad* (2011) intersperses text and visual experimentation to create the effect of a collage of impressions to weave together thirteen interrelated stories.

A student of mine once handed in an assignment that was a crumpled up piece of paper. Inside, I found a story of how the student's assignment had become a crumpled up piece of paper. Another assignment I received from the same student was an origami rose. The story was written on each petal of the rose and had to be peeled off until the reader/peeler reached the heart of the story, a heart-breaking poem about a woman named Rose who broke the student's heart.

Thinking visually about text is an innovative and exciting way of challenging the textual hegemony and dominant textual assumptions about the printed page.

'CONCRETE NOVEL' EXERCISE

Take a part of your novel or story that would lend itself to being manipulated visually and create a parallel or substitute visual text to accompany or replace it. For example, could your story be presented as PowerPoint slides, as Jennifer Egan does in *A Visit from the Goon Squad*?

Conclusion

Visual elements add another dimension to novels and ask our readers to read and think visually as well as conceptually. The tyranny of print can be subverted, enhanced and replaced with the visual arts to produce an innovative 'novel' idea and to engage readers in a richer experience of the text by asking them not to 'invisibilise' the words and read through them to an intellectual apprehension of meaning but to see the book as an object. Imagine a novel as a work of art much like a painting in a gallery, to be 'read' in many ways.

References

Barber, Nicolas. 2016. Watchmen: The Moment Comic Books Grew Up. *BBC*, 9 August. www.bbc.com/culture/story/20160809-watchmen-the-moment-comic-books-grew-up. Accessed 28 August 2018.

Bland, David. 1958. *The Illustration of Books*. London: Faber and Faber.

Brezzo, Steven L. 1986. *Dr. Seuss from Then to Now*. San Diego: San Diego Museum of Art.

Carroll, Lewis. 1993 (1865). *Alice's Adventures in Wonderland*. London: Dover Publications.

Cohen, Charles and Edward Wakeling (eds). 2003. *Lewis Carroll and His Illustrators*. Cornell: Cornell University Press.

Cohen, Charles. 2004. *The Seuss, the Whole Seuss, and Nothing But the Seuss: A Visual Biography of Theodor Seuss Geisel*. New York: Random House.

Disney, Walt (producer). 1951. *Alice in Wonderland* (movie). Walt Disney Productions.

Lanes, Selma G. 2003. *The Art of Maurice Sendak*. New York: Abradake Press/Harry N. Abrahams, Inc.

Metcalfe, Eva-Maria. 1996. Civilising manners and mocking morality; Dr Heinrich Hoffman's *Struwwelpeter*. *The Lion and The Unicorn* (Special Issue: Struwwelpeter and classical Children's Literature) 20, 2: 201–216, 301–302.

Noakes, Vivien. 2006. *Edward Lear: The Life of a Wanderer*. Sutton: Stroud.

Postman, Neil. 1994. *The Disappearance of Childhood*. New York: Vintage.

Ralph Caldecott Medal. 2013. Association for Library Service to Children. American Library Association. www.ala.org/alsc/awardsgrants/bookmedia/caldecottmedal/aboutcaldecott/aboutcaldecott. Accessed 28 August 2018.

12 INTERACTIVE NARRATIVE AND DIGITAL POSSIBILITIES

Multitasking

I am sitting in a lecture theatre, watching and listening to a lecture, with my laptop open. I am taking notes. But I also flick to Facebook every now and then to see whether anyone has posted on my page regarding the book launch. I then flick to the university website to see how many people have enrolled. I now and then check my email and reply to a few urgent emails. When the lecturer mentions the new Moreton Bay campus and tells us there is a website updating its progress, I type in the address and browse through the pictures and info there. Then I open Word and read an assignment from one of my students.

*

All this during a lecture. In the 'old days', I would be expected to concentrate on the monotask at hand. But even in those pre-digital-information overload days, I would probably doodle, write a poem that was insinuating itself on my creative left side, and make notes about things I had to do after the lecture.

*

And as I look around the lecture hall, everyone is multitasking like me. Is this the way we now interact with the world, schizophrenically, dissonantly? I've watched my son do homework the same way. He listens to music and communicates with friends who are helping him in real time with the assignment and he has multiple screens open which he flicks to constantly.

*

Is the way we read and write different in this age of technology and information? In 19th-century Victorian Britain, readers were prepared to sit motionless for many hours at a time, absorbed in novels that had long chapters, very little white space, and slow introductions. Now readers want immediate entry into the novel, short bite-size chunks to read. I read three to four novels at a time, dipping into each for short times. I prefer short bites and paragraphs because I do not have the time I used to.

*

Should our writing reflect this change of the way we read and absorb information?

*

Fragmentation

Ted Gioia, in *The Rise of the Fragmented Novel*, suggests that the novel's recent fragmented form is a response to the ever-increasing fragmented nature of media. 'In 1978, a typical 30-second TV commercial had a camera cut every 3.8 seconds. By 1991, these same commercials inserted a camera cut every 2.3 seconds... and music videos were adopting an ever more rapid pace, featuring a cut every 1.6 seconds' (Gioia, 2013, p. 9). Rather than bemoaning this fact, Gioia argues that this 'pleasing sense of dislocation' (ibid) is something writers should aspire to.

Similarly, in 'Fragmentary: Writing in a Digital Age', Guy Patrick Cunningham argues that modern reading, particularly in digital media, is an 'avant-garde literary approach that best fits our particular moment' (2012, n.p.): 'More and more, I read in pieces. So do you. Digital media, in all its forms, is fragmentary. even the longest stretches of text online are broken up with hyperlinks or other interactive elements (or even ads)' (ibid).

*

Even US Presidential decrees are issued now in tweets.

*

> ✏️ **FRAGMENTATION EXERCISE**
>
> Write the beginning of a novel that demands your reader multitask. Either present your narrative in discontinuous fragments or counter your narrative with another that disrupts the reading flow on the page.

The polyphonic novel

In a sense, the novel has always been fragmentary, dissonant and polyphonic (many-voiced). Mikhail Bakhtin first used the word polyphonic to describe the novel in 1934 when remarking on the voices in Dostoyevsky's novels. Such novels, Bakhtin claims, demand a multitasking reading practice. Polyphony is a feature of narrative, and the use of heteroglossia (many tongues or voices) allows the novel as a form to contain contradictory voices: characters, narrators and the author all compete for the reader's attention and reflect a type of refracted authorial intention (Bakhtin, 1981, p. 324).

David Lodge similarly sees polyphony as a feature of the novel in which 'a variety of conflicting ideological positions are given a voice and set in play both between and within individual speaking subjects, without being placed and judged by an authoritative authorial voice' (1990, p. 86).

But recently, novelists have been consciously taking up polyphony as a narrative technique and embracing contradiction, fragmentation, and Jean François Lyotard's 'petit recits' in an attempt to demonstrate how we multitask and accept dissonance, simultaneity and contradiction as part of our reading practice. Linda Hutcheon claims that 'postmodernism is principally an ironic mode, which simultaneously says or does one thing and another' (1988, p. 16). Thus, postmodern writers embrace polyphony as a means to reflect our fragmentary and multitasking practices. Polyphony can be consonant (each voice contributing to a narrative whole) or dissonant or disruptive (where voices contradict the narrative flow). Examples of consonant polyphonic novels are William Faulkner's *As I Lay Dying* (1930), in which each voice builds up a narrative whole, or Zadie Smith's *NW* (2012), in which four Londoners' stories weave together, or composite novels such as Jennifer Egan's *A Visit from the Goon Squad* (2010) (mentioned in the previous chapter), in which each chapter disrupts the previous one, changing character, plot and style. Egan employs a variety of forms, styles and viewpoints to create a pastiche of many voices. The novel 'distill[s] a medley out of its polyphonic, sometimes deliberately cacophonous voices', says one reviewer (Churchill, 2011). Egan switches from first to second to third person, from past to present tense, and from traditional forms of narrative to reportage to graphics to textspeak. The penultimate chapter is a PowerPoint slide show.

Similarly, David Mitchell's *Cloud Atlas* (2004) and Tim O'Brien's *The Things They Carried* (1990) present the reader with a challenge – to tie up all the polyphonic voices. Julio Cortázar's *Hopscotch* (1963) is set out non-sequentially, beginning with Chapter 73 and ending with Chapter 131, a puzzle for the reader to piece together. Dissonant polyphonic novels, however, do not tie narrative threads together so neatly. Examples are Italo Calvino's *If on a Winter's Night a Traveller* (1979), a series of first chapters of novels that are never completed, or Audrey Niffenegger's *The Time Traveller's Wife* (2003), in which the reader is also a time traveller.

J.M. Coetzee's 2008 polyphonic novel *Diary of a Bad Year* displays three parallel texts on each page, each in a separate voice. The primary text along the top of the page, 'Strong opinions', is a recognisable academic essay, an intellectual discourse, disembodied and objective. It is undermined by the second strand of discourse, which is the narrator's emotional narrative, his self-doubts, his account of his disruptive feelings for a woman whom he recruits to type his work and who criticises, even belittles, his 'strong opinions'. The third strand of narrative is even more disruptive – the dialogue between the woman and her husband, who plan to rob the narrator of his money and silence his strong opinions once and for all. What makes this a modern polyphonic novel is the reader's dilemma: do we read the strands simultaneously? What narrative is untold between strands? The form of the novel disrupts any conventional linear reading pattern and will not allow a monologic reading. We are constantly multitasking, flickering from one strand to the other, comparing, contrasting, and page-turning.

The modern reader should not be distressed by this undermining of the authorial voice, used as he or she is to contradiction, disruption, and simultaneous, competing discourse. See, for example, how used we are to comments on blogs and to reading counter narratives on Twitter during a television debate.

> ✏️ **POLYPHONIC EXERCISE**
>
> Write a piece that weaves together disruptive or contradictory voices of characters, narrators and the author, who all compete for the reader's attention. Aim for 'a variety of conflicting ideological positions [that] are given a voice and set in play both between and within individual speaking subjects, without being placed and judged by an authoritative authorial voice' (Lodge, op. cit.).

The multigraphic novel

Robert Coover, in his 1992 *New York Times* essay 'The End of Books', predicted that hypertext links would put 'venerable novelistic values like unity, integrity, coherence, vision and voice' in danger (1992, n.p.).

The first eBook readers were introduced in the late 1990s but did not become popular until the mid 2000s with the Sony Reader (2006) and the Amazon Kindle (2007). Now, eBooks can be read on a number of devices – iPads and iPhones – but specifically designed book readers are designed to imitate a paperback book (including a screen fashioned to look like real paper) and to be read even in direct sunlight.

At first, eBooks were simply imitations of 'real' books. But an eBook allows polyphony to occur in a literal sense. In a polyphonic novel, the phonic element is metaphoric. But now audio can weave its strands across the visual and the textual. In eBooks, readers can follow hyperlinks, look up words in dictionaries, decide narrative sequence, experience simultaneous multi-levels of narrative, or multitask by watching videos, listening to audio, and participating interactively with the narrative, characters and plot as part of the reading experience.

In his book *Creative Writing and the Radical* (2016), Nigel Krauth argues that the novel is no longer a 'monograph' but a 'multigraph' and that the novel needs to incorporate new technologies into its form and content, become interactive and thus address the modern reader's desire to access information instantaneously and in multiple ways. A multigraphic novel allows seemingly contradictory strands of discourses all at once.

Krauth cites an example of the brave new world of novel ideas: Michael Morpurgo's *War Horse* (1982) is an interactive novel designed for the iPad and includes text, audiobook read by the author, and a timeline of the historical context of the narrative, including all relevant media in video, photographs and scans of documents, and interviews. The novel is a polyphonic performance.

Writing a multigraphic novel demands that authors be more than monographers. Authors will need to play with the forms of new media, social media, design, video and audio; reflect on how they read and write; and incorporate this into both form and content.

> **'MULTIGRAPHIC FICTION' EXERCISE**
>
> Write an interactive paragraph with hyperlinks and embedded audio and video.

Interactive narrative

Imagine a storyteller sitting around a fire. The audience sits silently, spellbound by his or her story. Then he or she turns to the audience and says, so what happens next? Or you're now in the story. Do you cross the bridge or face the monster?

Interactive fiction invites the reader to be a player in a non-linear story that is not predetermined.

The earliest interactive narratives were 'Choose your own adventure' stories in which the protagonist (second-person 'you') was offered choices that allow several plot outcomes. In 1976, Edward Packard created the 'Adventures of You' series with *Sugarcane Island*, designed for a children/middle-grade readership, and the Bantam 'Choose your own adventure' series that followed proved to be one of the most popular children's series in the 1980s and 1990s. How the reader chooses is to select options and follow instructions. If you decide to go into the forest, go to page 8; if you decide to turn back, go to page 35, and so on. Typically, there were a range of endings (from 8 to 44).

With the advent of eBooks and electronic readers, interactivity opens up possibilities for even more interaction. The simplest way to become interactive is to create a non-linear story that the reader navigates by clicking links, and the readers 'choose their own adventure' by typing in commands. An eBook of this nature can be rewritten, amended and added to, and the reader can also become part of the creative process. Electronic writer Andy Campbell calls this a 'liquid canvas' (Campbell, 2011, n.p.).

As new technology accelerates, even as we try out new ideas, they become outdated. Hyperlinks, for example, are a thing of the past, and new technologies are providing opportunities for novel ideas to proliferate at a rapid pace. For example, the CAVE (cave automatic virtual environment) is a digital virtual three-dimensional space that opens up new frontiers for digital storytelling. Used by engineers, scientists, biologists and architects, the CAVE allows researchers to visualise complex, multi-dimensional data in a virtual space. How can creative writers use such a facility in terms of modelling other worlds, devising narrative strategies and transcending the limits of our monographic paradigms of reading and writing texts? What kind of writing can be produced? Brown University has a CAVE facility which Creative Writing students use to experiment. Robert Coover, the metafictional/experimental writer of the 1980s, initiated the program: 'Immersive technologies are apt to become a dominant art form in our culture', he says. 'What we're trying to do here is ensure that they develop as places for literature' (Baard, 2003, n.p.).

Modern 'readers' – and we may now have to find another word for this activity – who are used to interactive computer games, social media and polyphonous multimedia will demand more and more multi-sensory experiences in their 'reading' experiences. As Memmott suggests, 'we will need to expand and alter our concept of "novel" and "poetry"' (ibid).

As we have seen, the novel arose out of specific material and technological contexts, out of an oral and performative tradition. In this era of hyper-technology, the novel can once more embrace the complex narratives of the digital world.

References

Baard, Mark. 2003. Writing's on the Wall in 3-D Cave. *Wired* 15 February. www.wired.com/2003/02/writings-on-the-wall-in-3-d-cave/. Accessed 29 August 2018.

Bakhtin, Mikhail. 1981. Discourse in the Novel. In *The Dialogic Imagination: Four Essays*, ed. Michael Holquist, 259–422. Trans. Michael Holquist and Caryl Emerson. Austin, TX: University of Texas Press.

Campbell, Andrew. 2011. *Fiction of Dreams* [lecture 14 Dec]. Bangor, Wales, UK: Bangor University. Quoted in R. Lyle Skains. 2016. Creative Commons and Appropriation: Implicit Collaboration in Digital Works. *Publications* 4, 1. www.mdpi.com/2304-6775/4/1/7. Accessed 29 August 2018.

Churchwell, Sarah. 2011. *A Visit from the Goon Squad* by Jennifer Egan – review. *The Observer*, March 13. www.theguardian.com/books/2011/mar/13/jennifer-egan-visit-goon-squad. Accessed 29 August 2018.

Coover, Robert. 1992. The End of Books. *The New York Times*, June 21. https://archive.nytimes.com/www.nytimes.com/books/98/09/27/specials/coover-end.html?_r=1. Accessed 29 August 2018.

Cunningham, Guy Patrick. 2012. Fragmentary: Writing in a Digital Age. *The Millions*. https://themillions.com/2012/01/fragmentary-writing-in-a-digital-age.html. Accessed 28 August 2018.

Gioia, Ted. 2013. The Rise of the Fragmented Novel: An Essay in 26 Fragments. http://fractiousfiction.com/rise_of_the_fragmented_novel.html. Accessed 28 August 2018.

Hutcheon, Linda. 1988. *A Poetics of Postmodernism*. London & New York: Routledge.

Krauth, Nigel. 2016. *Creative Writing and the Radical: Teaching and Learning the Fiction of the Future*. Bristol: Multilingual Matters.

Lodge, David. 1990. *After Bakhtin: Essays on Fiction and Criticism*. London: Routledge.

CONCLUSION: WRITING INNOVATIVE FICTION

Ben Marcus, in 'Why Experimental Fiction threatens to destroy publishing, Jonathan Franzen, and life as we know it', identifies what he calls the 'reader's muscle' – Wernicke's area, in the left temporal lobe of the brain – which is responsible for complex linguistic abilities. This muscle needs to be exercised if it is to keep our cognitive abilities sharp and growing and keep our language agile enough to engage with the world around us in a focused way. Marcus argues that it is literary fiction (and poetry) that invigorates this muscle:

> Literary language is complex because it is seeking to accomplish something extraordinarily difficult: to engrave the elusive aspects of life's entanglements, to represent the intensity of consciousness, to produce the sort of stories that transfix and mesmerize (Marcus, 2005, p. 39).

The brain is, literally and metaphorically, as big as the universe in that it contains as many neurons as there are stars and neural pathways that are virtually infinite. If we stare up at the Milky Way, we are seeing what our brain (our 'self') looks like in all its vast wonder.

By reading and writing innovative fiction, we are literally going on a Star Trek, exploring new worlds and time and space travelling. This kind of travel, I believe, prevents brain atrophy, makes new neural connections and creates intelligence, meaning making, and self-actualisation. Far from being 'elitist' and obscure, literary and experimental/innovative fiction is doing a fundamental job: activating and exercising our brains. As writers, we have important work to do.

The novel is an exciting and ever-changing phenomenon that by its very nature is innovative and disruptive and dares us to constantly remodel our thinking and express ourselves in ways that allow our humanity to emerge in all its complexity and wonder.

The history of the novel is one of increasing awareness of our consciousness, of human potential, and of connection to others and the world around us. It challenges atrophied thinking and the status quo and embraces change.

Genre fiction is often a refuge from change, a reassurance that the world is as we see it, but genre fiction pushes boundaries and peels back layers of deception and false appearance to allow the 'truth' of what is underneath to emerge.

The innovative novel simultaneously builds on and breaks with tradition. It both inhabits and questions the boundaries of literary fiction and genre. It unsettles and stimulates and is not afraid of experimentation and discomfort. It breaks rules and invents new ones. It asks us to examine ourselves and reimagine our world, it takes risks, it is playful with language, and it performs a glittering dance with language.

In taking up the vocation of novelist, we join the great community of writers and artists through the ages who have grappled with meaning and self and other.

In Chapter 1, I spoke of the binary of 'experience' and 'authority' set up in *The Canterbury Tales* by the two first storytellers of the pilgrimage, the Knight and the Miller, who pit their diametrically opposed approaches to storytelling to the world. The Knight advocates for tradition, for *olde bookes*, and grounds his stories in the wisdom of his forebears (the Graeco-Roman literary tradition). We can learn from our writer ancestors and build on their knowledge. 'The Knight's Tale' is then an intertextual palimpsest.

Conversely, the Miller argues that stories emerge from the here and now, from direct personal experience and engagement with the contemporary world, and involve deconstructing those old myths and traditions and refreshing them. We write from our immediate engagement with the world.

As writers, we need both – no sense in reinventing the wheel. We can build on knowledge of novels and techniques and movements and established genres. In addition, we need to intellectually and emotionally and experientially engage with the world we live in.

Both tradition and experience are tools we need to write innovative novels. In this book, I have sampled only a few possibilities and led you along my personal journey of discovery. You will create your own paths. You can reverse time and visit the future and be other selves.

I look forward to seeing what you will do with the novel form and encourage you to throw your full self into your writing and show the world who you are and how big your universe is.

Every time the novel is declared dead, it is reborn. Perhaps this is what a novel is, a process of reincarnation, an ever-evolving form that reflects our evolving consciousness and leads the way to further possibilities of the self.

Reference

Marcus, Ben. 2005. 'Why Experimental Fiction threatens to destroy publishing, Jonathan Franzen, and life as we know it', *Harper's Magazine*, pp. 39–52, October.

INDEX

aesthetic delight 67–8
author intrusion 116
authors as characters 118–20
automatic writing techniques 76–9

beginnings (of novels) 120–1
binaries 143–4
breaking the fourth wall 117
bricolage 156
bricoleur 97, 156

cadaver exquis 77
calligraphy 181
CAVE (cave automatic virtual environment) 195
collage 98
concrete novels 186
corporeal feminism 154
countervoices 136–7
cultural appropriation 173
cut-up method 77

dark side, writing from the 136
death of the author 91
deconstruction 90, 106
dialogic epistolary writing 26
disgust 128
disruption 104
dissecting myths 10, 11
double consciousness 172
duck/rabbit figure 43

endings (of novels) 119, 122–4
epistolary 24
erasure 105

erotic and pornographic writing 19
essentialism 144, 169
exquisite corpse/cadaver 77

fancy versus plain prose 59
feminine sentence 146–7
fictional autobiography 53
fonts 181
fragmentation 103, 190
frame story 124
free indirect discourse 49, 50
freewriting 4

gendered writing 72
gothic 17
graphic novel 177, 185
grunge literature 134

haiku 59–60
handwriting 181
hybridity 172

iceberg theory 66–7
illuminated manuscripts 180
illustrated books 177, 182
imagism 60–1
innovation 7
interactive narrative 189, 194
interior monologue 49
intertextuality 99
ironism 95
irony 95

journal writing 3, 25
juxtaposition 96

INDEX

kafkaesque 79–80

language of the unconscious 76
l'ecriture feminine 142, 145–7, 149, 152
le mot juste 61–2
limerick 183
liquid canvas 194
literary fiction 9, 11

magical realism 75, 80
manga 179
manly writing 145–6
masculine prose 65, 69
masculine sentences 147
metafiction 109
minimalism 58
modernism 42
monologic epistolary writing 26
multigraphic novel 193
multitasking 189
muscular prose 65, 69

narcissism 110
nerve points 138
newspeak 71
non-subordinating style 49, 50–1
novel, 127
novella 6, 15, 44–5, 65, 128, 164, 170

omission 66–7
Orientalism 168
out-language 139

palimpsest 99
parody 97
pastiche 97
pathos 21
patriarchal language 149
petit recits 191
poioumena 94
polylogic epistolary writing 26

polyphonic novel 191
postcolonialism 161
postmodernism 87
priest of the imagination 5, 6

queer form 157
queer writing 155

realism 15, 30
relativity 42

sacred idiom 69
satire 36
schlock writing 153
sentimental novel 20
sex, writing about 130
Shakespeare's sister 146
social and domestic realism 37
sous rature 90
spectrum of truth 8–9
spontaneous prose 55, 77
stream of consciousness 46
style 62–3
subaltern 169
surrealism 76
surrealist automatism 76–7

taboos 127
third space, the 184
time 55
transgressive ecriture feminine 153
transgressive fiction 127

unconscious 54
under erasure 90

verfremdungseffekt 117
verisimilitude 32
Victorian realism 38
visual learning 178

writing LGBTQI+ 157
writing the body 142

Printed by Books on Demand, Germany